THE BATTLE FOR THE LAST DAYS' TEMPLE

Politics, Prophecy, and the Temple Mount

RANDALL PRICE

HARVEST HOUSE PUBLISHERS

EUGENE, OREGON

Cover by Terry Dugan Design, Minneapolis, Minnesota

THE BATTLE FOR THE LAST DAYS' TEMPLE
Copyright © 2004 by World of the Bible Ministries, Inc.
Published by Harvest House Publishers
Eugene, Oregon 97402
www.harvesthousepublishers.com

Library of Congress Cataloging-in-Publication Data
Price, Randall.
  The battle for the last days' Temple : politics, prophecy, and the Temple Mount / Randall Price.
      p. cm.
  Includes bibliographical references and index.
  ISBN 0-7369-1318-1
  1. Temple of Jerusalem (Jerusalem)   2. Temple Mount (Jerusalem)—History—Religious aspects—
Judaism.   3. Bible—Prophecies—Temple of Jerusalem.   I. Title.
  BM655.P75 2004
  296.4'82—dc22   2003021790

Printed in the United States of America

04   05   06   07   08   09   10   11   / VP-CF /   10   9   8   7   6   5   4   3   2   1

In memory of
Dr. S. Lewis Johnson, Jr.,
who taught me how to
labor in the Word of God
and showed me how to love
the God of the Word.
Soli Deo Gloria!

To Tommy Jenkins,
my spiritual father, who
for 35 years has ministered
to me and with me in the
Lord's service. Thank you
for being God's man in my life.

Acknowledgments

This book owes its inspiration to Bob Hawkins, Jr., president, and Carolyn McCready, vice president of editorial, and the publishers' committee at Harvest House Publishers. I wish to thank them for their foresight to address this critical aspect of biblical prophecy and Middle Eastern politics and for inviting me to present my research in this book. I also wish to thank Mrs. Ann Clark and her roommate Elizabeth for their hospitality during my time of research and writing in Jerusalem, and Mr. and Mrs. Gordon Whitelock and Mr. and Mrs. Don Barber of Camp Peniel, Inc., for the gracious provision of their speaker's cabin and their hospitality during the completion of my writing in Texas. I am especially grateful to Professor Eilat Mazar and MK Rav Benny Elon, who took time from their busy schedules to answer my questions about recent events related to the struggle for the Temple Mount, and to Gershon Salomon, who allowed me privileged access to his group's *Tisha B'Av* demonstration at the gate of the Temple Mount.

Thanks is also due to Mr. Robert Handley, who assisted me with research material, and Miss Angie Alvarez, who provided invaluable help with photography and videography in Jerusalem. I also want to thank Mr. Alexander Schick of the Bibelausstellung, Sylt, Germany, Professor Eilat Mazar of the Hebrew University, and Mr. Zachi Zweig of Jerusalem for their help in providing access to photographic archives, Israeli artist Larissa Lando for permission to reproduce copies of her prophetic art prints, and Mr. Zachary Vandermeer for photographic technical assistance and work on the indexes.

I am also immensely grateful to my congregation at Grace Bible Church in San Marcos, Texas, who has again granted me time away from our local ministry to minister at large and has encouraged me and prayed for me in the course of my writing. Gratitude is also expressed to Steve Miller, Betty Fletcher, Gary Lineburg, Corey Fisher, and Georgia Varozza of Harvest House Publishers for their fine assistance during the editorial and production stages of producing this book.

Finally, I could not have accomplished a word of this book without my wife Beverlee's loving support and crucial interaction, and the prayers, hugs, and gentle proddings of my mother, Maurine Price (who also worked on the indexes), and my children, Elisabeth (and her husband Eric), Eleisha, Erin, Jon, and Emilee. You are all the greatest!

Contents

A Word from the Author

For more than a decade I have researched and investigated the struggle that has continued over the Temple Mount in Jerusalem. The process began for me when, in 1989, I witnessed the beginnings of Temple activism in Jerusalem and was invited by Thomas Ice to write a book with him, setting these current events into the context of biblical prophecy. The book that resulted from that collaboration, *Ready to Rebuild: The Imminent Plan to Rebuild the Last Days Temple* (Harvest House, 1992) became a best-seller and was one of the first books to deal extensively with the Temple movement. A few years later I wrote *In Search of Temple Treasures* (Harvest House, 1994), which explored the rich tradition concerning the lost treasures of the Temple, especially the rabbinic tradition embraced by most of the Temple organizations in Israel that the Ark of the Covenant still exists beneath the Temple Mount and will be recovered once Jewish control of the site is established.

Over the next decade a host of literature on Temple activism was produced by secular, Jewish, Christian, and Muslim authors, including master's theses and doctoral dissertations. Political and prophetic novels also began to proliferate with the controversy over the Temple Mount as the major theme, and even a few movies were produced with the explosive issue of the Temple as a key ingredient in the plot. More importantly, those within the Temple movement in Israel began to generate their own publications and films explaining their convictions and intentions. In addition, those in Temple organizations, as well as many others, launched Web sites detailing their activities and began offering historical and theological studies on the Temple. Today, a computer search engine will call up a seemingly unending stream of such sites.

During this time I continued to dialogue with the Jewish and Muslim authorities involved in the struggle over the sacred site. I am grateful for the exceptional access and interviews those on both sides afforded me, despite the often tense relations that were experienced as I shuttled between political adversaries. My interactions with many of these individuals, as well as with many in the traditional Christian and messianic communities in Israel, challenged me to revisit the conventional ideas about the Temple that I had received in my Christian theological training and to undertake my own study of the subject from the original biblical, traditional, and historical sources. This study led to a published doctoral dissertation[1] in a department of Jewish studies at the University of Texas on a critique of Christian theological supercessionism (the belief that the church has fully and finally replaced national Israel in the purpose and plan of God), a view that has historically attempted to prove its case by pointing to the judicial destruction of Jerusalem and the Temple by the Roman army in A.D. 70.

My method in that work was to isolate the judicial element of Temple desecration and destruction pronounced against Israel in the Old and New Testaments and to identify it as a motif joined inseparably with the redemptive element of Temple restoration. Moreover, this motif was demonstrated to be an eschatological motif, indicating that its use in the New Testament held out a future for national Israel in accordance with a literal fulfillment of the Old Testament prophetic texts predicting redemption and restoration in the last days. I have also written two book chapters dealing with the theological supercession of Preterism in particular, an eschatological position that contends most or all of the biblical prophetic texts related to Israel—as well as those attending and including the second coming of Christ—were fulfilled in the first century, especially in connection with the fall of Jerusalem and the Temple (A.D. 70). These studies were published in *The End Times Controversy: The Second Coming Under Attack* (Harvest House, 2003).[2]

This present work follows a popular academic study, *The Coming Last Days' Temple* (Harvest House, 1999), which examined the theological purpose and prophecies of the Temple in the Old and New Testaments. In spite of the book's formidable size

(732 pages), it was well received by both Christian and Jewish audiences and led to the production of a documentary film by the same name.[3]

When the Al-Aqsa intifada began in September 2000 and was followed in September 2001 by the terrorist attack on New York's World Trade Center towers and the Pentagon in Washington, D.C., my response to these events was in the form of two books—*Unholy War* (Harvest House, 2001) and *Fast Facts on the Middle East Conflict* (Harvest House, 2003). These reported the historical, political, and religious issues behind these conflicts. Both of these works attempted to update readers in regard to the struggle over the Temple Mount—an insurmountable obstacle that caused the Oslo Peace Process to collapse, and which has become the feared flashpoint for inciting a greater future conflict.

My role in this history has simply been that of an observer and reporter. However, I have been accused of being considerably more. In April 2000, four months before the outbreak on the Temple Mount which became the Al-Aqsa intifada, The Free Press released Gershom Gorenberg's book *The End of Days: Fundamentalism and the Struggle for the Temple Mount*. In this work, which depicts Jewish, Christian, and Islamic fundamentalists equally as fearful figures who could bring about self-fulfilling prophecies of apocalyptic proportions on the Temple Mount, I discovered myself mentioned repeatedly as a member of this dangerous group. Recently, Christian authors Timothy Weber and Stephen Sizer have made similar accusations, warning the evangelical Christian community against supporting a Zionist agenda.[4] On another occasion while perusing a bookstore in Jerusalem, the manager recommended to me a controversial book by a Jewish author. Purchasing the book, I went back to my apartment to relax and read one chapter in the book that dealt with a so-called "Temple Mount plot." As I read about this alleged plot I learned that it had been orchestrated by members of the Quatuor Coronati Lodge (a Masonic order), including, according to the author, Prime Minister Ariel Sharon and former Hebrew University physicist Dr. Asher Kaufman, in order to "set the Middle East aflame through assaults on the Temple Mount." Imagine my surprise as I read further of a list of others linked with this Masonic order who were, according to the author, "determined to ignite the Final Days, no matter how many Jews die," and found *myself* named as a co-conspirator![5]

Let me assure you that I have not been nor am I now part of any Masonic order nor of any political activist group, nor do I wish for the deaths of anyone in the struggle for the Temple Mount—Jew or Arab. My writing on the subject of the Temple stems from my desire to help others set the content of the Bible into its proper historical context. Many errors in biblical interpretation have been made because the biblical text has been read by people simply in light of their religious traditions without regard for the text's original meaning. As one who interprets the biblical prophecies in a consistently grammatical, historical, and literal manner, a method that I believe best explains the text in its context, I have concluded that the Bible teaches there is to be a future restoration for national Israel that includes a spiritual return to the Lord and a physical return to the Land (Jeremiah 31:27-37; 33:7-9; Ezekiel 36:18-38; 37:14,23-28).

As part of this restoration, Israel's central institution, the Temple, is destined to return to finally fulfill its peaceful purpose to be "a house of prayer for all the peoples" (Isaiah 56:7; cf. Mark 11:17). The same prophecies that predict this restoration in the last days also reveal that it will take place only after "a time of distress" (Daniel 12:1; cf. Matthew 24:21), during which the nations will come against Jerusalem to do battle (Zechariah 12:3,9; 14:2) including desecrating the city's rebuilt Temple (Matthew 24:13; Mark 13:14; 2 Thessalonians 2:4; Revelation 11:2). Therefore, despite my own longing for the peace promised by the prophets, I must acknowledge that, according to the biblical text, it will not come except on the other side of war. Only when this Temple is rebuilt and filled again with God's presence (Isaiah 4:4-6; Jeremiah 3:17; Ezekiel 43:1-7) will all the nations be drawn to Jerusalem—not for warfare, but for worship—and the world will no longer learn war (Isaiah 2:2-4). Should not all who seek such peace pray for such a day?

Now, even if I were capable of the things which I have been accused of, I still would be powerless to bring to pass an apocalyptic event any more than have the fiercely opposed forces who have fought over the Temple Mount in the past and who continue to fight over the site today. According to the Bible, all the people of this world "are accounted as nothing" (Daniel 4:35) before the God of the universe. We mere mortals are in His almighty hand, who "does according to His will in the host of heaven and among the inhabitants of earth" (Daniel 4:35), and it is He alone who "has fixed [the times] by His own authority" (Acts 1:7). Such a conviction docs not exhibit fatalism, but encourages faith, for it gives assurance of a God who alone can bring the prophetic promises to pass.

Which brings me to the purpose behind this present book, *The Battle for the Last Days' Temple*. As the struggle over the Temple Mount has evolved into a conflict and threatens to turn into a war, it is necessary to understand the conflicting claims and provocative events that are propelling us toward the last days—in which both the days of distress and the promise of peace will be realized. As you read the details of the current conflict and impending battle, it is my hope that you will be able to discern the hand of God directing the many personalities and problems that have a part in His plan and that this awareness will settle your souls as you trust in Him who is our peace (Isaiah 9:6; Ephesians 2:14).

Randall Price
Jerusalem
Tisha B'Av 2003

The Focal Point of the Battle

If one would want to explain in a nutshell what all the strife at present is all about in and around Israel, spiritually speaking, then the answer would have to be this: There is an enormous battle about the possession of "who gets" the heart of the city of Jerusalem, the Temple Mount.

Jan Willem van der Hoeven
Director, International Christian Zionist Center

The Temple Mount in Jerusalem has today become the centerpiece of the political conflict in the Middle East. It is a holy site over which is threatened a holy war. In 1999, *Jerusalem Report* journalist Gershon Gorenberg wrote in his book *The End of Days: Fundamentalism and the Struggle for the Temple Mount,*

If there's any place in the world where belief in the End is a powerful force in real-life events, it's the Holy Land. The territory today shared and contested by Jews and Palestinians is the stage of myth in Christianity, Judaism, and even Islam. When a great drama is played out here, the temptation to match events with the script of the Last Days can be irresistible. For a century just such a drama has been acted out, compelling the world's attention—and firing the expectations in all three religions among those who hope for the End.[1]

Gorenberg's concern is that fundamentalist belief—particularly in relation to the role of the Temple Mount in end-time events—could stir a fear and fanaticism that, acted out in the political arena, could produce disastrous apocalyptic scenarios.

Gorenberg's book is also about the struggle for the Temple Mount, the battle for possession of that holy ground over which Islam claims exclusive sovereignty as its third holiest site and over which Israel (since 1967) has exercised sovereignty and upon which Orthodox Judaism believes a Temple will be rebuilt in the last days. It is a battle that is just beginning even though it has been brewing for decades. It is a battle whose roots stretch backward in time to the days of Israel's first monarchy and whose branches weave throughout the history of the nations to climax with the final kingdom on planet earth. It is a battle that today is being waged more often with words, but sometimes also with stones, tear gas, and guns. This battle is predominantly religious, yet it is inseparable from the political quest for peace in the Middle East. It is a conflict over a site in a city most people in the West have never seen; yet it is linked with the events of 9/11 that have now forced the West into a war against terrorism and committed western troops to the blood-soaked soils of these ancient lands. As such, it represents a clash of cultures birthed in the East but which have grown separately in power in both the East and the West, only to encounter one another at last in the East.

A Battle of Belief

Ultimately, this confrontation over a holy site is at the heart of a cosmic conflict—a battle of belief—that has been raging since the dawn of time and will be resolved only at the end of days. It is, therefore, a drama that has a place as much in prophecy as in politics and involves beliefs as much as bureaucracy. And because the future develops from the present, it is appropriate that we consider the prophetic events in light of present experiences. In contrast with Gorenberg's book, which dismissed the biblical predictions while warning of self-fulfilling prophecies from fanatics, this book takes seriously the prophecies made by Israel's prophets and expects their fulfillment in God's way and in God's time. However, I agree with those who express concern over "forcing the hand of the Messiah" with respect to the Temple Mount, which would have disastrous consequences for both Jewish and Arab peoples. Conversely, the recognition here is that God has, and will bring to pass, a purposeful program for the Jewish and Arab peoples—a purpose which, on the other side of the battle, will see the Temple Mount fulfilling their dual divine destiny (Isaiah 19:16-25; Zechariah 14:16-19).

The Two Sides

Since biblical times, religious Jews have prayed three times a day *toward* the site of the ancient Jewish Temple. But since the Mount came under the sovereignty of the Jewish state almost 40 years ago, no Jew has been officially permitted to pray *at* the site! Today, the Muslim authorities that were permitted by Israel in 1967 to control the Temple Mount now declare that no Temple ever existed there. They further claim that the city of Jerusalem, and even the entire Land of Israel, never had a Jewish history! Further still, they warn (as Mufti Ikrima Sabri has done repeatedly) that any attempt to counter these claims and impose a Jewish presence at the site will start a cataclysmic war with two billion Muslims worldwide.

Unquestionably, the focal point for Islamic terrorist groups, in their ongoing war with Israel, is the city of Jerusalem and especially the holy site of the Temple Mount. For example, during the U.S.-led war with Iraq, Hamas leader Abdel Aziz al-Rantisi (in the Gaza Strip) called for Iraqis to unite for a massive *jihad* in Jerusalem: "Send thousands of martyrs from Iraq, who will advance with their explosive belts against our enemies in Jerusalem and Palestine. Our enemies are the enemies of Allah....Fight them! Allah will chastise them at your hands, and he will lay them low and give you the victory over them! (*Sura* 9:14)."[2] Like the Bible, the Qur'an depicts the battle for Jerusalem culminating in an apocalyptic war, although with decidedly different outcomes.

Time for a Temple

Back in 1989, *Time* magazine reported that an Israeli poll had revealed that some 18 percent of the Jewish population wanted to see the Jewish Temple rebuilt. This was touted by some as an exceptional number and was criticized by opponents as unreliable. At the time, the first Palestinian intifada was taxing Israeli patience and there was a widespread hope that peaceful negotiation would soon restore order. While some Orthodox Jews warned that the negotiations to appease the Arabs would lead to a loss of the Temple Mount, most Israelis feared that controversy over the Temple Mount threatened a loss of peace. The subsequent decade and a half saw the Oslo Peace Process come and go with a second intifada birthed, according to the Palestinian Authority, by conflict over the Temple Mount, which has since led to some 1000 Israeli deaths (and twice as many Palestinian deaths). The result has been an almost complete polarization of the Israeli and Palestinian societies and a dramatic change in Israeli attitude toward the issue of rebuilding the Temple.

In July 2003, a survey commissioned by the Reform movement's Israel Religious Action Center and conducted by the Dahaf Institute revealed that 53 percent of those queried said they would like to see a third Temple on the Temple Mount.[3] The *Jerusalem Post* followed this survey with a poll of their own via their Web site. The result of some 1200 respondents was more than 80 percent in favor of rebuilding the Temple at the present time.[4] This poll confirmed earlier surveys that had shown a growing shift in the Jewish community in favor of the Temple Mount as a whole. These polls, conducted by the Guttman Institute of Applied Social Research of some 1500 Israelis, revealed that 99 percent felt the Western Wall was important, and 84 percent of the total sampling (and 73 percent of non-observant Jews) wanted to pray on the Temple Mount.[5] The next step was clear, as Yossi Klein Halevi observed in *The Jerusalem Report:* "winning the right to Jewish prayer is merely the activists' interim goal: the ultimate goal is a rebuilt Temple."[6] This shift has taken place most among secular

Jews, which is reflected, in part, by the advent of an organization called Secular Jews for the Temple, whose goal is to promote Jewish awareness of the Temple and the Temple Mount. One of their spokesmen has explained the need for their organization at the present time:

> The fact that the Arabs pray from there to Mecca, but at the same time don't let us go up there, makes the Temple Mount into a symbol of our Exile and humiliation....Historically, too, the Mount was not only a place of sacrifices, but also a place and a symbol of our nationhood. The Arabs, too, feel that as long as they control the Temple Mount, they have a chance to banish us totally from the Land.[7]

These religious, national, and historical feelings merge annually at the Jewish commemoration of the destruction of the First and Second Temples, which occurred on the same day—the ninth (*tisha*) of the Jewish month of *Av* (approximating the Julian calendar's month of August)—and is observed as a solemn

Photo by author

Knesset member and minister of tourism Rabbi Benny Elon leads Jewish marchers around the walls of the Old City during a *Tisha B'Av* commemoration. At this annual event, some 100,000 Jews march around the walls of the Old City.

day of fasting and reading of the book of Lamentations. On the eve of *Tisha B'Av,* Jerusalemites customarily circle the walls of the Old City, within which is the Temple Mount, in a march to proclaim Jewish sovereignty over the Temple Mount and to recognize it as the place for the coming Third Temple. This past year some 100,000 Jews (and some Christians) marched around the walls, led by Knesset member and minister of tourism Rabbi Benny Elon.

Yet while this multitude could proclaim sovereignty, they could not practice it. At that moment, and for 33 months previously, the Temple Mount had been closed to Jews by Islamic authorities and to everyone else (non-Muslims) by Israeli authorities. The point was proved the next day *(Tisha B'Av)* as a Knesset member attempted to demonstrate his right to visit Judaism's holiest site, the Temple Mount. Despite his possessing diplomatic immunity and supposedly unrestricted access throughout Israel,

Photo by author

Jerusalemites rally at the Western Wall on the eve of *Tisha B'Av* reading from the Book of Lamentations and praying for the speedy rebuilding of the Temple.

Israeli police barred his entrance, stating that his presence would be too great a provocation to the Muslims and would result in violent consequences.

The Calm Before the Conflict

In spite of the Israeli police's warning of dire consequences, one week later the Israeli government re-opened the Temple Mount for visitations. Islamic officials protested and Palestinian leaders threatened that Israel was "risking a backlash both in the country and throughout the Muslim world." Adnan Husseini, the director of the Islamic Waqf, which oversees the site, stated his belief that Israel was not trying to restore the status quo (of access to the holy places by other religions) but to allow religious Jews at the site in order to pray and eventually rebuild the Temple. He declared the official position of Islam and the Palestinian Authority when he said, "This is God's will for this to be a mosque. They [the Israeli government] have to recognize this. They should not make a war with Islam, with the Islamic world."[8]

Consequently, as Israeli Jews walked again on the Temple Mount and watched Arab children playing kickball among the olive trees and cypresses, their sense of calm belied the fact that dozens of police officers were at their sides with Plexiglas shields and riot gear stored nearby and at the ready. The police were well aware this could be the calm before the conflict, the lull before the storm—a storm they have faced before and expect to soon face again. What will the future hold? Is there on the horizon a climatic war over the Temple Mount? Will Jews return to the Temple Mount to rebuild their Temple, as many expect? What effect will the struggle for the Temple Mount have on the rest of the world? These are some of the issues we will explore together as we consider the political problems and prophetic promises surrounding the battle for the last days' Temple.

Part 1

THE BIBLICAL BATTLES

1

The Precepts of Prophecy

I doubt not through the ages, one increasing purpose runs.

ALFRED LORD TENNYSON

People will not understand these and related ideas until they happen, for they are hidden by the prophets.

RAMBAM

The present controversy that exists over the problem of the holy places in Jerusalem forms the center of the Middle East conflict today. Israeli Knesset member and minister of tourism Benny Elon affirms this when he says, "The Temple Mount is at the heart and is the most important issue in the conflict, even though the majority of Jews as well as others don't understand it."[1]

Given the recognition in this statement that the majority of Jewish people and others do not understand the place of the modern Temple Mount in the current conflict, we can also conclude that many people have no idea why a battle would be fought in the future for a last days' Temple or why this needs to concern them at the present time. Some might say, "If the Jews have gotten along well enough without a Temple for 2000 years, why do they feel the need to build another one?" Indeed, over the 19 centuries of Diaspora (Jewish exile outside of the Promised Land) the faith of most Jews has not been tied to a specific place but has been practiced in whatever foreign context the people existed. Why should this situation change now, since nothing else in Jewish experience has been changed? After all, wasn't the Temple just a symbol from the past? Why do some people want to set up an actual stone building? Do they want to bring back animal sacrifices as well? And with the Middle East situation so explosive, why would anyone want to provoke further violence from the Arabs or risk a religious war with Islam by arguing over the rights to a holy place? Surely no Temple is as important as a human life; why not just forget about it and live together in peace?

These are good questions, and certainly proper in light of the urgent need to resolve the Middle East conflict and bring peace to the Israelis and Palestinians. However, these questions reveal a shortsightedness that measures the present only by itself, for they fail to consider the prophecies of the past and their fulfillments in the future. Before we can develop fully-informed answers to these questions related to the ongoing Temple controversy, it is important for us to consider some precepts of prophecy about the Temple that will guide our understanding of the issues and will offer a foundation for understanding the current dilemma.

Understanding Unfulfilled Prophecies

First, it is necessary to recognize that *the Bible (both the Old and New Testaments) contains unfulfilled prophecies that will be fulfilled in the same way they were given.* The Old Testament is not out of date, but like the New Testament (itself 2000 years old), contains hundreds of prophetic statements that have yet to be fulfilled in the manner they were originally given. Consider the statistics: There are 23,210 verses in the Old Testament, and of these, 6641 contain prophecy (28.5 percent of the Old Testament). There are 7914 verses in the New Testament, and of these, 1711 contain prophecy (21.5 percent of the New Testament). All together there are 31,124 verses, of which 8352 contain prophecy (27 percent of the whole). This reveals that almost one-third of the Bible (Old and New Testaments) contains prophecy.

In the statement of these prophecies, the past provides the grounds for the realization of the future. Moreover, this future realization can be understood only if the grounds established in the past remain *unchanged*. Otherwise the realizations become not divine fulfillments (as the prophets predicted), but human fabrications made to fit our present reality. This, of course, means we must read the Bible as it was written and by methods that interpret its message based on human traditions, theories of literary criticism, or by a post-modern approach which reduces the Bible to personal experiences.

Some biblical scholars say the original writers of Scripture intended their messages to be understood metaphorically and never expected their readers to understand them literally. However, the majority of prophecies, while they may contain some figurative language, were given in an actual historical and geographical context for the apologetic purpose of confirming God's Word and comforting the recipients in real circumstances. No metaphorical message could accomplish this purpose. For example, the Jewish people suffering in exile were given prophecies of their return to the Land of Israel (Isaiah 44:26–45:3; Jeremiah 25:12-14; 27:21-22). Such prophecies had to be fulfilled literally to fulfill their purpose. Only if the Jews (and not some other people) actually returned to the Land of Israel, from which they were exiled (not some other place), could the prophecy make sense and offer real hope to a captive people. More important, there is no way that prophecies could offer a proof of the power of God to perform His promises, unless they were fulfilled as they were given. These exile-related prophecies were fulfilled literally in the past with the return of a remnant of the Jewish exiles to Jerusalem beginning in 539 B.C.

At one time, all biblical prophecy was unfulfilled, but through the ages, much has been fulfilled (depending on how one interprets and applies messianic prophecy). And the principle of literal fulfillment for past-fulfilled prophecies establishes the pattern for the literal fulfillment of future unfulfilled prophecies. For example, there are prophecies that promise to the Jewish nation a future restoration in the Land of Israel under a New Covenant with both spiritual and material blessings (Isaiah 2:2-4; Jeremiah 31:31-34; Ezekiel 36:24–37:28; Zechariah 8:3-23; 12–14). In these contexts, Israel is redeemed and spiritually observant of God's ways and is the dominant nation to which all the Gentile nations come to learn God's laws. There is no longer any war, and the Temple stands in Jerusalem as the spiritual center for God's restored presence as well as for all mankind. Clearly, these prophecies have not yet been fulfilled literally for Israel or the nations.

Because of this lack of literal fulfillment, some have tried to counter the accusation that these prophecies failed by developing various explanations that the prophecies actually *were* fulfilled, but not in a literal fashion, arguing the language of prophecy is idealistic or symbolic. In one scheme, fulfillment is with historical Israel and occurred within one of the past experiences of Jewish exile and return, the language of restoration being hyperbolic (exaggerated). In another, a different people and place find fulfillment (for example, with the church throughout the world). In yet another, the application is idealistic, being completely nonspecific and timeless (for any person in any age). In each of these schemes, the prophetic texts are interpreted partially or wholly in a nonliteral manner, with specific details, which might require literal fulfillment, read in the light of the whole.

This approach, however, contradicts the precedent set by prophecies that have already been fulfilled (e.g., Genesis 15:13-14; Exodus 12:29-36,40-41), and fails to satisfy the promised expectation of the original Jewish audience, for whom the prophecies were intended as a present comfort and justification for future hope. For example, Ezekiel prophesied about both Israel and the Temple's ruin (Ezekiel 4–24) and its restoration (Ezekiel 33–48). Because the ruin occurred historically in the events culminating in the Babylonian invasion and destruction in 586 B.C., the details of the text can be seen to have been fulfilled literally. Now, even though Israel returned from exile and rebuilt the Temple, the extent of the restoration and magnitude of the Temple described in the text have no complete correspondence with the past historical restoration. Are the prophecies of ruin to be interpreted literally and the prophecies of restoration to be interpreted nonliterally? How could a nonliteral promise of restoration offer comfort and confidence to Jews in a literal exile? Moreover, how could it offer, as it claims, *proof* to the more powerful Gentile nations of the almighty power of Israel's God (cf. Ezekiel 36:23-36; 37:21-28; 38:14-16,23; 39:6,21,25-29)?

The alternative, then, to the nonliteral approach is to interpret the text consistently and literally. Therefore, if a prophecy has not yet been fulfilled literally, its fulfillment must still be future. This approach alone offers both comfort for the present and confidence in the future, and holds out the real hope that God will demonstrate before the world His sovereignty on the stage of history.

Having said this, it is necessary to briefly note the different foci presented in the Old Testament and the New Testament respectively. The Old Testament focuses on the preparation of and purpose for Israel's calling as a nation. Within this program designed to make God known to the nations (the rest of the world), there is the prophecy of a glorious future Temple as part of the fulfillment of Israel's restoration through the messianic advent and under the New Covenant in the last days (Isaiah 2:2-4; Ezekiel 37:25-28; 40–48; Haggai 2:7-9; Zechariah 6:12-15; 8:3).

By contrast, the New Testament's focus is upon how the covenental basis for the fulfillment of this prophecy for Israel and the nations has been provided by Messiah. In the New Testament, Jesus came as the prophesied Messiah and fulfilled the *spiritual* requirements for Israel and the nation's redemption and restoration. In the future, Jesus will return to fulfill the *physical* requirements through His messianic rule. However, at the present time, both Jews and Gentiles can experience the spiritual blessings of the New Covenant through the bestowal of God's Holy Spirit.

Because of this universal spiritual emphasis and the postpone-
ment of the prophesied national blessings until the time of messianic rule, the New Testament rarely touches upon these benefits
(such as a glorious new Temple) promised to national Israel.

However, because the New Testament does acknowledge the
promise of Israel's future restoration (Matthew 8:11; 10:23; 19:28;
20:21-23; 25:31-32; 26:29; Mark 14:25; Luke 2:38; Acts 1:6-7; 3:20-21;
Romans 11:12,15,23,25-27), we must assume the Temple is a part
of this promise (cf. Matthew 23:38-39 with Psalm 118:22-26; Mark
11:17 with Isaiah 56:7). Even though the New Testament employs,
on occasion, spiritual elements of the Temple (a holy structure
where the presence of God dwelt) to explain the new nature of the
New Covenant believer—corporately as a spiritual body, the
church (1 Corinthians 3:16-17; 2 Corinthians 6:16–7:1; Ephesians
2:21-22), and individually as a physical body, the saint (1 Corinthians 6:19-20)—this does not imply that the New Testament does
not follow the Old Testament in recognizing the Jerusalem
Temple as essential to Israel's future destiny. Rather, this underscores the Temple's historic sanctity, a belief revealed by apostolic
action and assertion (cf. Luke 24:52-53; Acts 2:46; 3:1; 20:16; 21:26;
24:11-12,18; 25:8).

Understanding God's Promises to Israel

Second, we must recognize that *national Israel has not yet fulfilled her predicted purpose, and therefore has an abiding validity
as a people and as a national entity.* The Old Testament explains
the promises made to national Israel, while the New Testament
explains why these promises have not yet been fulfilled. Keep in
mind that Jesus and His disciples were Jews and belonged to
national Israel, as did most of the writers of the New Testament.
They shared the conviction that Israel had been chosen through
the Abrahamic Covenant (Genesis 12:3) to be God's instrument
of universal blessing: "It is you who are the sons of the prophets
and of the covenant which God made with your fathers, saying
to Abraham, 'And in your seed all the families of the earth shall

be blessed'" (Acts 3:25). This was to be fulfilled spiritually as the nation accepted its role as the "servant" of God and became a "light of the nations so that [God's] salvation may reach to the end of the earth" (Isaiah 49:6). Although Israel initially failed in this commission, through God's anointed servant, the Messiah, the nation will find redemption and fulfill its destiny (Isaiah 52:13–53:12; Luke 24:21 with John 4:42; Acts 13:23) and the Gentiles will receive God's light (cf. Matthew 4:14-16 with Isaiah 9:1-2; Matthew 12:17-21 with Isaiah 42:2-3; Luke 2:29-32 with Isaiah 42:6; 49:6) and realize the relationship of blessing promised them in the Abrahamic Covenant (Romans 11:16-18; Galatians 3:8-9,29). At this time of fulfillment, the Jewish people *as a nation* will also realize other blessings of this covenant, such as the prescribed territorial allotments given in Genesis 15:18-21.

Why make the distinction "as a nation"? Because, while *individual* Jews in this age of the church have believed and received spiritual blessings related to both the Abrahamic Covenant (Romans 2:28-29; 4:16-17; Galatians 3:6-7) and New Covenant (Hebrews 8:6-12; 10:16; 12:24), the unconditional promises of God made in both covenants was to the Jews *as a nation*. In Jeremiah 31:35-37, after Jeremiah prophesied about the conditions and characteristics of the New Covenant (verses 31-34), we read of God's confirmation of its fulfillment:

> Thus says the LORD, who gives the sun for light by day and the fixed order of the moon and the stars for light by night, who stirs up the sea so its waves roar; the LORD of hosts is His name: "If this fixed order departs from before Me," declares the LORD, "then the offspring of Israel [the Jewish people] also will cease from being a nation [the Jewish nation] before Me forever." Thus says the LORD, "If the heavens above can be measured, and the foundations of the earth searched out below, then I will also cast off all the offspring of Israel for all that they have done," declares the LORD.

In this passage the word for "nation" is the Hebrew term *goy*, a stronger term than the Hebrew word *'am*, which simply means "people." This term *goy* refers to Israel as a national entity, and indicates that the fulfillment of the New Covenant as promised in this context cannot simply be for individual Jews within the church, but contains the hope of national Jewish restoration to the Lord (spiritual) and to the Land (physical). Furthermore, the promise is clearly *unconditional* because the prophecy states it will be fulfilled despite "all that they have done" (verse 37). In the context of the book of Jeremiah, this includes the covenant unfaithfulness and spiritual apostasy for which the nation was punished with exile from the Land. By extension, it must also include the national rejection of Jesus as their Messiah, for which the nation also suffered exile (Matthew 23:37-39; Luke 19:41-44).

This understanding goes against the traditional replacement view of much of Christendom, which says that Israel, having rejected Jesus as its Messiah, has itself been rejected by God as His chosen people (nation), and the national promises formerly made to Israel have been transferred to the church. However, the apostle Paul, in the book of Romans, makes the opposite case. He states, "Then what advantage has the Jew? Or what is the benefit of circumcision [the sign of the Abrahamic Covenant]? Great in every respect....What then? If some did not believe, their unbelief will not nullify the faithfulness of God, will it?" (Romans 3:1-3). And again: "From the standpoint of the gospel they [Jews who have rejected Jesus as Messiah] are enemies for your sake, but from the standpoint of God's choice they are beloved for the sake of the fathers [the Abrahamic Covenant]; for the gifts and calling of God are irrevocable" (Romans 11:28-29). Therefore, the Jewish people, as a nation, have an abiding validity until they realize their purpose as promised by God—a purpose that He will fulfill in His time (Romans 11:25-27).

However, one point needs to be made that is often overlooked in our thinking about the Israel of the past that rejected her Messiah and the Israel of the future that will repent. There is also the

Israel of the present that, as the "remnant according to grace" (Romans 10:5), *has* embraced her Messiah. This "Israel of God" (Galatians 6:16) has continued to be the recipient of the promises of God through time and serves as a reminder that God is not yet finished with "His people whom He foreknew" (Romans 10:2). British author Rob Richards, chaplain at Lee Abbey in North Devon, explains this well when he says, "God has not replaced Israel. Quite the opposite. He had kept Israel because the remnant kept faith. Into believing Israel, we are grafted as Gentiles."[2]

Jesus understood this when, despite Jewish rejection of His messianic ministry, He told His disciples, "Truly I say to you, that you who have followed Me, in the regeneration when the Son of Man will sit on His glorious throne [the time of Israel's national restoration in the messianic kingdom, cf. Matthew 25:31-34], you shall also sit upon twelve thrones, judging the twelve tribes of Israel" (Matthew 19:28). Jesus must have believed that national Israel (the 12 tribes), though rejecting Him for the present, would continue in the divine program, for He expected Israel in the future to be under His messianic rule. Similarly, Paul, in his defense before Herod Agrippa II, declared, "I am standing trial for the hope of the promise made by God to our fathers; the promise to which our twelve tribes hope to attain, as they earnestly serve God night and day" (Acts 26:6-7). Paul did not deny to national Israel the validity of its promised hope because it had rejected its Messiah.

In like manner, Peter, during the festival of Shavuot (Feast of Pentecost), declared to the Jews who had rejected Jesus, "Repent and return, that your sins may be wiped away, in order that times of refreshing may come from the presence of the Lord; and that He may send Jesus, the Christ appointed for you, whom heaven must receive until the period of restoration of all things about which God spoke by the mouth of His holy prophets from ancient time" (Acts 3:19-21). The phrases "times of refreshing" and "the period of restoration" are both terms that refer to the future messianic kingdom. Note that Peter, in saying this, is speaking to Jews who, only weeks before, had approved Jesus' crucifixion (verses 13-15,17). Yet Peter still says this is the promise of God to them as a nation and that the coming messianic king is appointed for them (verse 20) because they are "sons of the prophets and of the covenant" (verse 25). While such statements are conditioned upon national repentance (verse 19), they nevertheless reveal the view of the apostles and the early church that national Israel had abiding validity.

Therefore, if national Israel has abiding validity, so does its Temple, which is prophesied to be central to the program of the fulfillment of Israel's national destiny under the Abrahamic Covenant (Isaiah 2:2-3; 56:6-7; 57:13c-d; Zechariah 8:3-23).

Understanding God's Promise About the Land

Third, it is necessary to realize that *the Land of Israel was chosen by God as the homeland of the Jewish people and remains their homeland today regardless of its occupation by other peoples.* This statement, while certainly echoed in the secular movement known as Zionism, is based on the biblical covenants that promised defined geographical boundaries to the Jewish people, such as found in Genesis 15:18 and 17:7-8:

> On that day the LORD made a covenant with Abram, saying, "To your descendants I have given this land. From the river of Egypt as far as the great river, the river Euphrates...."

> I will establish My covenant between Me and you and your descendants after you throughout their generations for an everlasting covenant, to be God to you and to your descendants after you. I will give to you and to your descendants after you, the land of your sojournings, all the land of Canaan, for an everlasting possession.

It is significant that although Abraham was the father of both the Jewish people (through Isaac) and the Arab people (through Ishmael), the covenant was established *only* with Isaac and his descendants (see Genesis 17:18-21). This means the Abrahamic

Covenant, and the land promise contained within it (Genesis 15:18-21), is exclusive to the Jewish people as the sole descendants of Isaac. This promise, in turn, was selectively passed on to Isaac's son Jacob (who was renamed *Israel*) and not his son Esau (Genesis 28:13-15; 35:12).

Esau and his Edomite descendants were rejected with respect to God's covenant and therefore appointed land outside the covenanted boundaries (Malachi 1:3-4). The psalmist, in Psalm 105:8-11, emphasized this chosen line when he wrote, "He has remembered His covenant forever, the word which He commanded to a thousand generations, the covenant which He made with Abraham, and His oath to Isaac. Then He confirmed it to Jacob for a statute, to Israel as an everlasting covenant, saying, 'To you I will give the land of Canaan as the portion of your inheritance.'" Later, the prophets declared that the territorial aspects of the Abrahamic Covenant (such as possession of the full extent of the promised boundaries and the universal blessing of all mankind) will be fulfilled in the last days (Isaiah 2:2-4; Hosea 3:4-5; cf. Ezekiel 37:24-28; Zechariah 8:7-8,11-13).

When Jesus and the New Testament writers acknowledged the Abrahamic Covenant, they also recognized the covenant's land provisions. So while the New Testament makes no direct statement concerning the Jewish people's inheritance of the Land of Israel, such is implied in its acceptance of the Abrahamic Covenant. We should also note that the duration of the land covenant is stated to be "everlasting" (Genesis 17:8) and "for all time" (Deuteronomy 4:40). This indicates Israel's possession of the Land was not meant to be temporary but remains in force today. To be sure, Israel has sinned and been punished with exile from the Land, but the unconditional nature of the Abrahamic Covenant requires that God's faithfulness ultimately overcome this problem and make possible a complete fulfillment for all the covenant people in the covenant Land (cf. Ezekiel 36:16-38; 37:1-14,21-28). Thus, the modern-day claim by the Jewish people to the Land of Israel rests on an ancient and unchanging divine promise.

In like manner, the future Temple, prophesied to be built in the Land during the last days, requires that the Jewish people be at home in their Land and in possession of the city of Jerusalem and the Temple Mount. In terms of the present preparation for the fulfillment of this prophecy, the wars between Israel and the Arabs in 1948 and 1967 resulted in the modern State of Israel (for the first time since the loss of its independence and the destruction of Jerusalem and the Temple in A.D. 70) regaining sovereignty over its historic homeland (including Judea and Samaria) and Jerusalem with the Temple Mount. The Davidic Covenant, which will be fulfilled during the messianic age, joins the prophecies of a restored Israel and Davidic dynasty with that of a restored Temple and priesthood. For example, in Jeremiah 33:14-18 we read about the promised Messiah who will accomplish this restoration of the government and the Sanctuary:

> "Behold, days are coming," declares the LORD, "when I will fulfill the good word which I have spoken concerning the house of Israel and the house of Judah. In those days and at that time I will cause a righteous Branch of David [the Messiah] to spring forth; and He shall execute justice and righteousness on the earth. In those days Judah will be saved and Jerusalem will dwell in safety; and this is the name by which she shall be called: the LORD is our righteousness." For thus says the LORD, "David shall never lack a man to sit on the throne of the house of Israel [2 Samuel 7:16]; and the Levitical priests shall never lack a man before Me to offer burnt offerings, to burn grain offerings, and to prepare sacrifices continually."

This promise of the fulfillment of the Davidic Covenant, like that of the New Covenant, is guaranteed by a repetition in verses 20-22, 25-26 of the unconditional pledge made previously in Jeremiah 31:35-37. Therefore, the Promised Land must be preserved for the fulfillment of these promises to its people and must be recognized as the perpetual homeland of the Jewish people today and forever.

Understanding Prophecy and God's Timetable

Fourth, with respect to the present condition of the Jewish nation (unbelief) and the secular nature of the Jewish state (unspiritual), we need to recognize that *the fulfillment of prophecy does not depend on human faith or spirituality, but on the eternal plan and promise of God.* The prophet Zechariah affirmed this when he wrote concerning the fulfillment of God's prophecy at the time of the building of the Second Temple: "'Not by might nor by power, but My Spirit,' says the LORD of hosts" (Zechariah 4:6). Likewise, in the New Testament, the apostle Paul summed up Israel's election in God's purpose when he declared: "So then it does not depend on the man who wills or the man who runs, but on God who has mercy" (Romans 9:16). Today, many Orthodox Jews believe the prophetic program for Israel has not yet been realized because the State of Israel is a secular state or because there is a low level of spirituality among Jews in general or because not enough Jews are committed to rebuilding the Temple.

Among Christians, it is often stated that because the Jews have not yet believed in Jesus as their Messiah (returned spiritually to the Lord), their return physically to the Land has no prophetic significance. However, the unconditional nature of the covenants regarding the Land instructs us that God's program, and especially His prophetic program, does not depend on human initiative, as though almighty God were waiting on mortal man to do something before He could act, but is determined by His own sovereign plan (Jeremiah 17:5-7; Ezekiel 36:22-28).

A statement of this fact—in the context of Israel's national restoration—was made in the New Testament by Jesus to His disciples on the Mount of Olives. In Acts 1:6-7 we read, "So when they had come together, they [the disciples] were asking Him [Jesus], saying, 'Lord, is it at this time [after the completion of spiritual redemption for Israel] You are restoring the kingdom to Israel?' He said to them, 'It is not for you to know times or epochs which the Father has fixed by His own authority....'" In other words, God the Father and Jesus were committed to act within a predetermined plan (which included a spiritual outreach to Israel and the nations during the present age, Acts 1:8). The Old Testament confirms this design for us in its presentation of the Abrahamic Covenant as unilateral and unconditional—terms that indicate its fulfillment depends upon God, not man.

The biblical prophets emphasized this aspect of the Abrahamic Covenant to Israel when, as a result of violating the Mosaic Covenant (which, by contrast, was multilateral and conditional), the nation was punished by exile from the Land (see Deuteronomy 4:26-27,40; Jeremiah 7:3-7). There are certainly conditional aspects in unconditional covenants, but the conditions (such as obedience) relate to the *temporal* fulfillment of the covenant by man, not the *eternal* fulfillment by God. This is because, as Deuteronomy 29–30 explains, in God's plan, the Land and Israel are joined in final fulfillment. Israel's disobedience and exile is predicted (Deuteronomy 29:30:2-4), but will be followed with an equally predicted return and restoration (Deuteronomy 30:1-10). To reiterate, the Abrahamic Covenant is unconditional because God initiated it and has personally assumed the obligation for its fulfillment. Restoration to the Land is therefore possible, for even sin on the part of the Jewish people cannot keep the promise of the covenant from being fulfilled (see Deuteronomy 4:29-31; Isaiah 41:8-9; Jeremiah 30:2-3,8-11; 31:35-37; 33:23-26; Ezekiel 36:18-28). These texts reveal that Israel will one day fulfill the conditional terms of the covenant because in the last days, every Israelite will "know the LORD" (Jeremiah 31:34) for God will have given them "a new heart and...a new spirit" and will put His Spirit within them and cause them to walk in His ways (Ezekiel 36:26-27).

Again, we have a precedent established for the literal fulfillment of yet unfulfilled prophecies by past-fulfilled prophecies such as Jeremiah 29:10-14, in which the Lord, at His appointed time, moved the Jewish people in the Babylonian captivity toward the repentance necessary for their restoration from exile:

> For thus says the LORD, "When seventy years have been
> completed for Babylon, I will visit you and fulfill My good
> word to you, to bring you back to this place. For I know
> the plans that I have for you," declares the LORD, "plans for
> welfare and not for calamity to give you a future and a
> hope. Then you will call upon Me and come and pray to
> Me, and I will listen to you.…and I will restore your for-
> tunes and will gather you…and will bring you back to the
> place [the Land of Israel] from where I sent you into exile."

As we keep in mind the plan of God, which accomplishes His purposes according to His timetable, let's now consider the present-day actions of some Israelis (as well as of some Christians) calling for the State of Israel to effect legislation in favor of Jewish prayers on the Temple Mount, to reinforce its sovereignty over the site, or even build a Third Temple. Should this be viewed as a provocation that will somehow force the coming of the end of days, as an Israeli journalist has feared?[3] If the Land of Israel, the city of Jerusalem, and the Temple Mount are in fact part and parcel to the fulfillment of Israel's purpose to bless the world, then actions that favor this purpose cannot be responsibly opposed by believers in the biblical prophecies. Moreover, no such actions in and of themselves force a premature conclusion to the present conflict, since the outcome of these events will lead ultimately to the fulfillment of God's prophetic promises, which are determined by His sovereign plan and purpose.

Therefore, we should recognize that no political action, however zealous or provocative, could affect the fulfillment of prophetic events. This is not to say that present political events, especially in the Middle East, might not reflect the progressive outworking of God's prophetic program as the stage is being set for future prophetic fulfillments.

Understanding Israel's Place in Prophecy

Fifth, and finally, it is necessary to understand that *the modern State of Israel is a part of the future fulfillment of the prophetic plan.* God's earthly program in the past focused on Israel with respect to its promise as a people, a place, and a purpose that would remain in perpetuity (Genesis 12:2-7). Prophetically, this program and focus continues into the future, for God has stated that He is not yet finished with Israel (Jeremiah 33:14-18; Romans 11:11-15,23-24). Because God controls history and is directing it toward the fulfillment of His program, events throughout history related to the Jewish people and their Land have prophetic significance, even if these events do not yet completely fulfill any specific prophecy. Just as the dispersion of the Jewish people among the nations (Diaspora) over the past two millennia has been deemed prophetic (of God's judgment), so the return of the Jewish people to Israel over the past century to reestablish an independent nation in the Land must also be considered prophetic (of God's restoration). And, in the same way, just as the dispersion occurred in successive stages over time (722 B.C., 586 B.C., A.D. 70, A.D. 115, et al.), so may the restoration also occur in stages today and in the future (before the Tribulation, e.g., 1897, 1948, 1967; and at the end of the Tribulation).

Since the loss of Jewish sovereignty over Israel in the first century A.D., Bible students have expected prophetic texts concerning Israel to have a literal fulfillment, that the Jewish people would have to return to their ancient homeland, "the Land of Israel," regain their national status as "the people of Israel," and exist in an adversarial relationship with the Gentile nations so that God could demonstrate He was "the Holy One in Israel" (Ezekiel 39:7). Furthermore, Jerusalem, as the central city of prophecy, would have to share in this fulfillment, returning to Jewish sovereignty but as the subject of international controversy.

The prophecy of Gog and Magog in Ezekiel 38–39 well illustrates these particular expectations. Set in an eschatological context (Ezekiel 33–48), the text specifically states that its fulfillment "shall come about in the last days" (38:16). At this time the people of Israel are described as living in "the cities of Israel" in "the land of Israel" (38:14,18-19; 39:9). According to Ezekiel 37:25 this Land is "the land that I [God] gave to Jacob [Israel] My servant, in which your fathers lived." Ezekiel 38:8 also notes that the Jewish people who had returned to the Land had been "gathered from many nations." By contrast, the historic restoration (regathering) of Jews from exile in 538 B.C. was from only one nation (Babylon). Only in our modern period have we witnessed a regathering of Jews to Israel from "many nations."

Moreover, in Ezekiel's Gog and Magog prophecy, the mountainous region that extends the length of the country is identified as "the mountains of Israel" (39:2,4,17). It was not until after the Six-Day War of 1967 that this region again became a part of the territory of the modern State of Israel and could be properly called "the mountains of Israel." Up to 1967, this region was under a succession of foreign rulers, and Jordan last controlled it from 1948–1967. Ezekiel 38:8,12 even notes that this mountainous land—before the Jewish people returned to it and restored it—had been under "the sword" (foreign dominion) and "a continual waste." History affirms that under foreign domination, and especially during the 400 years of Ottoman Turkish rule, the once-fertile mountain region (particularly in the north) had been denuded and had eroded into a wasteland.

Furthermore, it is significant that this territory of biblical Judea and Samaria, known today as the West Bank, is, like the rest of the Land of Israel, in a state of contention with the surrounding nations and even the nations of the world. Ezekiel 38–39 is a prophecy that uniquely details a future invasion of Israel by a huge alliance of foreign nations (38:3-13). Interestingly, Ezekiel's prophecy also provides the detail that at the time of this invasion, the people of Israel are living "securely, all of them" in a "land of unwalled villages" (38:8,11). This would not have been true of ancient Israel, where cities were typically surrounded by a defensive wall. But in our modern era, Israel's military has afforded the nation unparalleled security, and modern methods of warfare have made walled cities unnecessary—despite the new security fence (which does not affect this unwalled status).

Even though history confirms that the conditions predicted by Ezekiel are those that have characterized the birth of and continue to depict the current status of the modern Jewish state, this text cannot be pressed to reveal more than the conditions that must be present in Israel before final fulfillment is possible. How, then, can we know that the *present* State of Israel is the *same* Israel Ezekiel and the prophets predicted would exist in the last days? The answer may be provided in Isaiah 11:11-12, where the temporal order of predicted regatherings to Israel from the nations would seem to require that the present-day Israel is the Israel that will experience prophetic fulfillment. This passage reads:

> Then it will happen on that day that the Lord will again recover [regather] the second time with His hand the remnant of His people [the Jewish people] who will remain from Assyria [Greater Syria], Egypt, Pathros [Upper Egypt], Cush [Ethiopia], Elam [Iran], Shinar [Iraq], Hamath [Lesser Syria], and from the islands of the sea [Mediterranean coastlands]. And He will lift up a standard for the nations and assemble the banished ones of Israel, and will gather the dispersed of Judah from the four corners of the earth [universal regathering].

The context of this passage is eschatological, the setting being the ultimate period of fulfillment in the messianic kingdom. Verses 1-5 describe the second advent of Messiah in judgment to rule the earth, verses 6-9 depict the restoration and peaceful conditions under the New Covenant, and verse 10 introduces Israel's national repentance and return to the Messiah. Verses 11-12 continue this theme, revealing the time and extent of the end-time regathering. Notice that the universal regathering to the Lord is said to occur when "the Lord will again recover *the second time* with His hand" (emphasis added). This "second time" is obviously the "last time," as this restoration is the final one for Israel. If the "second time" is the "last time," then when is the "first time" implied in the text? Like the "second time," it too must be a time of international Jewish regathering to Israel by God's hand.

If we go back into Israel's history of regathering we find an exodus from Egypt and a restoration from Babylon. However, neither of these regatherings can satisfy the specific geographic and temporal conditions of this prophetic text because they were regatherings from only *one* place (not from "the four corners of the earth"), and each of them had a subsequent exile follow their return. How many regatherings can you have between a "first regathering" and a "second regathering"? The answer is none! According to Matthew 24:30-31, the last regathering of Israel to the Lord will be in national repentance at the time of His coming at the end of the Tribulation. This last time or "second time" regathering (according to Isaiah) is followed by the establishment of the kingdom for Israel and the judgment of the nations (Matthew 25:31-46), ending forever Israel's fear of exile. Notice that the "second time" regathering as a time of repentance indicates that prior to this regathering, national Israel existed in a state of unbelief (cf. Zechariah 12:10-14; 14:4; Romans 11:25-27). Moreover, the context makes it apparent that the nation was already in the Land of Israel. Therefore, the "first time" regathering must be sought immediately before this in a time in which Israel has returned to the Land in unbelief.

This fits the pattern revealed in many prophetic passages of the regathering of national Israel taking place in two phases or stages: the first to the Land before the Tribulation in unbelief, and the second to the Lord before the Millennium in belief. The first regathering of Jews to the Land of Israel in unbelief, and their reconstitution as a nation since their exile among the nations 2000 years ago, is the modern one.[4] And since there can be no further dispersion before the "second time" regathering, the present State of Israel *must* be the national Israel that will remain in the Land until it experiences the completion of physical regathering and the climactic spiritual regathering.

Morover, this interpretation requires us to accept that the modern return of Israel to the Land (even in unbelief) is a divinely ordained event ("by His hand") as a part of God's prophetic program. This means that despite the sometimes unjust actions of the Jewish state or the perceived arrogance of her leaders, as national Israel, the Jewish people are still the "people of God" and destined to be regathered again to God at the return of their Messiah. To be sure, Israel must also pass through the time of Jacob's trouble (Jeremiah 30:7), yet she will also inherit the kingdom promised by the prophets. For this reason, we who understand the plan of God as revealed in the prophetic Scriptures must respect His purpose for the Jewish people and pray for His will to be done through them, for His plan will result in rich blessings for the world (Genesis 12:3; cf. Romans 11:12,15).

We must recognize, however, that even among prophetic futurists there are those who doubt the prophetic significance of the present-day Jewish state. Objections range from an agnosticism (we can't know whether the Jewish return to Israel at this time is relevant to future fulfillment) to specific questions about the nature of the modern return and the current spiritual condition of the Jewish people. In relation to the agnostic objection, because futurism places prophetic fulfillment for Israel in the future (the last days/end times), and dispensational futurism in particular places fulfillment in an age distinct from and following that of the church (after the rapture of the church), there is a hesitancy to view current events with respect to Israel as having prophetic significance. However, significance does not require present fulfillment but only present *preparation* for fulfillment, for as has often been observed, (future) prophetic events can cast their shadows behind them (into the present).

In relation to the specific questions, objections are often made that the modern return of the Jewish people has been partial (part of the Jewish people to part of the Land), and is secular rather than spiritual in nature. However, it is not necessary that all of the Jewish people return to the Land at once as a singular event, for as we have shown, regathering appears to occur in stages. Reiterating this view, two regatherings of the Jewish people seem to be delineated in the prophetic texts—one before the Tribulation, and one before the Millennium. The first of these appears to be primarily a physical regathering to the Land, while the second appears to be characterized by a spiritual regathering to the Lord. If this first regathering is in spiritual *unbelief,* then we should expect it to be a secular and political movement, as is the modern Zionist movement that led to the establishment of the Jewish state. Furthermore, the lack of a spiritual motive for returning to the biblical Land would produce only a partial physical return from the Diaspora—that is, it would be comprised mostly of Jews from lands where they experienced persecution and forced exile, as has been the cause of immigration by the majority of Jewish immigrants to modern Israel.

Even so, the limited extent of this first regathering can still be demonstrated to have geographically taken place from "the four corners of the earth." The second regathering, then, which would follow a time of worldwide Jewish persecution during the Tribulation, will result not only in Israel's seeking physical deliverance but also spiritual (Luke 21:25-28).

With all this in mind, we are now ready to discover what the Temple is all about—its significant role in Israel's past and the central place it occupies in God's prophetic plan for the future.

My hope is that this overview of prophetic precepts will help you understand the purpose and relevancy of investigating the current struggle for the Temple Mount as well as the practical encouragement this struggle holds for those who look for the outworking of God's program within world affairs. In the next chapter, we will consider the purpose for which the Temple existed in the past, and the reason why its restoration today is so fervently sought by some and violently opposed by others.

2

Temple 101

For there was a tabernacle prepared, the outer one, in which were the lampstand and the table and the sacred bread; this is called the holy place. And behind the second veil, there was a tabernacle, which is called the Holy of Holies, having a golden altar of incense and the ark of the covenant...and above it were the cherubim of glory overshadowing the mercy seat; but of these things we cannot now speak in detail.

HEBREWS 9:2-5

On the eve of Passover in traditional Jewish homes, the family gathers together for the Passover Seder, a meal that commemorates the historical event of the Jewish people's exodus from Egyptian bondage to the Promised Land 3500 years ago. The meal begins with the head of the household reading the Haggadah, a retelling of the biblical account of the people's oppression and their deliverance from the Egyptian Pharaoh. This retelling of the story is accompanied by symbolic activities performed at the table. As the meal progresses, a time-honored ritual occurs in which the youngest son asks a series of four questions. These questions, elicited by the symbolic activities performed up to that point, set the stage for the explanation of the exodus as told through the Haggadah. The first of these questions is, "What makes this night different from all other nights?" Paraphrasing this initial question in relation to the Temple, we might ask, "What makes this place different from all other places?"

In answer to this question, let me invite you to participate in an introductory course on this subject: Temple 101. The logical starting point is to begin at the beginning by first considering the most basic concept concerning the Temple: its meaning.

The Meaning of *Temple*

In defining the concept of a *temple,* the languages of the Bible employ various terms. The general Hebrew term for *temple,* although rarely used in the Bible, is the word *hekal.*[1] This term probably derived from an original Sumerian word (*e-gal*), meaning "big house."[2] From another Sumerian term, *temen,*[3] comes the Old Greek term *temenos* ("precinct"), which denotes "a piece of land marked off from common uses and dedicated to a god."[4] These terms define a special place of theophany where a deity appeared as revealer, healer, or giver of fertility, but *did not dwell there.* Thus, the term may be generally used with reference to any ancient Near Eastern center of worship, whether pagan or Israelite. In this sense the term could be rendered in English as "shrine," and today has this meaning in modern Hebrew, as, for example, in *Hekal Ha-Sefer* ("the Shrine of the Book")—the name of Israel's museum of the Dead Sea Scrolls.

The Bible, however, preferred to describe the Jerusalem Temple as *Beit 'Adonai* (the "house of the Lord"), or *Beit 'Elohim* (the "house of God").[5] This expression better denotes the basic idea of the Temple as "a place where God dwells," a connotation expressed by the earliest Hebrew term for God's abode, *Mishkan* ("dwelling place," "Tabernacle").[6] Another biblical Hebrew term for the Temple (and the one used today in modern Hebrew)[7] is *Beit Hamikdash* ("the Sanctuary")—literally "house of holiness," but usually translated as "sanctuary," or simply *Mikdash* ("Holy [Place]," "Sanctuary").[8] This latter term appears in the Old Testament primarily with reference to the only legitimate Israelite

Temple in Jerusalem (Psalm 74:7; 96:6; Isaiah 63:18; Lamentations 1:10; 2:7,20; Ezekiel 5:11; 9:6). In this regard it may denote either the entire Tabernacle compound (Leviticus 19:30; 26:2), the entire district of the Temple (Ezekiel 43:21; 44:1,5,7-8), or exclusively the Holy of Holies (Leviticus 16:33). However, it could also be used of rival Israelite temples both inside and outside the Land (Isaiah 16:12; Amos 7:9,13).

The Septuagint (a Greek translation of the Old Testament) follows the Hebrew Bible in its understanding of *Beit Hamikdash* ("Sanctuary") by its selective use of the term *naos*, a noun derived from the verb *naio* ("to dwell" or "inhabit"). In classical Greek, *naos* referred to the "abode of the gods," with specific reference to the innermost part of a shrine, which contained the image of a god.[9] The Septuagint uses this term 55 out of the 61 times it appears to translate the Hebrew *hekal*, the nonspecific sense of a "palace" or "a temple." If the Septuagint had wished to indicate "*a* temple" in general, it might have used the Greek term *heiron* ("holy place").[10] As a result of this usage by the Greek Old Testament, the term takes on a technical significance referring exclusively to the "Temple of God" in Jerusalem.[11] This usage was adopted by the Greek New Testament[12] and often denotes the inner part of the Temple (the Holy of Holies) in distinction to the outer part of the Temple (the Temple complex) by the more common Greek word *heiron*, the general term for a sacred edifice. An example of this in the New Testament can be seen in *naos* being used as a metaphor for the church or the believer's body as "a temple." In these two cases, the term is used because the emphasis in the text is on the indwelling presence of God (within the Holy of Holies), which corresponds to the indwelling Holy Spirit. Further, in the book of Revelation, *naos* is used of both the earthly and heavenly temples, where in the latter reference, the Holy of Holies is usually indicated by God's presence, the mention of incense, or the Ark of the Covenant (Revelation 11:19; 15:8; 21:22).[13]

Our English Bible versions do not adequately reflect these distinctions that are apparent in the original biblical languages. They translate the primary Hebrew and Greek terms by the word "temple," which is itself derived from the Latin *templum* after the Greek *temenos*. While in most cases the English translation "temple" refers to the Jerusalem Temple, I prefer to capitalize this reference to distinguish it from references to rival Jewish and non-Jewish temples.[14] This capitalization will also be used with all references to the Jerusalem Temple as well as to the heavenly Temple and the Tabernacle (which, as a portable structure, was later incorporated into the Temple). Therefore, the term *Temple* has in view the permanent aspect of God's dwelling with His people, which includes all intermediate and future forms.

A History of the Past-Days' Temple

The history of the Jewish Temple begins with God's choice of Mount Moriah in Jerusalem for an altar and a place for the testing of Abraham's faith with his son Isaac, the heir of the Abrahamic Covenant (Genesis 22:2). Mount Moriah was established as the

Photo by author

The future site of the Temple in the days of King David—the barren hill above the city is Mount Moriah, where Solomon built the First Temple (10th century B.C.).

place where God would provide for His people through His provision of a sacrifice in substitution for Isaac, thus preserving the boy's life, upon which depended the future of the Jewish nation (Genesis 22:13-18). Next, the Lord delivers Israel from its bondage in Egypt and instructs Moses to take the people to the place established for His Sanctuary (Exodus 15:17). At Mount Sinai, Moses receives the heavenly blueprint for the Sanctuary and its vessels (Exodus 25:8-9,40). The Tabernacle is constructed as a portable and temporary dwelling place for God's presence (Exodus 40:36-38; cf. 2 Samuel 7:6) and remains Israel's Sanctuary for 485 years through the periods of the conquest of Canaan and the settlement in the Land.

This period of settlement ends in the time of King David, who destroys Israel's enemies and captures Jerusalem, making possible a political and spiritual center for the nation in the place of promise. David's desire to build the First Temple qualifies him to begin the financial preparations for the project (2 Samuel 7:2; 1 Chronicles 17:1; 29), but he was not allowed to build it because as a warrior, he was not a fitting symbol of God's peaceful program (1 Kings 3:3-14; 5:3). That privilege went to David's son Solomon. In contrast to the Tabernacle and Tent of Meeting,

Used with permission from Alexander Schick *Bibelausstellung Sylt*

Model of the Tabernacle, Timna Park, Israel.

Solomon's Temple was to be a *permanent* structure and habitation for God's glory (2 Chronicles 7:16). However, it seems that when the First Temple was constructed, the Tabernacle/Tent of Meeting was included within it (1 Kings 8:4; 2 Chronicles 5:5), probably in a chamber beneath the Holy of Holies.

Despite the plan that the Temple in Jerusalem was to be permanent, its existence was conditioned upon the nation's obedience (1 Kings 9:4-9). This meant that throughout Israel's history, the Temple could be removed and returned as often as Israel was fickle or faithful to the covenant. Spiritual decline in the form of idolatry, apostasy, and Sabbath violations began in the time of Solomon (1 Kings 11:1-13; 2 Chronicles 36:21) and climaxed in the time of Manasseh (2 Kings 21:7-14). As a result, after 374 years as Israel's Sanctuary, the First Temple was destroyed by the Babylonians in 586 B.C.

After 70 years of Babylonian exile, a Jewish remnant of about 50,000 returned to Jerusalem under Zerubbabel the priest to begin building the Second Temple (Ezra 1–6), which was completed and dedicated in 515 B.C. After another 500 years, the Second Temple was in severe need of repairs. The reigning Judean king, Herod the Great, refurbished it completely, doubling its height and greatly expanding its size. Yet despite its new appearance, it was still subject to the stipulations of the Mosaic covenant, which pronounced "curses" for Israel's disobedience. Therefore, the sins of Israel again doomed the Temple to divine judgment, and Jesus prophesied its imminent destruction (Matthew 24:2; Mark 13:2; Luke 21:6,20-24). The sentence was carried out 586 years after the dedication of the original Second Temple and 76 years after its reconstruction, in A.D. 70, by the Tenth Roman Legion under the command of Titus, son of the emperor Vespasian.

Although the Jewish people attempted to rebuild the Temple a number of times over the next 568 years, none were successful or lasting. Jerusalem was conquered by Islam in A.D. 638 and in 691, a Muslim shrine known as the Dome of the Rock was erected

Used with permission from World of the Bible Ministries

Model of the Second Temple (Herodian Temple) at the Holyland Hotel, Jerusalem.

upon the site of the Temple ruins. In 715 a Muslim mosque known as the Al-Aqsa Mosque was constructed at the southern end of the Temple Mount compound. Other mosques, prayer niches, and administrative buildings were added over the next 1200 years, turning the Jewish Temple Mount into the Muslim *Haram el-Sharif* ("Noble Enclosure"). In 1948 Israel became an independent nation again after 1878 years, and in 1967, Israel recaptured the site of the Temple Mount in eastern Jerusalem. Although the State of Israel maintained sovereignty over the Temple Mount it returned the administration of the site to the Jordanian-controlled *Waqf,* or Islamic Trust. In a compromise agreement between the Israeli authorities and the Muslim authorities, the site would be opened to visitors for tourist purposes, but no non-Muslim religious expression would be permitted at the site.

This status quo prevailed for 33 years, until in September 2000, the Palestinian-controlled Waqf (which took over administration of the site in 1994) banned Jews from entrance to the Temple Mount because Knesset member Ariel Sharon led a delegation of

Photo courtesy of Israel Government Press Office

Aerial photograph of the present-day Temple Mount with the Muslim Dome of the Rock at the center and the Al-Aqsa Mosque in the upper left corner of the platform.

Israelis into the Al-Aqsa compound, leading (according to the Palestinians) to the Al-Aqsa Intifada. As a result of security concerns associated with the Waqf's decision, the Israeli government extended the closure of the Mount to all non-Muslim visitors. In June 2003 the Israeli authorities reopened the site after a 33-month hiatus, permitting restricted visits by police-escorted tourist groups, in spite of protests by the Waqf. However, the ban continued on non-Muslim entrance to the Dome of the Rock and the Al-Aqsa Mosque.

A History of the Last-Days' Temple

The prophecy of a future Jewish Temple in Jerusalem is a key part of the biblical restoration promise made to national Israel for the last days. This promise was made by prophets who prophesied at the close of the First Temple period (Isaiah 1:24–2:4; 4:2-6; 11:1–12:6; 25–27; 32; 34–35; 40–66; Jeremiah 30–33; Ezekiel 36–48; Amos 9:11-15; Joel 2:28–3:21; Micah 4–5; 7:11-20; Zephaniah 3:9-20), and was renewed by the prophets who prophesied after the return from captivity (cf. Daniel 9–12; Haggai 2:5-9; Zechariah 8–14; Malachi 3–4). Therefore, just as the Second Temple was a restoration edifice to Israel as a result of national repentance, so the Third Temple will be a restoration edifice once a new national repentance is secured (Zechariah 12:10–13:2; Romans 11:25-27).

In continuity with the Old Testament promise of Israel's restoration, Jesus and the New Testament writers likewise expected a rebuilt Temple in Jerusalem as part of the eschatological restoration program. A future Temple may be implicit in New Testament texts that addressed Israel's national restoration (cf. Acts 3:19-26; Romans 11:1-32), but in passages that concern a Third Temple, the attention centers on the preparation for restoration and the conclusion of the period of Gentile domination. We also see in the Bible that during this time, the Third Temple is a focal point of the prophetic warnings of the end of the age (Matthew 24:15; Mark 13:15; 2 Thessalonians 2:3-4; Revelation 11:1-2). Based on Daniel's warning of the Temple's desecration in his 70-weeks prophecy (Daniel 9:27), Jesus reveals the Temple to be the signal event marking the transition into the Great Tribulation (Matthew 24:15; Mark 13:14). The apostle Paul also builds upon Daniel's prophecy in his depiction of the Tribulation Temple's desecration by the "man of sin" (2 Thessalonians 2:4). Similarly, the apostle John, who wrote concerning the coming Antichrist (1 John 2:18), describes the desolation of the Temple courts by Antichrist's Gentile forces during the last half of the Tribulation period (Revelation 11:1-2).

The future Temple is presented by the biblical writers as existing in "the last days," "the end time" and "the Day of the Lord." This is a period commencing with the seventieth week of Daniel's prophecy (which begins the Tribulation period) through the duration of the messianic kingdom. As the Temple is the symbol of both Israel's national and spiritual existence, this future program involves both desecration during the Tribulation (Isaiah 66:1-5; Daniel 9:27; 11:36-45) and spiritual restoration during the Millennium (Isaiah 2:2-3; 56:6-7; Ezekiel 37:25-28; 40–48; Haggai 2:7-9; Zechariah 6:12-15). Specific texts that speak about the Millennial

Temple are Isaiah 2:2-4, Jeremiah 33:18; 60:7,13, Ezekiel 37:26-28, 40–48, Haggai 2:9, and Zechariah 6:12-13; 14:20.

It is necessary to distinguish, in prophetic contexts that predict the Third Temple, whether the Temple in view is that which will be built in the "time of Jacob's trouble" (Jeremiah 30:7 KJV), a period known in the New Testament as the Tribulation (Mark 13:19), or that which will be built in the millennial kingdom (the time of Israel's national restoration). The Tribulation Temple will apparently be built by Orthodox Jews (Isaiah 66:1-6) and will be desecrated by the Antichrist (Daniel 9:27; 11:36-45), who will be judged by the Messiah when He comes to purify His Temple (Malachi 3:1-4; Revelation 19:19-20). This Temple may be destroyed at this time by the earthquake that splits the Mount of Olives (which overlooks the Temple Mount) in an east-west direction (Zechariah 14:4).

The Millennial Temple will be built by the Messiah, after His coming judgment on the nations (Zechariah 6:12-13; 14:3-4), as well as by redeemed Jews, and as a particular sign of restoration, representatives from the Gentile nations will help as well (Zechariah 6:15; Haggai 2:7; cf. Isaiah 60:10). It will be distinguished from the Tribulation Temple not only by its greater size but also by its greater glory, as the Shekinah glory of God will be restored to it (Ezekiel 43:1-7; cf. Ezekiel 10:4,18-19; 11:22-23) and the Gentile nations will worship in it (Isaiah 56:6-7; 60:6; Zephaniah 3:10; Zechariah 2:11; 8:22; 14:16-19). These physical and spiritual traits also distinguish the Millennial Temple from any previous historical Temple (the First Temple and Second Temple lacked Gentile worshipers, and the Second Temple lacked the Shekinah glory). In addition, the topographical and architectural dimensions and rituals of the Millennial Temple are historically unique (Ezekiel 40–48; Zechariah 14:10-11).

This Temple, around which the millennial saints are encamped (Ezekiel 45:1-7; 48; Revelation 20:7) will be attacked at the end of the Millennium (Revelation 20:7-9), but there is no indication that it will ever be destroyed. This may be because in the past, the destruction of the Temple was a sign of divine judgment, and this Temple will exist at a time when the curse has been lifted (Isaiah 65:25) and when a New Covenant will have replaced the old Mosaic Covenant (which contained the punishments for violation of the covenant), and because Israel's new nature will prevent it from sinning against the Lord and incurring His wrath (Jeremiah 31:31-34; Ezekiel 36:25-28; 37:23,26-28). At the conclusion of the Millennium, however, the Millennial Temple apparently will be removed with everything in the old order when a new earth is created (Isaiah 65:17; 2 Peter 3:10-13).

Although the New Testament does not deal directly with the Millennial Temple, it is implied in contexts where Jesus cites an Old Testament text concerning the future Temple (Matthew 23:39; Mark 11:17) and is assumed both in contexts that touch upon the period of Israel's restoration (Matthew 19:28; 25:31; Acts 1:6-7; 3:19-21) and which speak of the future millennial kingdom (Revelation 20:1-9). With this general survey of the Temple through time, we are now prepared to consider the specific purpose which the Temple serves in the divine plan for the ages.

3

The Purpose of the Temple

The key to understanding the Holy Temple's functioning in all its detail is a concept which takes in an entire worldview. The Temple is a microcosm, a cosmic blueprint. Within the Holy Temple, all forces unite to acknowledge Him who brought them all into being as the only reality, the Supreme Force which drives the universe.

RABBI CHAIM RICHMAN

For most Jews today, the Temple is simply a long-lost relic of antiquity, a historical footnote reminding them of a primitive period in their people's past when bloody sacrifices paved the way to a bloodthirsty God who punished them with epidemics and exile if they did not obey. For many Christians, the Temple is nothing more than a theological object lesson of Israel's sin—a shadow whose purpose has been eclipsed by a greater spiritual substance. For Muslims, the Temple, if it ever existed except as Israeli propaganda, was removed because of Israel's corruption and replaced by Islam as the final and pure revelation of God.

Unfortunately, these views represent the perspectives of the best-educated individuals in each of those religious groups, for the average Jew, Christian, or Muslim has little or no idea about the basic purpose, plan, or history of the past Temple, and even less concerning the prophecy of a future one. However, if God has a future for the nation of Israel in His plan, and that plan is to be realized in the same place as it was in the past, then the Temple, as a prominent symbol of that nation's past failure, should be expected to be a part of its future restoration. This indicates that God has had and still has a purpose for the Temple— a purpose that will conflict with all plans not submitted to His own and therefore bring about the battle for the last days' Temple. And what exactly is God's purpose for the Temple? A good place to begin is to look at God's plan for the Temple as first revealed to Moses.

The Plan for the Temple

God's plan for the Temple was first revealed at the foot of Mount Sinai. Concerning this historical event and its connection with the Temple, Rabbi Shmuel Bar Abba explained in the Jewish Midrash: "The Holy One, Blessed be He, desired to have an abode below, just as He has one above…and when Israel stood before Him at Sinai, He told them: 'There is only one reason I delivered you out of Egypt—in order for you to erect for Me a Tabernacle so that My presence will dwell amongst you'" (*Tanhuma Bechukoti* 65). The biblical text behind this statement is Exodus 25:8: "Let them construct a sanctuary for Me, that I may dwell among them."

As the Israelites camped at the foot of Mount Sinai and saw the all-consuming sacred fire atop the mountain, they became fearful and wondered, *How could mere man co-exist with such a God?* The fear the Israelites felt came from an innate consciousness that their lack of holiness distanced them from the Creator, whose very being defined holiness. But God's command had included the means for God and man to co-exist, and that means was to build a sanctuary that would keep God in their midst yet keep them from being consumed. With the construction of this holy structure the long exile from God's presence was ended, and a theocratic nation could exist with God ruling over His people.

This was God's plan for the Temple from the beginning—the restoration of a relationship so that a kingdom of priests could be formed to reflect God's holiness on earth (Leviticus 11:44-45; 19:2; 20:7). With this in mind, let us next consider…

The Purpose of the Temple

When King David charged the people of Israel concerning the preparations for the First Temple, he declared "…the work is great; for the temple is not for man, but for the LORD God" (1 Chronicles 29:1). This statement reflects the Israelite distinction that while the Temple would certainly be a place where the needs of man were met, it was first and foremost a witness to the fact of God's existence, His covenant with Israel, and His purpose through the nation of Israel as a kingdom of priests to manifest God's glory to the world. In order to fulfill this holy mandate, the Jewish people had to fulfill the terms of the covenant given to them (see 1 Kings 2:3). The commandments contained in this covenant have been numbered at 613. In order to accomplish these commandments in their entirety, the Temple and its service was required. Because at least one-third of these commandments depend upon a functioning Temple for their completion, one purpose of the Temple was to enable Israel to fulfill its function to be a kingdom of priests. In like manner, the prophecies of Israel's restoration, at which time the nation will fulfill its purpose to bless the world, depend on the existence of the Temple. This is particularly true about the messianic prophecies that describe the Messiah building the Temple (Zechariah 6:12-13) and coming to His Temple (Malachi 3:1).

In Scripture, we can discern at least eight aspects of God's purpose for the Temple:

1. *A Station of the Divine Presence*

While the concept of God dwelling in the midst of His people may have been symbolized in Eden (Genesis 3:8), the first historical promise of God's presence among His people through the

Temple occurs in the "Song of Moses," recorded in Exodus 15:17: "You will bring them and plant them in the mountain of Your inheritance, the place, O LORD, which You have made for Your dwelling, the sanctuary, O LORD, which Your hands have established." In time, the Temple in Jerusalem became the only place on earth where God's presence was manifested among His people.[1] Now the theological statement in Solomon's dedicatory prayer of 1 Kings 8:27 that God could not be contained on earth by any structure meant that God Himself could not be localized on earth. Thus the Temple stood as the visible station of God's invisible, though manifest, presence. For this reason, the divine presence was expressed by a circumlocution that He had caused His *Name* to dwell there (cf. Deuteronomy 12:11; 2 Chronicles 7:16; Ezra 6:12; Nehemiah 1:9; Jeremiah 7:12). Thus, while God Himself did not even temporarily dwell in the Temple, it was a fixed place where God, in His transcendence and incomparability, was accessible to man. The Jewish sages called this divine manifestation the *Shekinah* (from the Hebrew verb *shakan,* "to dwell"), explaining that this concentration of the divine presence in a given place did not imply divine reduction, for "the more limited the space, the greater is His might."[2] Jesus acknowledged this aspect of the Temple's purpose when He said, "Whoever swears by the temple, swears both by the temple and by Him who dwells within it" (Matthew 23:21). Eschatologically, the final portrait painted of the millennial Jerusalem in the book of Ezekiel underscores this reality: "…and the name of the city from that day shall be '*Adonai Shammah*" ("The LORD is there," Ezekiel 48:35).

2. A Sign of the Covenant

The Tabernacle and the Temple functioned as witnesses to God's covenants with Israel. The presence of God in the Temple presupposed a covenant relationship, based on the model of the Hittite legal arrangement between a sovereign ruler and subject people known as the suzerain-vassal treaty. In this relationship, God as the suzerain would conditionally protect and prosper

Israel as His vassals. The Temple was a witness to the Mosaic Covenant, for it had been built to house the Ark, which served as a repository of the tablets of the Law (Exodus 25:9 with 2 Samuel 7:2,5). Its placement on "the Mount of the Lord" in Jerusalem (the land of Moriah) was confirmation of the Abrahamic Covenant and God's promise to make spiritual provision there (Genesis 22:14). It was also confirmation of the Davidic Covenant and the promise of a son (Solomon) who would build God's house and whose house God would build until the messianic Son would establish His throne there forever (1 Chronicles 17:14).

The religious impact of the Temple was directly related to it being understood as a sign of covenantal security.[3] This is seen in the denunciations against covenant-breaking made in the prophetic literature,[4] as for example, in Jeremiah 7:7-15, where the prophet Jeremiah refers to the people's trust in the promises of the Abrahamic and Mosaic covenants that Israel would dwell in the Land forever (verse 7) as a *false* security because the promises were conditional, resting upon covenant obedience (verse 8). Each destruction of the Temple proved this point, since destruction was prophesied as a retributive judgment for violation of the covenants.

In the prophetic context of the last days (Isaiah 2:2-3; Micah 4:2-3), the Temple will again serve as the place to which the world will come to learn God's law as the basis of millennial government:

> The mountain of the house of the LORD [the Millennial Temple erected on the Temple Mount] will be established as the chief of the mountains...and all the nations will stream to it...many peoples will come and say, "Come let us go up to the mountain of the LORD [the Temple Mount] to the house of the God of Jacob [the Temple]; that He may teach us concerning His ways and that we may walk in His paths. For the Law will go forth from Zion and the word of the LORD from Jerusalem" (Isaiah 2:2-3).

During this future age, the Temple will serve as a sign of the New Covenant and Israel will be protected and prosper under its terms (Isaiah 59:20-21; Jeremiah 31:27-40; 32:37-40; Ezekiel 16:60-63; 37:21-28), but this time *without* threat of covenant violation, since the people will all have "a new heart and…a new spirit" to obey the Lord (Ezekiel 36:26). This prediction of covenantal fulfillment through the Temple reminded Israel that each new beginning of the Temple marked the end of exile from both the Land and the Lord.

3. *A Signal of the End of Exile*

Israel's experiences of exile and Diaspora, whether in Egypt, Assyria, or Babylon, ended only when she was able to establish or restore her central worship center. The motif of national rest in relationship to entrance to the Land and the establishment of a central sanctuary is presented in Deuteronomy 12:9-11:

> You have not as yet come to *the resting place* and the inheritance which the LORD your God is giving you. When you cross the Jordan and live in the land which the LORD your God is giving you to inherit, and He gives *you rest* from all your enemies around you, so that you live in security, *then* it shall come about that the place in which the LORD your God will choose for His name to dwell, there you shall bring all that I command you: your burnt offerings, and your sacrifices, your tithes and the contribution of your hand, and all your choice votive offerings which you vow to the LORD (emphasis added).

In verse 9 the *promise* of "rest" is found with the definite article (indicating a specific rest ("the rest"), and is paired with "the inheritance" as a gift from the Lord.[5] With verse 10, the *time* of "rest" is connected with settlement in the Land, and in verse 11 the *place* of rest is connected with building of the Temple. This relationship to the Temple is confirmed in Solomon's dedicatory prayer[6] found in 1 Kings 8:56: "Blessed be the LORD, who has given *rest* to His people Israel, according to all that He promised; not one word has failed of all His good promise, which He promised through Moses His servant." These words connect the building of the Temple with the fulfillment of the "rest" envisioned by Moses for the nation as stated in Deuteronomy 12:9.[7]

Moreover, the biblical prophets announced an *eschatological* rest, which was expected, since the exile had interrupted the promise of a permanent rest within the Land, and the destruction of the Temple had removed the symbol of that rest which is connected with the presence of the Lord, the giver of rest.[8] Isaiah anticipated a future "rest" for Israel after her last exile (Isaiah 11:10; 14:3-4,7; 28:12; 32:17), and associated the longing for it (in remembrance of the former "rest") with a spiritual purification that will bring eschatological restoration and rest (Isaiah 63:11-14). This rest will be maintained, according to Ezekiel, through the restoration of the Temple and its priestly service, literally "to rest in blessing" (Ezekiel 44:30). As the destruction of the Temple caused a loss of rest, so its rebuilding would restore that rest.

4. A Sociopolitical Institution

The Temple was not only prominent to the Jewish people as a religious institution, but it also played a considerable role in the political life of the people (especially during the Second Temple era). In addition, the Temple was extremely important to Jewish national unity, and Jews in the Diaspora have long fought for the right to send their monetary support and contributions to Jerusalem, despite many attempts by others to deny them that right. In fact, to the Jews, all other institutions, even those unrelated to the Temple service, gained moral stature from their association with the Temple.[9]

The Temple, therefore, governed the daily life of the Jew. This life was lived in view of the festivals, the pilgrimages, the sacrificial rites, and Torah reading and study—all of which revolved around the Temple. Though later (and especially after A.D. 70) the synagogue, which probably began in the Temple court, took precedence, it was with the Temple that the synagogue, and all other institutions, were organically connected. The Temple was the channel by which the religious institutions of Israel became a part of the life of the people. Stipulated hours of prayer were set according to the times of sacrifices (cf. Acts 3:1), and even those in the Diaspora were to turn their faces toward Jerusalem and the Temple. All legal matters were decided by the Sanhedrin, who had their full prerogatives of office only when seated in the Temple, and only when the sacrificial system was operational.[10] We will touch more upon the significance of the Temple to Jewish life in later chapters, but for now, it is sufficient to recognize the importance of the institution—an importance that will now be seen in the religious, historical, and cultural continuity that was imbued in the concept of the Temple.

5. *A Symbol of National Sovereignty*

The Temple was also a symbol of Israel's national sovereignty. This was evident when Israel's enemies, who had her under hegemony and considered her guilty of political disloyalty, demonstrated their (and their gods') "sovereignty" by ending Israel's independence through the destruction of the Temple. This is also seen by the Israelites' desire to rebuild the Temple and their enemies' desire to thwart rebuilding (such as in Ezra 4), and the Romans' exercise of control over the Jewish nation through political appointments to the office of high priest.[11]

The Temple was also essential to establishing and preserving national unity. The Davidic-Solomonic state united, for the first time, the political and spiritual centers in one capital, through the construction of the Temple. This act not only unified the tribal groups inhabiting the highlands from Upper Galilee to the Northern Negev, but also extended its domain to the surrounding regions of Syria and Transjordan. Thus, the Temple brought a unique measure of stability to Israelites throughout the Levant. The people's recovery from exile, which was a disunifying experience, was not complete until the Temple was rebuilt. That's because the Temple stood as a unifying institution for the nation, as well as a national rallying point in times of distress.

Even though Israel's political independence has been achieved today through the Zionist movement and military might, spiritual independence has not yet been realized because Jews are still forbidden access to the Temple Mount for prayer or religious activity of any kind. Those in the present-day Temple movement contend that the lack of unity among Jews today (the schism between secular and religious Jews as well as the schisms among the religious factions) is a result of the Temple's absence. They believe once the Temple returns, its presence will unite world Jewry as well as all the peoples of the earth.

The Millennial Temple, when built, will serve as a symbol of national sovereignty (under King Messiah) and bring about a unity among the people. In Ezekiel 48:1-35, we see this unity attained as the Land of Israel is allotted to the tribes of Israel in such a way that the Temple is the central reference point. This orientation will also provide unity through the river of life, which will flow to and refresh all the Land (Ezekiel 47:1-12), and ultimately this orientation will serve as the focal point for the nations who yearly assemble in Jerusalem for the Feast of Booths (Zechariah 14:16).

6. *A Source of National Blessing*

When the foundations for the Second Temple were laid during the Persian period, the prophet Haggai announced, "Consider from this day onward. before one stone was placed on another in the temple of the LORD....consider. Is the seed still in the barn? Even including the vine, fig tree, pomegranate and olive tree, it has not borne fruit. Yet from this day on I will bless you" (Haggai 2:15,18-19). This connection between the Temple and national blessing is well defined in Solomon's dedicatory prayer upon the completion of the Temple (1 Kings 8). The prayer reveals a cause-effect relationship between the Temple and the bestowal of rain, relief from famine, military security, and help in foreign distress (verses 35-49, cf. 2 Chronicles 6:24-30). In the parallel account in 2 Chronicles 7:12-14, a passage often misapplied to the American nation, fidelity toward God through the Temple is the immediate cause of national prosperity or its lack. So in the familiar words of verse 14 we read, "[If] My people who are called by My Name humble themselves *and pray [toward the Temple]*, and seek My face and turn from their wicked ways, then I will hear from heaven [i.e., the heavenly Temple], will forgive their sin and *will heal their land*" (emphasis added). Non-Israelite temples were places where people, through a ceremonial service, could meet the physical needs of their gods. By contrast, through the Jerusalem Temple, God was able to meet the needs of man. Because the Lord is at the center of the nation at the Temple, those who look toward the Temple via prayer will find protection (individually), as will the nation (corporately).

In the millennial kingdom, the blessings of restoration will include the renewal of the Land exemplified by the river flowing from under the altar of the Temple (Ezekiel 47:1-12; Zechariah 14:8) and agricultural blessings connected with the divine bestowal of rain (Zechariah 14:16-17). This rain, so vital to an agrarian society, will be provided based on Israelite and non-Israelite faithfulness to worship at the Temple at the appointed feasts. Thus, the national blessings secured by the future Temple will extend internationally to all the inhabitants of the kingdom, fulfilling the mandate of the Abrahamic Covenant that through Israel all the families of the earth would be blessed (Genesis 12:3).

7. A Source for Worldwide Blessing

Solomon, in his dedicatory prayer in 1 Kings 8, indicated that the Temple was to be a source of universal appeal and blessing. In verses 41-43 we read,

> Concerning the foreigner who is not of Your people Israel, when he comes from a far country for Your name's sake (for they will hear of Your great name and Your mighty hand, and of Your outstretched arm); when he comes and prays toward this house, hear in heaven Your dwelling place, and do according to all for which the

> foreigner calls to You, in order that all the peoples of the earth may know Your name, to fear You, as do Your people Israel, and that they may know that this house which I have built is called by Your name.

While the potential for such blessing existed during the First and Second Temple periods, the covenantal failure of Israel left this promise unfulfilled.

The biblical prophets depicted the Millennial Temple as the fulfillment of international blessing. In such texts as Isaiah 2:2-4; 11:1-11 (cf. 65:25) and 60–66, Zechariah 8:23; 14:16, and Micah 4:1-5, the Temple is envisioned as the center of world renewal, drawing all nations and peoples to the covenant people and to Temple worship.[12] In Isaiah 56:6-7, the prophet Isaiah boldly declared the Temple would serve as a sacrificial center and a "house of prayer for all the peoples." Jesus Himself employed this passage against the money-changers in the Temple, realizing that their cultic violations threatened the fulfillment of this great purpose (Matthew 21:12-13; Mark 11:15-17; Luke 19:45-47; John 2:13-16).

8. *A Structure for the Focus of Prayer*

Because Israel's God is the true God, the God of the covenant, and because only He can answer prayer, those who wanted to have prayer answered had to come to the Temple (or pray toward the Temple). Based on 1 Kings 8:48-49 and Daniel 6:11, the Mishnah stated that prayer should be made by directing the heart towards the Holy of Holies. The last Tannaitic sages had a difference of opinion concerning the interpretation of these Mishnaic instructions concerning the Holy of Holies: "To which Holy of Holies? R. Hiyya Rabba said: 'Towards the heavenly Holy of Holies;' R. Simeon b. Halafta said: 'Towards the earthly Holy of Holies.'"[13] This divergence was reconciled by the Amora R. Phinehas bar Hama, who said, "They do not disagree: the earthly Holy of Holies faces the heavenly Holy of Holies."[14] Thus, when a person orients himself toward the earthly Holy of Holies, he orients himself at the same time to the Holy of Holies in the heavenly Temple.

The variations in interpretation by the rabbis after the destruction of the Temple reflect on the problem created for Israel with regard to prayer. During Temple times, the only access for both Jew and non-Jew to the divine presence on earth was through association with the Temple. Without the regular Temple service, there was no direct link between people and their God, and no longer any possibility of atoning for sins, as one of the sages observed after the destruction of the Second Temple: "Since the day that the Temple was destroyed, an iron wall has intervened between Israel and their Father in heaven" (*Berakot* 32b; cf. Isaiah 59:2). In like manner, Simeon the Just underscored the pivotal position of the Temple for Jewish life: "the world is based upon three things: the Torah, *Avodah* [the Temple service] and the practice of *gemilut hasadim* ['charity']" (*Pirke Avot* 1.2). Given this perspective, the destruction of the Temple undermined one of the pillars of the Jewish universe—Temple service—and caused a complete imbalance in the life of the religious Jew, whose very existence was determined by the Temple's order.

This explains the rabbinic concept that the earthly Temple faces the heavenly Temple. If prayer depended upon orienting oneself towards the *Shekinah*, whose presence was within the Holy of Holies, then even after the destruction of the Jerusalem Temple, prayer could be continued (especially the Eighteen Benedictions) in the direction of the desolated Sanctuary.[15] Later, however, Amoraim argued, based on Song of Songs 2:9, "Behold, he is standing behind our wall," that the *Shekinah* never left the Temple Mount, and remained at the Kotel (Western Wall), which is a remnant of the Sanctuary site.[16]

While prayer is not specifically mentioned in those texts that describe the Millennial Temple, prayer is nevertheless a part of the worship that is indicated to take place there. In Zechariah 14:17 the command for all "the families of the earth" to ascend to the Temple Mount to "worship the King, the LORD of hosts" parallels the earlier function of the Temple as the place to which all earthly prayer was to be directed (1 Kings 8:29,41-43). And just as the blessing of rain once depended on this orientation to the Lord (1 Kings 8:35), it will do so again in the future (Zechariah 14:17-19).

A Purpose to Be Performed

Today, almost six million of the Jewish people have ended their physical exile in the Diaspora and returned to the Land of Israel. According to the biblical prophets, one day, all the Jewish people will be regathered to Israel and end their spiritual exile (Isaiah 27:12-13; 59:20-21; Ezekiel 36:24-28; Matthew 24:31; Romans 11:25-26). At that time, the Messiah will come and the divine presence will return (Zechariah 14:4; Ezekiel 37:1-4; Matthew 24:27; Luke 21:27). Then Israel will be established as a political and religious entity in the Land under the New Covenant (Jeremiah 31). All these future events are in accord with the various aspects of the Temple's past purpose, and therefore it is evident that the Temple must, in future history, return to serve its purpose.

It's important to note that whenever conditions have developed to permit the building of the Temple, opposition has also been present to prevent such fulfillment. Our brief and general overview of the Temple's purpose and history past, present, and future has now prepared us for a more specific look at the history of these battles over the Temple through time.

4

Ancient Battles for the Temple Mount

Many different men other than Jews have sat
[in Jerusalem] in the seat of power—Jebusites,
Egyptians, Babylonians and Persians; Hel-
lenist Greeks and Romans; Byzantines, Arabs,
Crusaders, Mamelukes, Turks and British. But
throughout the flux of these thousands of years
there runs one constant thread—the unique
attachment of the Jewish people to Jerusalem
and the site of their holy Temple. History has
no parallel to this mystic bond, and without it
there would have been no state of Israel today.

JOAN COMAY

During a recent stay in Jerusalem, I followed with interest the daily news reports on two Knesset members (MKs), Inbal Gavrieli and Yehiel Hazan, who were publicly waging their private battle for the Temple. At issue was the abrupt closure of the Temple Mount (which had just reopened two months before after a 33-month closure) for the annual observance of *Tisha B'Av,* the traditional day of mourning over the loss of the Temple. If any day seemed appropriate for a Jew to visit the Temple Mount, this, the MKs argued, should be the day.

As governmental officials, these two bore parliamentary immunity, giving them the right to enter—without restrictions—any site under Israeli sovereignty. Both stated they were determined to exercise their right as Jews to go to Judaism's most holy site and declared it was "a matter of principle" since, as they stated, the site was closed only because the State of Israel was afraid of Arafat's threats and no real security situation existed. When the police announced they would not permit the MKs' entrance, the two became more resolute and demonstrative about visiting the site, despite police opposition. The expected showdown on the Temple Mount immediately catapulted the two MKs into the media spotlight.

On the evening before the fateful day of confrontation, the two were being interviewed on Israel's Channel 2 television program *Café Tel-Ad*, a popular pop-quiz show.[1] At the outset of the interview, the two MKs stated that the Temple Mount was "in their hearts and souls." Then the host, in typical pop-quiz fashion, began to ask them the most basic questions about the history of the Temple. When asked, "Who built the First Temple?" Hazan answered "Aaron the priest," and Gavrieli conceded she "didn't know." The interviewer had to tell them the answer was actually King Solomon. Likewise, neither could say who built the Second Temple. When asked, "What important event happened on the Temple Mount in the past?" the two were again stumped. Even when the host gave them the hint "…on Mount Moriah," still neither had an answer. So the host said, "Abraham's near-sacrifice of Isaac." Then the host sarcastically quipped, "But the Temple Mount is in your hearts and souls!" His next question was, "Who destroyed the Temples, and when?" By now the MKs realized this embarrassing line of questioning was to their disadvantage, so they stopped the interview.

The moral of this humiliating account is that one should not go boldly to battle over something they know little or nothing about. Yet before we judge the MKs too harshly, let us ask ourselves: How well would *we* do if asked these same questions about the Temple? Before we begin to explore our main topic, the battle for the last days' Temple, let us prep ourselves with a historical review of the battles of the Temple through time.

A Record of Conflict

From the time Jerusalem became the capital of Israel in 1004 B.C., no less than 69 battles have been fought over the city. Once the Temple was constructed in Jerusalem (967–960 B.C.), it became the central object in worship and in warfare, depending on how faithfully the Jewish nation followed God's law. A warning about the potential for the destruction of the Temple was issued at the time of its first dedication in 960 B.C. In 2 Chronicles 7 we are told that after the two-week-long dedication celebration had concluded, the Lord appeared one night to Solomon, the builder of the First Temple, with this message:

> For now I have chosen and consecrated this house that My name may be there forever, and My eyes and My heart will be there perpetually....But if you turn away and forsake My statutes and My commandments which I have set before you, and go and serve other gods and worship them, then I will uproot you from My Land which I have given you, and this house which I have consecrated for My name I will cast out of My sight and I will make it a proverb and a byword among all peoples. As for this house, which was exalted, everyone who passes by it will be astonished and say, "Why has the LORD done thus to this Land and to this house?" (verses 16,19-21).

According to this warning, covenant violation would result in divine discipline in the form of expulsion and exile. The evidence of Israel's severed relationship with God would be the destruction of the Temple, or the visible symbol of God's presence with His people. The traditional Jewish reason given for the destruction of the past Temples is that of "baseless hatred" among Jews or national disunity. However, from this biblical text it is evident that national disunity was a symptom, not the cause. This warning was put into action for the First Temple with the Assyrian exile of the northern kingdom of Israel (722 B.C.) and the Babylonian exile of the southern kingdom of Judah (605–586 B.C.) and destruction of Jerusalem (586 B.C.). The Second Temple was destroyed by the Roman army in A.D. 70 and this destruction was followed by expulsion and exile (A.D. 70–135). The divine warning against covenant violation, then, serves as the basis for the battles of the Temples.

However, the history of the Temples reveals a much more extensive record of conflict through time. This may come as a surprise to those accustomed to thinking only in terms of the destruction of the First and Second Temples and may ideally imagine peaceful periods of uninterrupted priestly service and Israelite worship in between. In reality, the struggles that have centered on the Temple Mount have been long and continuous, and embody the ongoing spiritual conflict between Israel and the nations—a conflict that will culminate in the battle for the Last Days' Temple.

The Preparation for the Temple

If we go back to the preparatory years of the Temple, during Israel's earliest presence in Jerusalem, we already find a setting of conflict. When Abraham came to Salem (Canaanite Jerusalem) to bring tribute to the ruling priest, Melchizedek, he did so after a battle with an alliance of eastern armies (Genesis 14:1-18). Abraham's gift of a tenth of the spoils from that battle was in response to the divine intervention that resulted in his victory over his enemies and for the sanctuary God's priest had given him and his men in the city. This initial encounter between the father of the Jewish nation and a priest of God in a "city of peace" sets the stage for Jerusalem as the chosen place for the Israelites to bring their tithes to the Temple after they have experienced rest from all their enemies (Deuteronomy 12:10-11). This significance is enlarged in Abraham's return, at God's command, to Jerusalem's Mount Moriah to offer his son Isaac (Genesis 22:2). In this incident, Abraham's spiritual conflict over obedience to God's command to sacrifice his son was resolved by divine intervention that saves Isaac, a sacrificial offering being made to God, and a renaming of the place as *'Adonai Yireh* ("the Lord will see to it") in testimony to the Mount as the place of future divine provision.

This provision was made possible to the nation of Israel when David conquered Jebusite Jerusalem and began preparations for the building of the Temple (1 Chronicles 28:11-19). However, David, as a man of war, was not permitted to build the Temple, which was to be a place of peace. This task would go to David's son, Solomon, whose Hebrew name *Shlomo* means "His peace." Again, the Temple is seen rising out of conflict to be the place where man can meet in peace with God. It's important to keep this in mind as we trace the history of the Temple Mount through time and consider the rebellious Israelites and pagan nations who have waged war with God.

The Biblical-Era Battles over the Temple

The beginning point in the battles over the Temple was the civil war that divided the Jewish nation between the north (Israel) and the south (Judah). The seeds of this revolt had already been sown in the time of King Solomon with his conscription of Israelites to construct the Temple, its court and equipment, and a complex of other structures (1 Kings 11:28; 12:4,11), and began to bear its bitter fruit with his personal spiritual defection (1 Kings 11:1-13). The prophet Ahijah predicted that Solomon's sin had set in motion a process that would ultimately tear the kingdom in two (1 Kings 11:29-35). When the kingdom of Israel seceded from Judah, the spiritual consequence was that Israel lost access to the Lord's presence at the Ark in Jerusalem within the kingdom of Judah (1 Kings 12:27). Although spiritually the northern tribes could have continued to make pilgrimage to the Temple as they had in the past, politically, such continued allegiance to the southern kingdom could not be permitted by the new king of the north, Jeroboam. To satisfy Israel's need for a sanctuary, then,

Jeroboam constructed alternate worship sites at Dan and Bethel, located at the northern and southern borders of the northern kingdom (1 Kings 12:28-29). By this action, Israel perpetuated the spiritual decline begun by Solomon, which led to the fall of their kingdom and exile at the hands of the Assyrians in 721 B.C.

Before the Babylonian invasion of the southern kingdom occurred, spiritual apostasy had already resulted in repeated minor battles on the Temple Mount. The division of the united kingdom under Solomon's son Rehoboam (c. 926 B.C.) had left the weakened kingdom of Judah open to invasion. Only five years into Rehoboam's reign the opportunity to invade was seized by the Egyptian pharaoh Shishak (Sheshonk I), who had given sanctuary to Jeroboam, the rebellious head of Solomon's conscripted laborers and who was targeted for assassination by the king. Shishak attacked Rehoboam's royal palace and the Temple complex, plundering both the Temple treasuries (1 Kings 14:26a), which contained the wealth collected by King David for the Temple's maintenance and utensils for the Temple service (1 Kings 7:51), and the king's house, which contained 200 gold shields made by Solomon (1 Kings 10:16).

As divine discipline continued, the Temple became the scene of repeated spiritual violations. Around 843 B.C. the wicked Queen Athaliah, who had erected in Jerusalem a temple to the god Ba'al, attempted to destroy the Davidic dynasty (2 Chronicles 22:10). However, one member of this dynasty, the child Joash, was hidden away in the Temple for six years until he was old enough to be crowned king. But Joash later abandoned the Temple and "served the Asherim and the idols" (2 Chronicles 24:18). God sent the priest Zechariah (son of the high priest Jehoiada, who had hidden Joash in the Temple) to rebuke the king in the Temple court, but the king had him executed, committing further a sacrilege against the Temple by carrying out this act within these sacred precincts (2 Chronicles 24:17-27). Joash's son, Amaziah, followed him as king of Judah and in worshiping foreign gods (2 Chronicles 25:14). Amaziah's challenge to the Israelite king

Jehoash (785 B.C.) resulted in his own capture, part of the walls of Jerusalem being torn down, and the plunder of Temple treasure and utensils from the Temple and of the treasuries of the king's house (2 Kings 14:12-14; 2 Chronicles 25:23-24).

Some 60 years later the Judean king Ahaz, a follower of the god Ba'al (2 Chronicles 28:2-4), appealed to the Assyrian king Tiglath-pileser III (745–727 B.C.) for military assistance, but instead received Assyrian hegemony and the demand of tribute to be paid by the Judean monarchy (2 Chronicles 28:16-20). In order to pay the tribute, Ahaz himself looted the king's palace and Temple treasuries and sent the payment to the Assyrian overlord. He also destroyed the Temple vessels and closed the doors of the Temple (2 Kings 16:10-18; 2 Chronicles 28:21,24). In 729 B.C., Ahaz's son, Hezekiah, who had restored the Temple service, was still faced with paying the Assyrian tribute money. At first he stripped away gold from the Temple in order to make this payment (2 Kings 18:15-16). But then he refused to make further payments. So in 715 B.C. the Assyrian army besieged Jerusalem (2 Kings 18:9-37; 2 Chronicles 32:1-19; Isaiah 36). God spared the city and the Temple from destruction at this time because Hezekiah humbly prayed for deliverance (2 Kings 19; 2 Chronicles 32:20-22; Isaiah 37). However, his subsequent foolish action in giving Babylonian emissaries a tour of the Temple treasuries betrayed Jerusalem and the Temple Mount to later invasion and destruction by the growing Babylonian empire (2 Kings 20:12-18; 2 Chronicles 32:31; Isaiah 39:1-7).

The final act of spiritual defection was performed by Hezekiah's son Manasseh, which resulted in the most serious desecration the Temple had yet encountered. Previous invasions had only raided the wealth of the Temple, but Manasseh's act stole its sanctity. He turned the Temple Mount into a pagan sanctuary, erecting altars for the two hosts of heaven in the Temple courts, and removed the Temple vessels and put a carved idol in the Temple itself—an act referred to in the biblical text as "the abominations of the nations" (see 2 Kings 21:2-7; 2 Chronicles 33:2-7). This act climaxed the apostasy of the southern kingdom, and was directly responsible for the Babylonian invasions and deportations (605–589 B.C.) that reached their pinnacle with the destruction of the Temple and final exile to Babylon in 586 B.C. During the Babylonian razing of the Temple, the Temple vessels were removed and transported to Nebuchadnezzar's palace in Babylon, while other valuable articles were burned (2 Kings 25:9,13-17; 2 Chronicles 36:18-19; Daniel 5:2-3).

After the Jews were in exile for 70 years, the Babylonian empire was overthrown (in 539 B.C.) and Jews from tribes in the former northern and southern kingdoms were permitted by the Persian king Cyrus to return to Jerusalem with the Jewish priests Shesbazzar and Zerubbabel to rebuild the Temple (Ezra 1:2-4). A second return occurred in 458 B.C. during the seventh year of the reign of the Persian king Artaxerxes I Longiminus (Ezra 7:8). When this Jewish remnant attempted to build on the Temple Mount, opposition arose from the resident Samaritan population that had been transplanted to the area by the Assyrian monarch Esarhaddon during 681–669 B.C. (Ezra 4:1-2).

This foreign element, which had intermarried with the refugee Israelite population, had created a syncretistic form of Judaism and sought legitimacy through involvement with the Jews in the covenantal act of rebuilding the Temple (Ezra 4:2). After they were rejected by the Jewish leadership, they wrote letters to the Persian kings Ahasuerus (Xerxes) and his son Artaxerxes Longimanus, who succeeded him (Ezra 4:6-16), and received an order to stop the Jewish reconstruction of Jerusalem and the Temple Mount (verses 17-22). According to the biblical account, the Samaritans then "went in haste to Jerusalem to the Jews and stopped them by force of arms" (Ezra 4:23). This battle on the Temple Mount caused a delay in the restoration of the city and Sanctuary until the second year of King Darius. The provincial governor of the region, Tattenai, appealed to Darius to search the royal archives for a copy of Cyrus' original decree, and once it was discovered, the edict causing the delay was reversed (Ezra 6:1-11). A similar "battle" occurred during Nehemiah's repair of Jerusalem's walls when San-ballat the Horonite, Tobiah the Ammonite, and Geshem the Arab opposed the work (Nehemiah 2:19-20; 4:1-3). So while the Israelites were carrying on the construction work, they had their tools in one hand and their weapons in the other (Nehemiah 4:7-18).

After the Temple was built, Jerusalem came under the control of a succession of Greek rulers (Alexander the Great, Egyptian Greeks [Ptolemies], and Syrian Greeks [Seleucids]). Under the reign of the Seleucid ruler Antiochus IV Epiphanes (175–164 B.C.), who is called "a despicable person" in Daniel 11:21, two Jewish factions, orthodox (strict Jewish culture) and Hellenist (pro-Greek culture), contended for the high priesthood. As a promoter of the Greek culture, Antiochus sided with the Hellenistic party and appointed the high priest Onias III ("the prince of the covenant" of Daniel 11:22), who permitted pagan worship in accord with Antiochus's decrees. In 170 B.C. Antiochus invaded Jerusalem and many Jews were killed and the Temple was plundered. He further desecrated the Temple by sacrificing an unclean animal, a pig, on the Brazen Altar and by erecting nearby a pagan statue of Zeus Olympias. Antiochus's actions were predicted by the prophet Daniel (Daniel 8:23-25; 11:21-35) and served as a partial fulfillment of the type of desecration Daniel and the New Testament predicts the Temple will suffer under the Antichrist (Daniel 7:24-26; 9:24-27; 11:36-45; Matthew 24:15; Mark 13:14; 2 Thessalonians 2:2-4). It is also believed that Antiochus IV took the veil that separated the Temple's Holy Place from the Holy of Holies and sent it as a tribute to the temple of Zeus at Olympia.[2]

The Post-biblical Battles over the Temple

In the year 63 B.C. a three-year siege against Jerusalem by the Roman army came to an end and successfully crushed Jewish resistance to Roman rule. When the Roman general Pompey entered the city in triumph and turned his horse toward the Temple, thousands of Jews threw themselves to the ground before the general and begged him not to enter the Holy Place. Although they could not battle any longer for their city, they offered their lives to prevent the Temple's desecration. This display of concern only served to convince Pompey that the Temple must contain great riches or some hidden secret, and so not only did he enter the Holy Place, but he tore away the veil of separation and went into the Holy of Holies itself. The Roman historian Tacitus recorded the act and its revelation as follows: "By right of conquest he [Pompey] entered their Temple. It is a fact well known, that he found no image, no statue, no symbolical representation of the Deity: the whole presented a naked dome; the sanctuary was unadorned and simple."[3] As a result, when Pompey ordered the destruction of the walls of Jerusalem, he not only left the Temple intact, but commanded that its sacrificial service should continue. Despite this act of Roman clemency, just nine years later, the second Roman governor of Jerusalem, Crassus Dives, robbed the Temple treasuries.

In 19 B.C., Herod the Great, appointed by Rome as king of Judea, turned his attention toward restoring the Temple as a means of gaining influence with the Jewish religious leaders in the Sanhedrin (which consisted of priests) and impressing the Roman authorities. The Jews, however, feared this was a ruse and that Herod was secretly staging an attack on the Temple. For this reason they would not permit him to remove one stone from the old Temple until all the building stones for the new construction were brought to the Temple Mount. However, Herod did not attempt to avoid conflict over the Temple, especially when his actions favored Roman custom over laws of Jewish sanctity. In one instance he confiscated the high priest's vestments as a demonstration of superior (Roman) authority. In another and more famous incident, in a show of loyalty to Rome, he installed a golden eagle over the eastern entrance to the Temple. As a bird of prey, the eagle symbolized Rome, but to the Jews, it corrupted the character of the Temple as a place of peace. In the first place, the eagle was, according to Jewish law, an *unclean* bird (Leviticus 11:13). Moreover, its display violated the Mosaic injunction against the making of graven images (whether of men or animals). Because of this desecration, a riot occurred in 4 B.C., which was led by the high priest Matthias. A group of some 40 Jews tore down the hated image and hacked it to pieces. This defiant act on the Temple Mount resulted in the removal of the high priest and the burning alive of his co-activists.

Herod died soon afterward, but his son Archelaus continued his father's vendetta against Jewish nationalists by killing some 3000 people in the Temple area at Passover. That same year, riots in the city by nationalist groups ended with the burning of the Temple cloisters. In A.D. 28, Pontius Pilate, the Roman-appointed governor over Judea, also engaged in an attack on and in the Temple, taking money from the Temple treasuries to construct an aqueduct and then massacring a number of Jewish zealots in the Temple courts during a protest (cf. Luke 13:1-2).

During the time of Jesus' ministry, the Temple, having been the center of frequent nationalist demonstrations, had made the Roman authorities fearful of the potential threat of a large-scale uprising led by a messianic figure. In this heightened atmosphere of conflict (cf. John 11:48-50), it is understandable how Jesus' disruptive actions in the Temple precincts (John 2:14-16; Matthew 21:12-13; Mark 11:15-18; Luke 19:45-48), messianic claims (Matthew 21:14-16; John 10:22-39), and statements concerning the Temple's destruction (Matthew 24:1-2; Mark 13:1-2; Luke 19:41-44; John 2:19-20) would be viewed with concern at His Jewish trial (Matthew 26:61-66; Mark 14:56-58,61-63; Luke 22:67-71) and Roman trial (Luke 23:2,5; John 19:7-8,12). The Romans' fear increased as Jewish nationalistic ambitions intensified after the time of Jesus. When in A.D. 40 the Roman emperor Caligula commanded his statue be erected and worshiped in the Jerusalem Temple, the Judean king Herod Agrippa I appealed to him and asked him to rescind his order to prevent a major Jewish uprising.

However, in A.D. 44, the death of Agrippa placed the whole of the country under direct Roman rule, further supressing any hope of renewed Jewish independence. Mounting Roman oppression, the siding of Roman authorities with the non-Jewish element in the Land, and repeated violations of the Temple's sanctity created the atmosphere for revolt. In A.D. 53 the Roman procurator of Judea bribed Jews to murder the high priest Jonathan in the Temple, leading to a succession of murders during feast days at the Temple (Josephus, *Antiquities* 20.8). In April of A.D. 66, when the Roman governor confiscated 17 talents from the Temple treasury, Jewish nationalists staged a revolt, seized the Temple, stopped the daily sacrifices which had been made in tribute of the Roman emperor, and captured the stronghold of Masada. This led to the First Jewish Revolt, which culminated in the Roman destruction of the Temple in A.D. 70.

The Roman Destruction of the Temple

The First Jewish Revolt, also known as the Great War, was unique in the history of the region because the Jews were the only people in the ancient Near East to launch a revolution on such a scale against the Roman Empire. It is also significant that the beginning and end of this conflict centered on the Jewish Temple.

In response to the Jewish insurrection, which was staged primarily in Jerusalem, Rome's leading commander, Vespasian, was dispatched to quell the uprising with four legions comprising a total of some 50,000 soldiers. Vespasian's plan of attack began in northern Israel, which, unlike Jerusalem, offered little resistance to his legions. One example was the Galilean fortress of Jotapata, which was defended by the forces under Josephus. The Jewish families at the fortress committed suicide rather than surrender, and Josephus defected to the Roman side. He then went on to become a court historian for the Romans and recorded the details of the fall of Jerusalem and the Temple. After Jotapata, the Roman legions marched on the city of Gamla in the Golan Heights, which, in the fall of A.D. 67, had attempted to prevent the Roman advance toward the Holy City. The Roman legions decimated the city and slaughtered some 4000 Jews. Rather than allow their families to fall to Roman savagery, some 5000 Jews took their own lives, plunging off the nearby cliffs to their deaths.

By the summer of A.D. 70, Vespasian's Tenth Legion had made its way to Jerusalem and placed the city under siege. Because of the influx of refugees from other Jewish cities destroyed by the Romans, as well as the influx of the Judean population fleeing in advance of the legions, the city's population had increased to at least three times its normal size. Jerusalem's reputation as one of the largest cities of the ancient world and as an impregnable one at that made it a significant challenge to the already-wearied Roman soldiers. Yet, its role as the center of Jewish political and spiritual authority and the Temple's place as the center of the Jewish Revolt required the city to be the foremost example of Roman punishment.

At the time of the Roman siege, two of the most militant factions among the Jewish nationalists, the Zealots and the Sicarii, had gained control of the Temple Mount. This had been accomplished with the aid of Idumean mercenaries (descendants of the Edomites) who had ruthlessly killed the more moderate Sadducaic and Pharisaic elements in charge. The aim of the militant factions, from the beginning, had been to crush the Roman occupation of Israel and drive the Romans from the Land. Now that the war had come to the Holy City, the nationalists were determined to fulfill their purpose or perish. To assure that the Jewish populace would not flee but fight to the death, the Zealots destroyed the city's storehouses of food and proclaimed the divine inviolability of Jerusalem. This meant the only way out of the city was in a coffin, and in fact, a leader of the Pharisaic sect, Rabbi Yochanan ben Zakkai, escaped by hiding in one and surrendering himself to Vespasian. Upon being delivered to the general, he addressed him as emperor, stating that God would allow only a great ruler to capture His city. According to tradition, a messenger from Rome arrived at this very minute announcing to Vespasian that the emperor had died and he had been crowned as the successor. Impressed by the rabbi's prophecy, the new emperor permitted him to safeguard the Torah scroll and its sages in the city of Yavneh. Thus, while the Temple was destroyed, the Torah was not, and though Jerusalem was spoiled, Judaism was spared.

Vespasian then returned to Rome to assume his duties as emperor, and gave his son Titus the command of the Tenth Legion and the charge to complete the siege against Jerusalem. Despite the widespread famine inside the walls of the city, the Jews celebrated a last Passover with their Temple and prepared for the Roman attack. It came days later with a catapult barrage that continued for two months until the Romans finally breached the walls. Advancing house by house, the Romans set fire to the city, slaughtering every Jew in their wake. One archaeological testimony to the fierceness of the fighting is the "Burnt House" within the present-day Jewish Quarter of the city. Here can be seen the debris of one of the houses destroyed by the Romans in A.D. 70, with the remains of a woman holding a spear, lying on the doorstep where she was felled in the attack.

Though weakened by hunger, the Jewish defenders held back the Roman assault from the Temple Mount for some three weeks. Then, on the ninth of the Jewish month of Av (our August), the Roman invaders reached the Second Temple compound. This was, providentially, the very day the First Temple had been destroyed by the Babylonians 656 years earlier. The Roman historian Dio Cassius describes the final opposition of the Jews nestled around the sacred precinct with the populace stationed below in the court and the elders on the steps and the priests in the Sanctuary itself. When part of the Temple was set on fire, the priests went to their deaths willingly, some throwing themselves on the swords of the Romans, some slaying one another, others taking their own lives, and still others leaping into the flames. Dio Cassius adds that for them the event did not seem to be destruction, but victory and salvation and happiness as they perished along with the Temple.

The Romans next plundered the Temple, taking out every item of value. After the destruction, these Temple treasures were displayed in Rome during a victory procession and carried by thousands of Jewish slaves. The image of this event remains to this day in the Roman Forum, on a relief etched on the monument known as the Arch of Titus' Triumph. After the Temple was ignited, the Romans chopped down the trees in the area to form a huge bonfire around the structure. This caused the moisture in the limestone blocks that comprised the Temple to expand and blow the stones apart, helping to collapse the Temple in a single day.

Later Roman Battles over the Temple

In A.D. 130 the Roman emperor Hadrian came to Jerusalem to begin the erection of a Roman colony on the ruins of the Jewish city. He renamed the city *Aelia Capitolina* in honor of the family name of the emperor and the Capitoline triad of deities (Jupiter, Juno, and Minerva). To make matters worse, on the very day that commemorated the Temple's destruction, the Ninth of Av, the Roman governor of Judea, Tinneius Rufus, ceremoniously plowed up the remains of the Sanctuary on the Temple Mount and its environs in the name of the emperor (see *Eruchin* 27a; Ta'anit 29a; Eusebius, *Ecclesiastical History* 4:6,1). Also, during the next two years, Hadrian issued harsh decrees that offended Jewish life and religious observance by prohibiting circumcision, public assembly, Jewish ordination, and any regulation of the religious calendar.

As a result, in A.D. 132 a Second Jewish Revolt against Rome erupted under the leadership of Shimon ben Kosiba, largely, it is believed by most historians, because of Hadrian's unkept promise to rebuild the Temple.[4] This Second Revolt was successful in liberating Jerusalem and, in recognition of the victory, the leading sage of the time, Rabbi Akiva, heralded Shimon as the Messiah and renamed him *Bar Kochba* ("Son of the Star"), a messianic title based on the prophecy in Numbers 24:17: "...a star shall come forth from Jacob, and a scepter shall rise from Israel, and shall crush through the forehead of Moab, and tear down all the sons of Sheth." From Jewish reckoning, Shimon seemed to fit this role, for he not only had managed to repulse the Roman garrisons, but he also ruled as king of an independent Jerusalem for the next three years. He, too, was apparently convinced of his messianic status, for he announced that his conquest of Jerusalem had begun the messianic era and he began a new calendar system of counting the years from the date of his victory. However, the capstone of messianic identity, as later the sage Maimonides would affirm (*Melochim* 11:4), was the rebuilding of the Temple.

According to the nineteenth-century Lithuanian rabbi Samuel Shtrashun (R'shash), who claimed his source was the Roman historian of the period, Dio Cassius, Bar Kokhba rebuilt the Temple and resumed the sacrificial system (commentary on *Pesachim* 74a). Rabbi Leibel Reznick, who has published a reassessment of the historical and theological events of the Bar Kokhba era,[5] believes there may have been a Bar Kokhba dynasty that lasted 21 years and that Shimon ben Kosiba led the Second Revolt under the rule of the emperor Trajan and built the Third Temple, or Bar Kokhba Temple. He then believes that Trajan quelled this revolt after a few years and sacked Bar Kokhba's Temple treasury. However, a Third Revolt (second Bar Kokhba uprising) occurred under Hadrian, and the Bar Kokhba Temple was rededicated and sacrifices resumed until Hadrian recaptured Jerusalem in A.D. 135. The emperor then issued restrictive edicts against Jewish study of the Torah, and made all Jewish observances or religious practices a capital offense. In order to demonstrate that the Jews had not succeeded in saving their people or their Temple, Hadrian destroyed the Bar Kokhba Temple.[6] This act of desecration was preserved in the Midrash: "Hadrian, may his bones be turned to dust, came and dashed the Temple stones" (*Deuteronomy Rabbah* 3:13). In its place on the Temple Mount, Hadrian erected a temple to the Roman trinity of Juno, Jupiter, and Minerva, along with an equestrian statue of himself.[7]

Upon the death of the first Christian emperor, Constantine, in A.D. 361, Constantine's nephew Flavius Claudius Julianus, or Julian, became the undisputed ruler of the Roman Empire at the age of 30. Julian had been raised as a Christian and educated in Christian truth by the renowned bishop of Caesarea, Eusebius. But upon his ascension to the throne, Julian revealed what he had been keeping a secret for years—that he had converted to paganism around his twentieth birthday. Seeking to promote paganism and counter Christianity, he observed that Judaism was opposed to Christianity and offered sacrifices, as did pagans. Moreover, Julian became aware of a pivotal debate between the Jews and Christians over the subject of the destroyed Jewish Temple. Christians claimed that its destruction was permanent and served as evidence of the supercession of the Jewish religion. Jews believed the Temple would be rebuilt again as a sign from God that His covenant with the Jewish people had not ended. Julian, therefore, decided to make Jerusalem a Jewish city and to rebuild the Temple for the Jews in an attempt to falsify the Christian claims.

The drama that unfolded saw Julian's construction engineer Alypius beginning work at the site while a host of Christians were praying in the Martyrium of the Church of the Holy Sepulchre. Their prayer was that the reconstruction would be halted. All at once, an explosion rocked the city at the construction site, killing the workmen and stopping the work. According to the accounts left to us by historians of the period, an earthquake interrupted the building plans and destroyed the site materials. Philip Hammond, in studying this earthquake, which also destroyed the Nabatean city of Petra, describes what happened:

> The stones were piled and ready. Costly wood had been purchased. The necessary metal was at hand. The Jews of Jerusalem were rejoicing. Tomorrow—May 27, 363 A.D.— the rebuilding of the Temple would begin!...Suddenly, and without warning, at the third hour of the night...the streets of Jerusalem trembled and buckled, crushing two hundred years of hope in a pile of dust. No longer would there be any possibility of rebuilding the Temple.[8]

The Roman historian Ammianus Marcellinus, who may have personally witnessed the incident, stated that "terrifying balls of flame [*globi flammarium*] kept bursting forth near the foundations of the Temple," burning some of the workers to death.[9] Apparently the earthquake ignited reservoirs of gasses trapped underground, or volatile materials were being used in the construction work and somehow were ignited into a violent explosion. Julian's death, shortly thereafter, forced any attempt to renew the project to be abandoned.

Almost a century passed without another recorded incident at the Temple Mount. Jews had been under a ban to not approach the Temple Mount except on *Tisha B'Av*. Then, in A.D. 438, Empress Eudokia, wife of Theodosius II, gave Jews in Jerusalem permission to pray on the Temple Mount on other holy days as well. The Jews therefore gathered on the Temple Mount during the celebration of Succoth (Feast of Tabernacles), waving palm branches as they made a procession around the ruined site. However, this act enraged the Syrian monk Bar Sauma, who incited his disciples to stone those who participated in the procession. They killed many Jews and threaten to kill the empress if she intervened.

In A.D. 629 the Persians (Sasanian Parthians) invaded Jerusalem, massacred its population and, according to some, attempted to reconstruct a temple on the ruined Temple Mount. Less than a decade later, a Muslim army led by Caliph Omar conquered the city and took the Temple Mount. In 691 Caliph 'Abd al-Malik ibn Marwan completed the construction of the Dome of the Rock over the supposed site of the Temple, followed in 715 by the construction of the Al-Aqsa Mosque, which was erected over the Christian basilica of Saint Mary, which had been built by Justinian a century before. These acts of Islamic supercessionism turned the Temple Mount into a new battleground for both Judaism and Christianity. Further, the Muslim ban on Christian pilgrimages to Jerusalem and its holy sites ignited a pietistic movement in Christian Europe to liberate the Holy Land, resulting in the Crusades. In 1099, after a bloody massacre by the

Crusaders of both the Jewish and Muslim populations of Jerusalem, the Latin kingdom of Jerusalem began. The Dome of the Rock was converted into a Christian church, the *Templum Domini* ("Temple of the Lord"), with a cross affixed to the top of the dome and an altar constructed on the rock inside. The Al-Aqsa Mosque was converted into the headquarters of the Order of the Knights Templar, whose adherents entered the tunnels beneath the Temple Mount in search of mystical relics. Almost 100 years later, in 1194, the Kurdish Muslim Caliph Saladin, defeated the Crusaders, removed the cross on the dome, and changed the Dome of the Rock and Al-Aqsa back to Muslim mosques. In 1541 Sultan Suleiman I "The Magnificent" closed the gate in the eastern wall of the Temple Mount, known as the Golden Gate, to prevent the fulfillment of a Jewish and Christian prophecy that the Messiah would use this gate to enter and conquer the city. From this time to the nineteenth century there was relative calm as Islam continued its domination of the site.

This prepares us to look at the history of the battle for the Temple in the modern period (1917–present). This overview will equip us to understand the specific concerns addressed in the upcoming chapters and prepare us for the greater history yet to unfold as we move toward the advent of the last days' Temple.

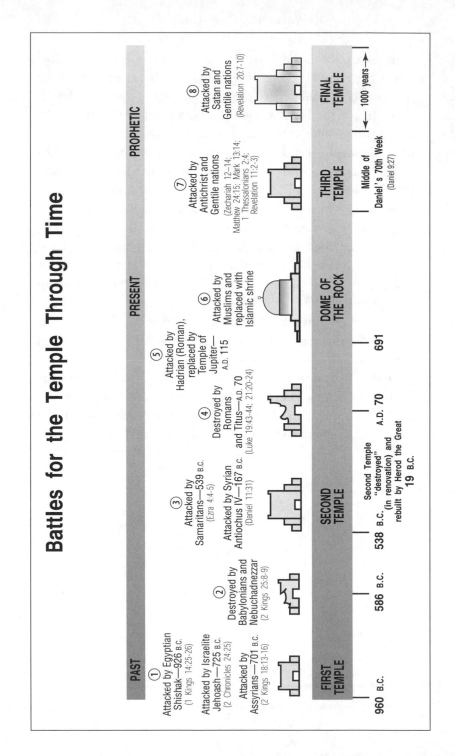

Battles for the Temple Through Time

PAST

PRESENT

PROPHETIC

① Attacked by Egyptian Shishak—926 B.C. (1 Kings 14:25-26)

Attacked by Israelite Jehoash—725 B.C. (2 Chronicles 24:25)

Attacked by Assyrians—701 B.C. (2 Kings 18:13-16)

② Destroyed by Babylonians and Nebuchadnezzar (2 Kings 25:8-9)

③ Attacked by Samaritans—539 B.C. (Ezra 4:4-5)

Attacked by Syrian Antiochus IV—167 B.C. (Daniel 11:31)

④ Destroyed by Romans and Titus—A.D. 70 (Luke 19:43-44; 21:20-24)

⑤ Attacked by Hadrian (Roman), replaced by Temple of Jupiter—A.D. 115

⑥ Attacked by Muslims and replaced with Islamic shrine

⑦ Attacked by Antichrist and Gentile nations (Zechariah 12–14; Matthew 24:15; Mark 13:14; 1 Thessalonians 2:4; Revelation 11:2-3)

⑧ Attacked by Satan and Gentile nations (Revelation 20:7-10)

FIRST TEMPLE

SECOND TEMPLE

DOME OF THE ROCK

THIRD TEMPLE

FINAL TEMPLE

960 B.C.

586 B.C.

538 B.C.

Second Temple "destroyed" (in renovation) and rebuilt by Herod the Great 19 B.C.

A.D. 70

691

Middle of Daniel's 70th Week (Daniel 9:27)

← 1000 years →

Part II:

THE RELIGIOUS AND POLITICAL BATTLES

5

Modern Battles
for the Temple Mount

*Scripture informs us that eventually the enemy will
battle against us if we just leave and go away.*

Rashi
on Deuteronomy 20:11-12

I t is sometimes thought that as man progresses forward in time, he learns to progress farther in temperance. However, the history of mankind has not been kind to such theories of social evolution. This has been particularly disappointing in the case of the world's holy sites, where restraint as a virtue of religion might be most expected. And that is especially the case with respect to the Temple Mount, which above all other sites in the world, has the imprimatur of God's holy purpose upon it.

As we witnessed in the previous chapter, Israel has become used to a long history of threats and oppression with respect to the Temple Mount. The day the Roman Tenth Legion stormed the Temple Mount and set fire to the Sanctuary ended Jewish sovereignty over the site. Over the next 1879 years, Jerusalem was conquered by many different nations, but always the Temple Mount remained outside of Jewish control. Wars between other nations were provoked by the site, such as the Crimean War (1853–56), which broke out as a result of a conflict over contradictory claims to the guardianship of the holy places by Russia and France. But the Jewish people remained outside of these conflicts, for the holy site continued to remain inaccessible to their worship, much less their control. For example, Saladin had imposed a ban on non-Muslim access to the Temple Mount in 1187 when he expelled the Crusaders from Jerusalem. This ban persisted for the next 668 years, until in 1855, the Duke of Brabant became the first non-Muslim to tour the Dome of the Rock. Despite this lack of access to the Temple Mount, Jews since medieval times have sought and fought for access to an exposed remnant of the Temple compound known in Hebrew as the *Kotel* ("Wall") and in English as the Western Wall or Wailing Wall.

War Begins at the Wall

This section of wall was not a part of the walls of the Temple itself, but was part of the retaining wall or great "box" Herod the Great had constructed to surround Mount Moriah and support the Temple Mount platform. Other parts of this wall have been accessible in times past, such as the southwestern section, where a Jewish inscription was placed in the sixth century in connection with the hopeful rebuilding of the Temple by emperor Julian, an underground section located in the present Western Wall Tunnel, where Jews of the Middle Ages met secretly to pray, and the *Kotel Qatan* ("Little Wall"), a small section of the Western Wall located between Arab shops and houses in the Muslim Quarter.

Yet the Western Wall has been the most prominent and accessible section of the wall to Jews through the ages, especially on *Tisha B'Av,* the date on which Jews mourn over the destruction of the two Temples. For centuries this was the only date and the Western Wall the only place where Jews were permitted to enter the city and express their sorrow over the loss of their Temple. For this reason, the name Wailing Wall became attached to the site. For a long time, Jews were restricted to a small alley in front of the Wall, while Muslims prayed at the mosques on the 35-acre platform above. During the nineteenth century, waves of Jewish immigrants caused the Jewish population to grow significantly, and Arab leaders became concerned. Jerusalem has always had a resident Jewish population, but in 1866, Jews became a majority in the city for the first time since 614. In 1827 the Egyptian ruler Muhammad Ali had refused to honor Jewish appeals for repairs to the Western Wall pavement. But when the Jewish population became a majority, Sir Moses Montifiore was able to go ahead and make extensive renovations.

Under the British Mandate, which began in 1917, the religious rights of Arab Muslims who visited the site were afforded special protection because the Arab world had been and continued to be seen as a greater strategic asset to the British. As a result, while Muslims were able to freely worship on the Temple Mount, including sounding out their five-time daily calls to prayer, the Jews below at the Wall were unable to even blow a shofar or make any audible noise that might disturb Muslim prayers. Under these restrictive conditions Jews continued to carry out their religious obligations in the narrow Western Wall alley, all the while being taunted by Muslims who attempted to disrupt their prayers. On August 23, 1929, following a year of constant harassment over

Photo courtesy of Alexander Schick, *Bibelausstellung Sylt*

The Western Wall area in the 1920s. At the time, the area near the wall was covered with Arab buildings, leaving only a narrow alley for Jewish worshipers.

the issue of Jewish prayers at the Wall and whether partitions, benches, and holy (Torah) arks could be placed at the site to facilitate services, thousands of Arabs rushed out of the Temple Mount compound and attacked the Jews.

The 1948 Battle for the Temple Mount

Fierce riots between Arabs and Jews over access and control of the Western Wall was one of the factors forcing political intervention in the problems in Palestine. The Islamic Grand Mufti of Jerusalem, Hajj Amin Al-Husseini, an Arab nationalist leader, directed anti-Jewish riots in Jerusalem between 1919–1940, and during World War II he collaborated with Adolph Hitler against the Jews and was the Third Reich's chief propagandist to the Arabs, aiding the Nazi program to exterminate the Jewish people.[1] Although Israeli independence was granted on May 14, 1948, Jordan took possession of East Jerusalem and permitted no Jewish access to the Western Wall or the Temple Mount. On May 25, 1948, after weeks of desperate fighting, the resident defenders of the Jewish Quarter and about 80 Hagganah soldiers found themselves outnumbered and outgunned by the Arab Legionaries. To save the more than 2000 elderly Jews who still lived in that part of the city, these defenders surrendered and the eastern section of Jerusalem fell to the Jordanians. For the next 18 years, Jordan forbade Jews access to their places of worship in this part of the city, including the Western Wall, which had been the focus of Jewish prayers for almost 2000 years.

Terrorism on the Temple Mount

At the time the Temple Mount came under Jordanian control, Abdullah I was Jordan's king. He was deemed too friendly with the Zionists and British, and he weakened his power base by placing Palestinian Arabs into governmental positions. He became unpopular, especially amongst the Arab nationalists led by the militant Jerusalem Mufti Hajj Amin Al-Husseini. As a result, upon entering the Al-Aqsa Mosque one day for prayers, he was assassinated by henchmen of the Mufti—a mere three years after Jordan had taken the Temple Mount. The event was witnessed by Abdullah's teenage grandson Hussayn bin Talal (Hussein), who would later succeed his mentally ill father Talal as king in 1953. And, just as his grandfather had lost control of the holy places to a Palestinian terrorist (Husseini), so the grandson, who became King Hussein, would also lose control of the site to another Palestinian terrorist, Yasser Arafat (a relative of Husseini).

It is also important to note that this terrorism and violence occurred between *Muslims*, within an *Islamic* holy site, and at a time when the Temple Mount was *exclusively* under Muslim control. Such facts call into question the supposed sanctity with which Muslims regard the site as well as how the present heirs of these terrorists, who now control the Temple Mount, could keep the site free of violence, even if they exercised sovereignty over it.

Jordan's "Battle" for the Temple Mount

The Hashemite Kingdom of Jordan has had a battle of its own over the Temple Mount. In 1949 Jordanian troops had managed to capture what is known as the West Bank, which included the eastern section of Jerusalem with the Temple Mount and the Jewish Quarter along with Jewish institutions such as Hadassah Hospital and the Hebrew University. Jordan had occupied the territory as part of an aggressive war and had illegally annexed it in 1950, renaming itself from Trans-Jordan to Jordan, since the idea of *trans* ("beyond [east of]") no longer applied. For almost two decades thereafter, no Jew in the western section of Jerusalem was allowed access to the Temple Mount—not even to the Western Wall.

In 1988, months after the PLO (Palestine Liberation Organization) had successfully launched its intifada ("uprising") against Israel, the Arab League decided to recognize the PLO as the official representative of the Palestinian people, and that Jordan must renounce its claims to territory that would have to house the future Palestinian state. This was a significant change, for Jordan had never given up hope of re-occupying the West Bank and East

Jerusalem after 1967, and its own relations with the PLO had been marked by conflict. To prevent the PLO intifada from spilling over into Jordan, on July 31, 1988, Jordan's King Hussein made an official royal speech in which he formally relinquished his claim to the West Bank. Yet Jordan retained its claim to administer the Islamic holy places in Jerusalem. For this reason, when Israel entered into a peace agreement with Jordan in 1994, Jordan alone was recognized as the protector of the shrines on the Temple Mount. Article 9 of the Israel-Jordan Peace treaty of October 26, 1994 states this recognition as follows: "Israel respects the present special role of the Hashemite Kingdom of Jordan in Muslim Holy shrines in Jerusalem. When negotiations on the permanent status will take place, Israel will give high priority to the Jordanian historic role in these shrines."[2] The next year, King Hussein followed through on his commitment by installing a Jordanian mufti in Jerusalem and beginning the restoration of the Dome of the Rock.

However, before the restoration project was completed, Yasser Arafat usurped the Jordanian mufti by installing his own Palestinian mufti, who then ordered Palestinians to ignore any religious dictates but his own. Thereafter, King Hussein acquiesced the site to Palestinian control, although he (and later his son–successor Abdullah II) continued to maintain their claim to be the protector of the Jerusalem holy shrines.

The 1967 Battle for the Temple Mount

On June 5, 1967 King Hussein joined other Arab states in an attack on Israel. During this Six-Day War, a battle for the Temple Mount resulted in Jordanian Arabs fleeing the Temple Mount as the Israel Defense Force seized the site.[3] It was then that Israeli troops came to realize the rampant desecration and destruction of everything Jewish on the Mount. Under Jordanian rule, 58 Jewish synagogues had been destroyed, the Western Wall had been turned into a garbage dump, with stones from the wall being used to build private houses, and Jewish gravestones had been used to construct latrines. The Temple Mount itself, although still in use for Islamic prayers, had not been maintained. The Al-Aqsa Mosque and the Dome of the Rock had deteriorated, and clumps of wild grass and weeds covered the stones of the sacred platform.

The Israeli soldiers who had triumphantly taken the Mount hoisted the Israeli flag to the top of the Dome of the Rock. But within hours of the first day of conquest, their leader, Moshe Dayan, ordered the flag to be taken down. This action revealed the course that would be followed with respect to the Islamic holy places. Dayan feared there would be a reprisal by the Arab world over Jewish control of the Temple Mount, and returned the jurisdiction of the site to the Muslims. According to later reports, the Waqf was prepared to accept only the area of the Al-Aqsa Mosque, believing the Israelis wanted to retain control of the area of the Dome of the Rock where the Jewish Temple had stood. However, Dayan had never thought in such terms, but had wanted freedom of access for all religions at the site under Muslim jurisdiction. Eventually, he was forced to accede to the Waqf's demand that Islamic law forbade any non-Muslim access to the Temple Mount for religious purposes (see chapter 9). Thus the Waqf resumed control of the whole of the Haram and began to exercise strict control over Jews whom they reluctantly had to admit to the site as tourists. This arrangement has perpetuated the Israeli government's concession to the Waqf ever since, controlling political decisions with the Arab states and the Palestinians, in the fear that any change that affected the agreed-upon status quo would result in a war with the Arab world.

Yet the Israeli victory did mean Jews could return to the Western Wall at the foot of the Temple Mount. Unfortunately, on August 23, 1969, Australian tourist Denis Michael Rohan, a member of a group considered to be a cult, according to fundamentalists and evangelical Christians, set fire to the Al-Aqsa Mosque, believing this act would hasten the coming of Christ. In response, Muslims demonstrated and accused the Israeli government of deliberately setting the blaze in order to create opportunity to rebuild the Temple. The Islamic Waqf then closed the Temple Mount to non-Muslims for two months.

Photo courtesy of Oren Gutfield

On June 7, 1967, the Dome of the Rock and Temple Mount are captured by Israeli Defense Forces and Israel regains sovereignty over the Temple Mount.

Photo courtesy of Israeli Government Press Office

Israeli Defense Forces chaplain Rabbi Shlomo Goren blows the shofar at the liberated Western Wall, which was finally back in Israeli hands after 2000 years.

In February of 1976, legislation was proposed that would permit Jews to pray on the Temple Mount, and Arab East Jerusalem schools and shops closed and strikes and riots ensued in protest against the legislation. Then in March 1979, a rumor that a Jewish prayer service might be held on the Temple Mount provoked a general strike among West Bank Arabs, and 2000 Arab youths brandishing stones and staves rioted at the Temple Mount. In August 1981 the discovery and excavation of a gate in a tunnel dating from the Second Temple era incited a riot among the Muslims. In protest, Arab schools and shops again closed, and Islamic authorities demanded that Israeli authorities permanently seal the ancient gate, even though the rabbis who found the gate contended the Ark of the Covenant was buried within the area behind the gate.

More riots occurred in January 1986 when an Israeli Knesset member attempted to pray on the Temple Mount. On October 8, 1990, when more than 20,000 Jewish worshipers were assembled at the Western Wall for prayers during the Feast of Tabernacle services, 3000 Palestinian Muslims on the Temple Mount hurled stones down upon the Jewish crowd below. The riot that followed left 18 Arabs dead and brought a missile attack against Israel from Saddam Hussein of Iraq, who had championed the Palestinian cause. At the end of October 1991, at the Middle East Peace Conference in Madrid, Spain, Syrian foreign minister Farouk Al-Shara accused Israel of attempting to blow up the Al-Aqsa Mosque and proclaimed there would be no free access for Jews to the religious sites on the Temple Mount unless Israel returned all of East Jerusalem (including the Temple Mount) to the Palestinians.

On September 15, 1993, the day the Israeli-PLO Declaration of Principles was signed, PLO Chairman Yasser Arafat announced that soon all the mosques, churches, and sacred sites in East Jerusalem would be under the Palestinian flag. And in response to a shooting in the Hebron mosque in February 1994, the Temple Mount was temporarily closed to non-Muslims. In September 1995 the opening of an exit tunnel for tourists who went into the Western Wall Tunnel sparked Muslim riots on the Temple Mount. These riots spread to outlying Arab villages, and 58 people died in the turmoil. During 1996–1997, any attempt by Jews to openly pray on the Temple Mount stirred additional riots and caused closure of the Temple Mount for brief periods.

In 1998, Muslims appropriated the Huldah Gate area behind the southern wall of the Temple Mount and built a mosque, despite Jewish protests. The mufti stated that Islamic sovereignty over the sacred sites would not be compromised. During the first few months of 1999, more than five attempts to attack the Temple Mount were thwarted by Jerusalem police, and the Palestinians came to assume greater control over the Temple Mount in view of the plan for East Jerusalem to become the capital of an independent Palestinian state. The mufti also threatened Jewish activists, saying that a Jewish presence on the Temple Mount was an offense to Islam and would not be tolerated. The Hamas spiritual leader Sheik Yassin and the Palestinian mufti Ikrima Sabri have declared that three billion Muslims worldwide will defend the sacred area to the last drop of blood.

Secrets of the Six-Day War

When Israeli forces captured the Temple Mount in June 1967, most of the Arab world expected Israel to demolish the Muslim mosques and rebuild the Temple. After all, when Islam captured the same site in 638, the Muslims erected their mosques over the site of the Jewish Temple. This is also what the Arab armies would have done in 1967 had the circumstances been reversed. Incidentally, this religious reasoning continues to cause Muslim leaders to misinterpret certain actions of the secular Israeli governments toward the Temple Mount as attempts to destroy the mosques and rebuild the Temple. In light of these expectations and fears in the Arab world, Israel returned jurisdiction of the Temple Mount to the Muslims. However, many Israelis have since contended that the Arab world would not have warred against Israel if Israel had kept control of the Temple Mount. At the time, the Arab armies were decimated, and Israel's military ruled the region. So when the Israeli government gave up control of the site, it actually appeared weak in the eyes of the Arab world, and Israel's concessions, in fact, failed to avert war with the Arab nations.

The Secret of Motta Gur

Over the last few years, several prominent figures connected with the Six-Day War have died—figures who had agreed to a code of silence about controversial events that transpired with regard to the Temple Mount. These deaths have made public some of the "secrets" of the Six-Day War. It had always been stated by the Israeli government that it had no designs in the war on the Temple Mount, but that the Mount fell into their hands unexpectedly. One of the "secrets" is that Israeli colonel Motta Gur, commander of the Reserve Paratroop Brigade that captured the Old City and liberated the Temple Mount, had acted on his own to seize the opportunity and reverse its 2000-year-long occupation by Islam. Abraham Rabinovitch, author of *The Battle for Jerusalem*, recalls that Colonel Gur had been hoping for the chance to attack the Old City and regain the Temple Mount at the very outset of the threat of war in May. However, as a man under command, he could not act independent of his orders. Chief Army chaplain (and later chief rabbi) Rav Shlomo Goren appealed to him to "ignore orders" and goaded him by saying, "You're not afraid to take chances? We could fix it up afterwards!" Although Gur did not immediately take the rabbi's advice, Rabinovitch records: "Gur...had in fact been thinking of that very thing! What would history say, he wondered, if Israel turned away from this moment? What would history say about him as the commander who failed to seize this historic opportunity?"[4] So on June 7, Colonel Gur seized his opportunity, and the Temple Mount came into Israel's hands.

When Gur and his troops entered the Temple Mount, they would never have believed that their government would again relinquish possession of the site. Gur's comments on that day reveal this conviction: "The Temple Mount! Mount Moriah... we're on the Temple Mount! The Temple Mount is ours!...We are in Jerusalem to stay."[5] Interestingly, Moshe Dayan, commander of the Israeli forces, who joined Colonel Gur's paratroopers at the newly won Western Wall, make a similar statement: "We have united Jerusalem, the divided capital of Israel. We have returned to our holiest of holy places, never to part from it again...."[6]

Secrets of Moshe Dayan

As we learned previously, Moshe Dayan was responsible for returning the administration of the Temple Mount to the Jordanian-controlled Waqf, and it has usually been assumed that Dayan acted under orders of the government. However, Rabbi Goren told me in 1994 that Dayan had acted alone on his own authority without even discussing with the government what he was about to do. After the deed was done, no one in the government dared to reverse his decision. According to Rabbi Goren, he was the only one who confronted Dayan about his action, stating to him, "You gave away the Holiest of the Holies to the enemies of yesterday and tomorrow!"

Photo courtesy of Israel Government Press Office

Moshe Dayan (with eyepatch) arrives at the newly captured Western Wall on June 7, 1967.

There are many factors that contributed to Dayan's action. From a personal standpoint, as a secularist who had grown up with Arabs and had a special affinity toward them, he was disinclined to hold on to the Temple Mount on religious grounds and was inclined to demonstrate to the Arabs his good intentions. From a military and political standpoint, he believed the West Bank and Sinai, which had also been captured in the war, should be held in view of future bargaining with the Muslims for peace, whereas Jerusalem and the Temple Mount held a special religious status for Muslims and would invite only war if Jews asserted their rights there. Dayan felt Israel could not justify maintaining Jewish sovereignty over the site in view of this greater threat from the Arab world.

Moreover, Dayan had been told by the chief rabbinate of Israel that Jewish *halakah* (religious law) would not permit Jews on the site. Therefore, Dayan saw no reason to further incite the Islamic world over a site held for 1300 years by Muslims and to which the majority of rabbis had banned Jewish visitation. Indeed, a month later, the chief rabbinate supported Dayan's decision and issued a ruling forbidding Jews to enter the Temple Mount for fear they would inadvertently desecrate the Holy of Holies.[7] Yet Dayan also knew that other Orthodox rabbis, such as his own Defense Forces chief chaplain Rabbi Shlomo Goren, did not believe that Jews should be forbidden from the entire Temple Mount. He knew Goren had a team of army engineers survey the site immediately after the war and had come to the conviction that it was permissible for Jews to enter a certain defined area. He knew that Rav Goren had even opened a synagogue within this area on the northern end of the Temple Mount. But religious opinions didn't concern Dayan because he had already decided on his course of action. Ten days after the capture of the Temple Mount, Dayan entered the Al-Aqsa Mosque, sat on the Muslim prayer carpets in stocking feet in a meeting with the Waqf, and, to their surprise, returned control of the site to them.

Secrets of Rabbi Shlomo Goren

Rav Goren became renown as the first rabbi to lead prayers at a Jewish-controlled Western Wall after 1330 years. Goren blew the shofar, recited prayer, and announced that the taking of Jerusalem had begun the messianic era. This belief motivated him to undertake a plan of action that would return Jewish worship to the Temple Mount and one day see the Temple rebuilt. Almost immediately after the capture of the Mount, he ordered a team of army engineers to survey the site so they could establish the perimeters of access without violating the rabbinic injunction against violating the holiness of the site by treading inadvertently in the Holy precincts, below which he believed the Ark of the Covenant still lay preserved within a secret chamber. This belief would later lead him and Rabbi Getz, Rabbi of the Western Wall, to undertake in 1991 a clandestine excavation, tunneling beneath the Temple Mount from within the inner recesses of the newly discovered Warren's Gate (deep within the Western Wall Tunnel) in search of the holy Ark.[8]

In May 1998 it was revealed for the first time that only hours after Israeli soldiers captured the Temple Mount, Rabbi Goren begged Israeli command to blow up the Dome of the Rock. Goren's remarks were quoted in an interview that retired Major General Uzi Narkiss, who led Israel's capture of Jerusalem's Old City, gave to the Israeli newspaper *Ha'aretz* before his death.[9] According to the interview, Rabbi Goren said, "Uzi, now is the time to put 100 kilograms of explosives into the Mosque of Omar so that we may rid ourselves of it once and for all!" When Narkiss rebuked him, Goren persisted: "Uzi, you will go down in history if you do this!" When Narkiss again refused, Goren is said to have pleaded, "You don't grasp what tremendous significance this would have. This is an opportunity that can be taken advantage of now, at this moment! Tomorrow it will be too late!" At this point Narkiss said he told Goren that if he didn't stop, he would have him put in jail. With that, Goren turned and walked away in silence.

However, Goren's former aide, Rabbi Menahem Hacohen, who was present at this discussion, gave a slightly different account of the story to Israel's Army radio. According to him, "The rabbi told Uzi that if, during the course of the war a bomb had fallen on the mosque and it would have, you know, disappeared, that would have been a good thing. Uzi said, 'I am glad that did not happen.'" Hacohen also said Goren "did not suggest using explosives," and "Uzi never told him not to do it." Army radio, however, has a tape of a speech Goren made in 1967 at a military convention, in which he called it a "tragedy" that Israel had left the Temple Mount in control of the Muslims. On the tape, Goren also said, "I told this to the defense minister [Moshe Dayan] and he said, 'I understand what you are saying, but do you really think we should have blown up the mosque?' and I said, 'Certainly we should have blown it up! It is a tragedy for generations that we did not do so…! I myself would have gone up there and wiped it off the ground completely so that there was no trace that there was ever a Mosque of Omar there!'"

Rav Goren was not alone in his enthusiasm for liberating the Temple Mount. Since those momentous days in 1967, a number of battles have been waged at the site and thus are key to our historical survey of the battle for the last days' Temple.

Activists Battle for the Temple Mount

The Temple Mount came under Israeli sovereignty only through military action, and Jewish activists understand that force will be the only way to again regain control of it from the Waqf. Almost immediately after the site was relinquished by Dayan, activist groups began planning to remove the Arab occupants and recover the Mount for Israel. The main goal of all of these groups is to prepare the site for the building of the Third Temple. Some believe this can be accomplished by human effort, while others believe only the coming of the Messiah will achieve their end.

Fire on the Temple Mount!

The first significant act of aggression against the Muslim structures on the Temple Mount did not come from Jews, but from an Australian member of a cult. In the early morning hours of August 23, 1969, Dennis Rohan, believing that his actions would hasten the return of Christ, set fire to the Al-Aqsa Mosque (see photo). The fire ravaged parts of the inner and outer structure and completely destroyed a rare sixth-century A.D. wooden pulpit that had stood in the mosque. The Arab reaction was not pitted against the psychologically unstable young perpetrator nor Christianity, but against the State of Israel. Waqf officials blamed the Israeli government and accused it of being behind a plot to destroy the Islamic holy places in order to build the Third Temple. Four days later the Waqf closed the Temple Mount to non-Muslims for two months while thousands of angry Muslims in the Old City called for *jihad* against Israel.

Even though the Israeli government denounced the action and swore it had no designs on the Temple Mount, the official Waqf inquiry into the arson placed full blame on the Israeli

Photo courtesy of World of the Bible Ministries, Inc.

The Al-Aqsa Mosque burning from a fire set by a cultist who wanted to see the Temple rebuilt.

government. One proof, according to the Waqf, was that Israeli firefighters had purposely delayed their arrival at the site, and when they got there, some witnesses claimed they were spraying gasoline on the fire, not water! Today, Arab opinion of this incident remains unchanged, and accusations against Israeli incursions on the Temple Mount frequently reference the "fire set by the Jews" as indicative of the Israeli government's true intentions.

The First Battle of the Western Wall Tunnel

Another riot on the Temple Mount occurred on August 28–30, 1981. Chief rabbi Goren and workers of the ministry of religious affairs found a leaking cistern, and, as a result, discovered one of the original entrances to the Temple Mount known as Warren's Gate. Joined by Rabbi Yehuda Getz, the two began a year-and-a-half-long excavation in secret, tunneling through this gate and underneath the Dome of the Rock in search of a hidden chamber they believed might contain the Ark of the Covenant. When the media leaked news of the dig and its purpose, the Arabs rioted in protest and sealed the gate, preventing further entrance to the excavation's tunnel. On September 2–4, Jewish seminary students, under orders from Rabbi Getz, broke down the Arab wall that sealed the gate, leading to a clash with the Arabs and their arrests by the police. The Supreme Muslim Council ordered a general strike be observed by all Arab schools and shops in East Jerusalem (on September 4) to protest the excavation efforts under the Temple Mount, and on September 10, the Waqf and the Israeli authorities jointly sealed the entrance.

Sabotage at the Temple Mount

An attack came again on April 11, 1982 when an American immigrant in the Israeli army, Alan Goodman, opened fire on the Temple Mount as he said, "To liberate the spot holy to the Jews!" Although he was ruled mentally unstable by the Israeli courts and sentenced to life imprisonment, the incident set off week-long Arab riots in Jerusalem, the West Bank, Gaza, and even drew international criticism against Israel. Then a mere two weeks later, Kach Party member Yoel Learner (who later became head of the Sanhedrin Institute, an organization that sought to return the government to a theocracy), attempted to sabotage a mosque on the Temple Mount. He was arrested and sentenced to two-and-a-half years in prison. And Jewish activists were not the only ones storing weapons on the Temple Mount; on December 9, 1982, Geula Cohen, a member of Israel's Knesset, raised the charge that the Muslims had caches of ammunition sequestered on the Temple Mount in preparation for the next war.

Three months later, on March 10, 1983, Rabbi Yisrael Ariel and a group of more than 40 followers sought permission to pray on the Temple Mount at the Solomon's Stables area adjacent to the Al-Aqsa Mosque. But after four youths connected with the Yamit Yeshiva were found breaking into the area, weapons and diagrams of the Temple Mount were recovered in a police search of Rabbi Ariel's base of operations, and many arrests made. Then on January 27, 1984, Temple activists were again arrested for planning to blow up the mosques when a Temple Mount guard discovered a cache of explosives.

The Temple Mount "Massacre"

Three years later the Palestinian intifada began and the Temple movement worked to oppose the threat the intifada posed to the Temple Mount. In October 1989, demonstrations at the Temple Mount by the activist organization the Temple Mount Faithful resulted in minor riots at Arab schools—riots that would have spread to the Western Wall Plaza had the group not been stopped by Israeli police. The next year, the group repeated their demonstration, and once again members were prevented by police from entering the site.

The Israeli police assured Muslim authorities that the group would not be allowed access to the Temple area, but on October 8, 1990, the Temple Mount Faithful held a parade outside the walls of the Old City, carrying with them a cornerstone for the Third Temple, and violence erupted. Arabs began throwing stones from

Palestinian reaction to Temple Mount Faithful demonstration (October 1990). Stones were thrown at Western Wall worshipers, and Israeli police (below) respond with tear gas.

the Temple Mount down to the Jewish worshipers at the Western Wall. The police first attempted to quell the rioting by firing tear gas and rubber bullets, but were forced to resort to live rounds to stop the Muslim attackers, who outnumbered police by as much as 100 to 1. By the time the violence had ended, at least 21 Palestinians had been killed and the tragedy had been labeled the Temple Mount "Massacre" by the media.

Later investigation of the event revealed that the violence did not erupt spontaneously as a result of provocation by the Temple Mount Faithful, but had been carefully planned by the PLO's Intifada Command. The Palestinian rioters had, in advance, stockpiled rocks, iron bars, broken glass, and knives. Before the investigation of the riot could be completed, the United States sponsored a U.N. resolution condemning Israel for the incident. What's more, Iraqi dictator Saddam Hussein used the incident to divert attention from his invasion of Kuwait (which had taken place only two months earlier) to the Palestinian plight. Championing the Palestinian cause, Hussein announced that he "would not get out of Kuwait until the Jews got out of Palestine" and launched more than 37 Scud missiles against Israel (with most landing in Tel Aviv). The United States pressured Israel to not retaliate, but still a nervous media wondered aloud if this were not the beginning of Armageddon. Here, for the first time in modern history, an incident at the Temple Mount had stirred the possible beginnings of an international conflict.

The Second Battle of the Western Wall Tunnel

The Palestinian intifada precipitated some new discussions about peace, which raised hopes that a peace like that with Egypt could be negotiated with the Arab countries bordering Israel (Lebanon, Jordan, Syria) and with the Palestinian Arabs in the West Bank and Gaza. From the outset, however, it became clear that the price of such a peace would be too high, for both sides could not agree on each other's demands regarding the division of Jerusalem and the possession of the Temple Mount. On October 31, 1991 at the Middle East Peace Conference in Madrid, Spain, when Syrian foreign minister Farouk Al-Shara accused Israel of attempting to blow up the Al-Aqsa Mosque, he proclaimed that there would be no free access to the religious sites on the Temple Mount unless Israel returned all of East Jerusalem to the Arabs. Such rhetoric was repeated in all the speeches made by Yasser Arafat and his representatives.[10] That the Arabs felt so

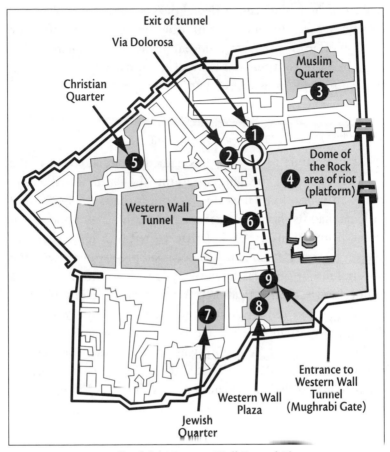

Details of the Western Wall Tunnel Riot

strongly on these matters was evident in September 1995 when the Israeli government opened an exit for tourists for the Western Wall Tunnel. The Waqf and Yasser Arafat publicly charged Israel with attempting to destroy the Islamic holy places and rioting took place on the Temple Mount and throughout the West Bank, leaving some 80 people dead. Later, on May 14, 1998, an arsonist set fire to one of the heavy wooden gates guarding the Temple Mount area. Internal security minister Avigdor Kahalani reported that a firebomb had been hurled at the door, setting it ablaze and damaging several stones surrounding the gate.[11] And after the election of prime minister Ehud Barak and on into the new century, the Waqf continued to view all attempts by Jews to pray on the Temple Mount as invasions of sovereign Arab territory and vowed that bloodshed would be the result.

The Battle for Al-Aqsa (the Al-Aqsa Intifada)

The Palestinian Authority has named the most recent of the modern battles for the Temple Mount "the Battle for Al-Aqsa." This battle, also known as the Al-Aqsa Intifada or the Second Intifada, had its flashpoint occur on September 28, 2000, when Israeli prime minister Ariel Sharon visited the Temple Mount. Sharon's purpose for making the visit, all pre-arranged with the Muslim authorities, was to escort a committee from his Likud political party to investigate reports that construction of a new mosque on the Temple Mount, undertaken by the Waqf, had damaged important archaeological remains at the site.[12] Although at this time the Temple Mount was open to visits from Jews as well as tourists, the Waqf had not allowed either archaeologists or the media into their construction sites. They had also warned Sharon about making the inspection. While the pretense for this warning was linked to challenging Islamic authority over the site, the real fear was that some action might be taken by the Israeli authorities with respect to the new mosque. This concern is reflected in a threat that was issued by Hasan Tahboub, head of religious affairs in the Palestinian Authority: "There will be massacres if there is any attempt to stop the opening of the mosque."[13] Likewise, Sheik Ahmed Yassin, the Islamic spiritual leader of the militant Palestinian organization Hamas, declared that any attempt by Jewish militants to seize control of the Temple Mount or to destroy Islamic shrines would lead to a bloodbath: "They will start a fire in which they shall perish."[14]

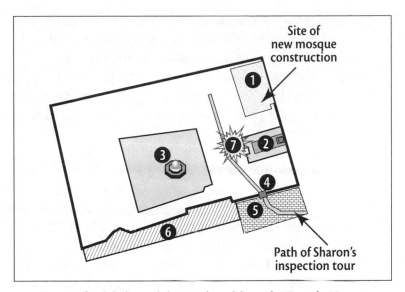

Route of Ariel Sharon's inspection visit to the Temple Mount

1. Solomon's Stables
2. Al-Aqsa Mosque
3. Dome of the Rock
4. Mughrabi Gate
5. Western Wall
6. Waqf buildings
7. Site of conflict with police the next day

Such statements only convinced Sharon that it was necessary to remind the Waqf and the Palestinian Authority that Israel was still sovereign over the Temple Mount and that Jews had the right to enter the site. Yet Sharon restricted his visit to the Temple Mount and did not enter any of the mosques so as to not provoke the Muslim authorities. Throughout his tour at the site he was accompanied by Arab MKs and representatives of the Waqf and some 1000 armed guards. The visit went peacefully and Sharon left without incident. The next day, a Muslim cleric delivered a fiery sermon at the Temple Mount mosque and denounced Sharon's visit, claiming that the Jews had defiled the mosque. The Muslim worshipers then swarmed out of the mosque and called for Muslims everywhere to "come and slaughter the Jews" and to "come and defend the mosques." The Muslims threw stones down on the Jewish worshipers at the Western Wall, and a riot was under way. Israeli police responded, and though they did not enter the Al-Aqsa Mosque, where the rioters had fled, the very presence of the police in the area provoked accusations that the Jews had entered the mosque (see diagram on previous page).

Yasser Arafat responded to the riot by calling for a renewal of the intifada, which he said was justified by Sharon's aggressive actions and the Israeli government's failure to heed the warnings of the Palestinian Authority and forced entry to the mosques. The Waqf responded by banning all Jews from entrance to the Temple Mount—a clear violation of the 33-year status quo arrangement permitting access to people of all religions, which was accepted by both sides in 1967. The Israeli government chose not to deal with the religious violation and political usurpation of the site because it was already suffering in the international media and from a U.N. Security Council Resolution that condemned Sharon's visit. Instead, the Israeli government closed the site to all non-Muslims, citing security concerns, since Israeli officials stated they could not guarantee the safety of visitors in light of the mounting tensions generated by the renewal of the intifada. This standoff continued for the next 33 months while the intifada

Photo by author

Jewish activists marching to the Temple Mount area.

claimed Israeli lives through homicide bombings and Palestinian lives through Israeli retaliations. Then in June 2003 the Israelis began to reassert their sovereignty over the Temple Mount and reopened the site to restricted visits, but not to the mosques.

A Sensitive Dilemma

It is clear from the recent struggles over the Temple Mount that Muslims are very assertive in claiming their authority over the Temple Mount, and are quick to resort to violence at the slightest perceived provocation. The Temple Mount has also proven to be one of the most sensitive issues in all the peace talks to date. What circumstances and developments in past history contributed to the Muslim perspectives of today? That's the subject of our next chapter—the Islamic claims to the holy site.

6

Muslims on the Mount

The mosques on the Temple Mount were built by the order of God [Allah]...Our sovereignty is not subject to compromise.

ADNAN HUSSEINI,
director of the Waqf

It started like most pleasant days in Jerusalem, where Israeli Arabs—Arab citizens of the State of Israel—go to jobs in the Israeli capital to work seemingly peaceably alongside their Jewish neighbors. However, this day would betray a different reality to the Jewish population. For on this morning, some 50,000 of these Israeli Arabs assembled on the Temple Mount for a rally organized by the Islamic Movement, an often-militant organization that operates freely under the protection of Israeli democracy.

Ostensibly, the purpose of the gathering was to address the theme "Everything for the Child of Islam." However, it soon became clear that the message did not concern the poverty of Palestinian children, but was a Muslim call to conquer the country and to control Jerusalem and the Temple Mount. Raed Salah, the leader of the Islamic Movement in Israel, shouted, "Palestine belongs to the Muslims and not to the Jews!" while young girls dramatized this call for *jihad* dressed up as homicide bombers with green headbands bearing the words *Islamic Movement* and

Shahid ("martyr"). He was joined by Sheikh Kamal Hatib, the second-in-command in the movement, who declared, "The Al-Aqsa Mosque—its foundations, walls, and buildings—belongs solely to the Muslims and not to any other religion. We warn the Jews that they will burn if they try to destroy the Al-Aqsa Mosque!"

This demonstration by Arab *citizens* of Israel—not radical Palestinians from the refugee camps—again reminded the Jewish citizenry that no amount of social, economic, and political benefits attached to citizenship matter when two peoples are divided in a religious war. Moreover, the demonstration brought to the surface once again Muslim demands for exclusive sovereignty over Jerusalem and its Temple Mount. Only by examining Islam's claims concerning the city and its holy site will we understand the reason for the increasing militancy displayed by the Arab Muslim population, how it has led to recent violent confrontations with a largely secular Israeli society, and how it will lead Israel to its most significant crossroad in history on the Temple Mount in the days to come.

The Nature of the Islamic Claims

Muslims have been on the Mount for the past 1300 years. Over this long history the site has come to be so defined by a Muslim presence that for Muslims, as well as for the uninformed masses, the site has no other meaning. The Muslim scholar Aref el Aref has stated that "the only text needed for a study of the history and present structures of the Temple Mount are the [Muslim] buildings themselves and the Arab inscriptions that both adorn and explain them."[1] With this kind of reasoning, Islamic officials at the site have come to deny any historical reality other than that which their religion can explain. When asked about ancient structures that obviously pre-date the Muslim arrival in Jerusalem, the standard answer is that these are "pre-Islamic." Things that are "pre-Islamic" are never anything more than this, and in fact, are of no real consequence to the devout Muslim. Moreover, nothing can be proved concerning that which is "pre-Islamic," since, to the Muslim mind, Islamic tradition is the basis for accepting a matter, and Islam has already accepted the Temple Mount—the Haram al-Sharif—as the Qur'an's "Al-Aqsa," the point from which the prophet Muhammad ascended to heaven in his famous Night Journey (*Sura* 17). Since these religious claims drive the battle for the Temple Mount from the Muslim side, and since most people are unfamiliar with the Islamic claims concerning the Temple Mount and with the historical sources that respond to these claims, let's look at these claims and responses here.

The Importance of Jerusalem to Muhammad

Muhammad's knowledge of and interest in Jerusalem appears connected to his desire to influence the Jewish community of Medina to accept his role as a prophet and adopt Islam. In an effort to attract Jews, he initially ordered his followers to pray toward Jerusalem, changing this practice and facing the Ka'aba in Mecca only after the Jews rejected him. From this it is possible to see that Muhammad regarded Jerusalem only because he recognized it was the city of greatest importance to the Jews. However, neither Jerusalem nor its Temple Mount were ever regarded by him as a place of Islamic pilgrimage. Rather, as Emanuel Winston, Freeman Center Middle East Analyst, points out, "Mohammed, in his time, had made Jerusalem literally a forbidden place to Muslims. It is not mentioned once in the Koran. If a Muslim had to go to Jerusalem for trade, it was called a '*zhu*' (journey)—not a religious '*haj*' as when Muslims make their mandatory pilgrimage to Mecca."[2]

If Jerusalem had had sanctity or significance for Muhammad, it is impossible that it would not have been mentioned by name in *Sura* 17:1, which describes the locations of Muhammad's Night Journey. Instead, we find reference only to *al-masjid al-haram* ("the holy shrine") and a cryptic reference to *al-masjid al-aqsa* ("the distant shrine"). There was no need to explain the reference to "the holy shrine," as every Muslim knew this to be the Ka'aba in Mecca. However, what of the "distant shrine"? In time it came to be identified with Jerusalem, but was this the original understanding of those who first read the Qur'an? Paul Fregosi, assuming a literal interpretation of *Sura* 17:1, notes that in the religion's beginning, Jerusalem had no historical association with Islam: "The stopover in Jerusalem [during the Night Journey to paradise] was probably the only occasion during his life that Muhammad ever visited the city, *previously sacred only to Christians and Jews*. After the Night Journey it also joined Mecca and Medina as holy cities of Islam [emphasis added]."[3]

Given the emphasis in the Qur'an on Mecca and Medina in order to preserve their status as holy cities, it is improbable that if Jerusalem were, as it is claimed today, "the third holiest city in Islam," that it would escape mention. Rather, given the significance of Mecca and Medina and the reference to the "holy shrine" as Mecca, it would be expected that "the distant shrine" would be Medina. Some Islamic scholars also state that at this time the *al-masjid al-aqsa* ("the furthest mosque") was thought to be either in Medina or al-Giranah on the Arabian Peninsula.[4] At any rate, there is no direct reference by Muhammad to Jerusalem in the Qur'an, and therefore no direction given by the founder of Islam regarding Jerusalem's holy places.

If there is no direct reference to Jerusalem in the Qur'an, and only one undesignated reference can be deduced by the Muslim for it, what then is the source for making Jerusalem the third holiest city in Islam? Jewish historian Shlomo Dov Goitein explains that "most of the traditions about Jerusalem and its sanctuary were local and largely of foreign origin and had no foundation in old Muhammadian stock."[5] Professor M.J. Kister has shown that the tradition whereby Jerusalem has been fixed as the third holiest city by Islam is a later development of an original tradition that spoke of Mecca as the *only* holy Islamic sanctuary. For four centuries, most Islamic scholars rejected Jerusalem as having a sacred significance for Islam. For example, the noted

Arab geographer Yakkut wrote in 1225 that Jerusalem was "holy to Jews and Christians," whereas "Mecca was sacred to Muslims."

One explanation for the sanctity eventually ascribed to Jerusalem by Muslims is the influence of Arab politics. Some scholars propose that 'Abd al-Malik, the first caliph after the Muslim conquest of A.D. 638, boosted the sanctity of Jerusalem in order to compete with Damascus, the new and expanding capital of the Islamic empire as well as with a rival caliph in Mecca, Ibn al-Zubayr. According to the ninth-century historian Ya'qubi, 'Abd al-Malik built the Dome of the Rock to attempt to divert the crowds of Muslims making the *hajj* (Muslim pilgrimage to Mecca) to Jerusalem.[6] I. Goldziher, in 1890, explained this diversion as the result of the campaign of 'Abd al-Malik against Ibn al-Zubayr,[7] but S.D. Goitein reexamined the theory and refuted it in 1966.[8] It is no longer accepted in modern scholarship, even though it was recently revived by a Muslim writer in an official Egyptian publication.[9] This does not mean, however, as Emanuel Winston points out, that Muslim reverence of Jerusalem and the Temple Mount was not originally fostered for political reasons:

> The Dome of the Rock was built by Caliph El Malik 70 years after Mohammed's death in the year 632 CE. Malik's goal was to turn Muslim "*Quibla*" (direction of prayer) away from Mecca, towards Jerusalem and him. This was a political move to bring pilgrims to Jerusalem in order to increase his power in the areas under Malik's control and make himself heir to Mohammed. He had no religious motivation, just geo-political ambition....Malik did not succeed in his goal to bring Muslims to Jerusalem or to himself. The Dome of the Rock was virtually ignored by the Muslim and Arab world as it fell into ruin....At the time of Mohammed's death, there was no mosque on the Jewish Temple Mount. It wasn't until the 12th century that the Kurd, Saladin, mounted a large propaganda campaign to claim that the mosque named "*al Aksa*" was where Mohammed had flown on his mythical night flight. Saladin

used this as an excuse to justify his attack against the Christian Crusaders who then had control of Jerusalem and the
Jewish Temple Mount. Saladin's goal was to whip up the
religious hysteria of the disparate tribes—much the same as
Arafat does today.[10]

Other scholars maintain that the motive was religious competition with the pre-existing Jewish traditions and Christian
churches that adorned the city of Jerusalem. Miriam Ayalon, professor of Islamic art and archaeology at the Hebrew University,
wrote,

> The first and foremost of these considerations is undoubt-
> edly the religious associations of ideas and events with the
> city prevailing among both Jews and Christians. Indeed,
> the fact that Jerusalem was already important to the two
> monotheistic faiths from earlier times, and the fact that
> Islam considered itself as the last of the revelations...
> made it legitimate for Islam to absorb and identify with
> former beliefs obtaining there. Jerusalem could not be
> ignored. The Temple area, which had been abandoned
> after the destruction of the second Temple and turned
> into the municipal dung center as a deliberate policy of
> the Byzantines, offered an ideal space to establish the
> monuments of the new rulers. Moreover, the very fact that
> some of the preexisting Byzantine buildings remained in
> Jerusalem and could provoke admiration, or eventually
> jealousy, required a Muslim response.[11]

The tenth-century historian of Jerusalem, al-Muqaddasi,
appears to confirm this assessment when he wrote, "Caliph 'Abd
al-Malik, noting the greatness of the Dome of the Holy Sepulchre and its magnificence, was moved lest it should dazzle the
minds of Muslims and so erected the Rock, the Dome....During
the building of it they had for a rival and as a comparison the
great Church of the Holy Sepulchre...and they built this to be
even more magnificent than the other."[12]

This act of supercessionism (or theological replacement) explains why the Dome of the Rock was erected 60 years after the Muslim conquest of Jerusalem. Islam lacked an established culture and monumental architecture to rival that of centuries-old Byzantine Christianity. This was especially true in Jerusalem, where from the time of Constantine, magnificent churches, basilicas, and monasteries had been erected to the glory of Christ. The original primitive wooden structure built to house the Rock was satisfactory to the first generation of Muslims who were accustomed to the simplicity of Muhammad's mosque in Mecca. However, the splendor of the Christian churches that filled Jerusalem and that were built in close proximity to the Temple Mount elicited a competitive response from second-generation Muslims who had grown up as conquerors. This also explains why the cupola inside the Dome of the Rock is covered with Islamic polemics against Christianity. Although Jesus is seen as a prophet in Islam, the impressive adornments throughout Jerusalem's churches magnified Jesus' divinity, a practice forbidden as *shirk* (the highest form of apostasy) in Islam.

Why Muslims Built the Dome of the Rock

According to Muslim tradition, the conquering Umayyad caliph Umar Omar ibn al-Khattab took Jerusalem without a struggle in A.D. 638, its surrender negotiated by the city's Byzantine patriarch Sophronius. Upon entering the city it is said Umar requested from the patriarch to be taken to "the *mihrab* ('place of prayer') of David." However, according to the account of the Byzantine chronicler Theophanes, "[Umar] donned the mask of hypocrisy. He wanted to see the temple of the Jews that Solomon had built, so that he could turn that site into a place of worship for his infidels."[13] At first Sophronius showed Umar the Church of the Anastasis (Resurrection), but refusing this identification, Umar was eventually taken with difficulty to the Temple Mount. The difficulty lay in the fact that during the time of Byzantine rule, the Temple Mount had been turned into the city's garbage dump.

After a stinking ascent through tons of refuse, Sophronius pointed to a large heap of trash and declared, "Here is that appalling abomination, as prophesied by Daniel, standing on the holy site!"[14] Beneath the centuries of debris was a large rock mass that tradition had taught was the foundation stone that had been within the Holy of Holies in the First and Second Temples. Sophronius' derisive statement reflected the preterist perspective that interpreted Jesus' statement in the Olivet Discourse (cited from the prophet Daniel) of an "abomination of desolation" to refer to the Second Temple that had been destroyed by Rome in A.D. 70. Byzantine Christianity's treatment of the Temple Mount had followed this line of thinking and by turning the Jewish site into a dunghill, sought to demonstrate God's irrevocable rejection of the Jews and its replacement by the church. This seemed to the church to be an appropriate way of symbolizing the Mount's abominable status to the largely illiterate resident population.

Umar was appalled not by the fact that this was a Jewish holy site, but by the Christian desecration that had taken place. According to Muslim tradition, he immediately ordered the site to be cleared, astonishing his subjects by taking the initiative and removing some of the accumulated filth from the sacred rock with his own hands. He then supposedly ordered the building of a "house of prayer" at the site. However, for over 60 years, no structure was erected for this purpose. When Umar's son Caliph 'Abd al-Malik (685–705) finally built a wooden edifice known as the Dome of the Rock (Arabic, *Qubbat al-Sakhra*) in 691 to enshrine the outcrop of bedrock believed to be the "place of the sacrifice" on Mount Moriah, it was for the sole purpose of displaying Islamic hegemony over Jerusalem and its Jewish and Christian holy places. In other words, the purpose was polemical and initiated an ideological battle against the long-established cultures in the city that had only recently been conquered by Islam and over which Muslim teaching proclaimed superiority. It is for this reason that the design of the wooden edifice was basically Byzantine—double-octagonal ambulatories encircling the

Holy Rock. Al-Malik wanted his architectural masterpiece to rival the existing Byzantine structures in Jerusalem. Therefore, the Dome of the Rock is an architectural expression of the ascendancy of Islam over the city. Inside the structure, the drum and dome contain ornate Qur'anic inscriptions affirming that God is one and not three, and that Jesus was an apostle of God and not His Son. These statements were designed to help Muslims counter the influence of Christian theology in the city.

Umar also symbolically demonstrated his conquest of Christianity by praying inside the Christian basilica of Saint Mary, located at the southern end of the Temple Mount, an act that obligated Muslims to turn the structure into a mosque. In 715 'Abd al-Malik's son, Caliph al-Walid I, fulfilled this obligation and erected the Al-Aqsa Mosque, its name being derived from a Qur'anic term attributed to the entire compound, over the site of the church. The remains of this can be seen in the "old Al-Aqsa" located beneath the present mosque. The Dome of the Rock, by contrast, was constructed as a shrine and not a mosque, for no caliph prayed there.

According to traditional Islamic accounts, when the command to build a mosque on the Temple Mount was given, a Jew (a convert to Islam?) named Ka'b al-Ahbar tried to get the caliph to establish it north of the Rock, proposing that this arrangement would allow worshipers to face Mecca in the south and simultaneously face the Rock (a direction of prayer Muhammad had once accepted). Umar rejected the proposal on the grounds that it would imitate Jewish religious practice. Based on this, Islamic scholar Moshe Gil concludes, "This anecdote provides clear-cut evidence of the fact that, in the initial phase of their rule, the Muslims did not assign any sacred status to the Temple Mount, and, indeed, regarded the assigning of such status as being contrary to the principles of Islam."[15]

Moreover, even though the teaching that the Dome of the Rock was the site of Muhammad's Night Journey would have benefited the caliph's polemical and political cause, he was unable

Photo by Paul Streber

The Muslim Dome of the Rock (after 1994–1996 restoration).

to use it for his purposes because no such connection in Islam had yet been made. "Yet," as Berel Wein has observed, "it is precisely because of its importance to Jews and Judaism that it has become one of the red lines of the Muslim world."[16] This, of course, became of greatest importance once Islam lost control of Jerusalem and its Islamic holy sites and they and Muslims came under the domination of non-Muslims after 1967. This turn of events was viewed by the Muslim world as a crime that needed to be avenged and the sacred property recovered through *jihad.* That is why the Palestinian Authority is so preoccupied with wresting the Temple Mount from the control of the Jewish State and how the Palestinian Authority's current destruction of ancient Jewish remains on the Mount and construction of new Islamic mosques helps achieve this goal.

The Islamic Destruction of Sacred Sites

While Islam fiercely contends for its own mosques and shrines, it has often been intolerant of the holy places of other religions. Throughout Islam's history of conquest, it has destroyed or altered historic sacred structures in the lands it has added to the Islamic empire. Sometimes the purpose for the destruction was punitive, such as Sultan Mahmud Ghaznavi's invasion and destruction of the temple of Somnath because the people of Somnath refused him passage or refused to pay the agreed-upon war booty. At other times, the motive was to replace previous religious traditions and bolster Islam's claim to be the final, superior religion. For example, in Turkey, Islam transformed the most important church of Eastern Christianity, the Hagia Sophia, into a mosque, and changed the name of the city of Constantinople to Istanbul. In 1009 the Fatimid ruler al-Hakim attempted to destroy Christianity's most holy site, the Church of the Holy Sepulchre in Jerusalem (the traditional site of the tomb of Jesus). A more recent example of Islamic intolerance was the Taliban's wanton destruction of ancient Buddhist statues in Afghanistan.

On the Temple Mount, both the Dome of the Rock and the Al-Aqsa Mosque were built over the ruins of Jewish synagogues or Byzantine churches, as well as the ruins of the Jewish Temple that preceded them. Although Islamic tradition states that the Al-Aqsa Mosque was built 40 years after Abraham and Ishmael constructed the Great Mosque in Mecca (some 2000 years before Solomon built the Temple), history records that the emperor Justinian had erected a Christian basilica on the Temple Mount a century before the arrival of Islam in Jerusalem that had the same dimensions as the later Al-Aqsa Mosque. The architecture of the old Al-Aqsa, below the present structure, also conforms to the Byzantine pattern of such a basilica. The octagonal shape of the Dome of the Rock, common to Christian architecture, was followed by the Muslim caliph 'Abd al-Malik because Islam at that point had not yet developed its own architectural style. Another example of Islamic construction meant to counter the influence of opposing faiths was the placement of a Muslim cemetery in front of Jerusalem's Eastern Gate (Golden Gate). This was intended to prevent the entrance of the Jewish (and Christian) Messiah to the site to rebuild the Temple. Modern Islamic practice in Jerusalem, and especially Palestinian practice, has continued to demonstrate an ongoing intolerance of the holy sites of other religions.

Photo courtesy of Alexander Schick *Bibelausstellung Sylt*

The Islamic Temple Mount in the late 1800s, with the Dome of the Rock at the center and the platform area in the foreground.

Photo courtesy of Alexander Schick *Bibelausstellung Sylt*

The Al-Aqsa Mosque as it appeared on a postcard in 1930.

Palestinian Muslim Supercessionism

In the 1920s, Jerusalem mufti Haj Amin el-Husseini used Jerusalem and the holy places as an instrument to provoke riots and foster Arab nationalism. After 1948, and especially after 1967, supercessionism became an important political tool to counter the influence of Jewish traditions in Jerusalem. From 1948 to 1967 Jordan controlled the eastern area of the city, which include the Jewish Quarter and holy places. The mostly Palestinian population destroyed everything Jewish in the Jewish Quarter and exercised exclusive control over Jewish holy places such as the Wailing Wall, even though it largely abandoned administrative functions in the rest of the city. Since 1967, Arab political demands for a return of the city have increasingly denied all historical Jewish claims to the city and denied the past existence of a Jewish Temple.

To this day, Palestinian Muslims under the Palestinian Authority continue to desecrate both Jewish and Christian holy places. In 1997, Palestinians took over Abraham's Oak Russian Holy Trinity Monastery in Hebron, evicting its monks and nuns. In Jerusalem, Palestinian Authority officers endangered the walls of the Church of the Holy Sepulchre (traditional site of the crucifixion and tomb of Jesus) by attempting to construct a latrine on its roof. At the outset of the Al-Aqsa intifada, Palestinian Muslims attacked and burned the Jewish synagogue in Jericho and the traditional Jewish tomb of the patriarch Joseph in Nablus. Despite protests by Israeli authorities and requests by the Orthodox Jewish community to the Palestinian Authority to restore the site, further desecration of the inner tomb has occurred, and today it is a trash dump. Since 2000, the Palestinian Authority has regularly stationed artillery and sharpshooters in Christian towns near churches to either shield their gunmen or bring Israeli fire down on places of worship.

In Nazareth, the ancient boyhood home of Jesus and a modern Israeli-Arab city with a large Christian population, Palestinian Muslims began construction in 2000 of a mosque in front of the Basilica of the Annunciation, the traditional site of the angel Gabriel's message to Mary that she would bear the promised Messiah. The mosque was erected on the pretense of the site having a connection with Shihab al-Din, a Muslim hero who allegedly fought the Crusaders on a nearby hill. Slated to be the largest mosque not only in the Middle East but the entire world, its foundations were erected despite protests by Pope John Paul II and President George Bush. Christians saw the presence of the mosque as an Islamic attempt to change the nature and character of the city and as a religious declaration that the era of Christian Nazareth was over. Israeli courts ruled that the construction was illegal and in July 2003, Israeli wrecking crews leveled the massive foundations, while Muslim clerics and Palestinian Authority officials threatened reprisals.

The destruction of Christian communities in the West Bank also coincides with the destruction of the Jewish and Christian holy places. When the Palestinian Authority first assumed autonomy over Bethlehem, Yasser Arafat seized a Greek Orthodox monastery near the Church of the Nativity to serve as his occasional residence. Shortly thereafter Palestinian Muslims converted the formerly Christian Manger Square into a mosque and area for Muslim prayer and began oppressing the resident Arab Christian population. Reports have circulated of Christians being beaten, raped, and murdered as collaborators with Israel, and charged by protection rackets. While very few complaints are filed with authorities about these bigoted acts, locals with whom I am familiar voice their fears in private. Moreover, the Al-Aqsa intifada forced the closure of Christian and tourist sites such as the Herodium and the shepherds' fields, severely affecting Arab Christian merchants who made their living from tourism. Furthermore, the Palestinian Authority incorporated 30,000 Palestinians into the municipality of Bethlehem, changing the Christians' 60 percent majority to a minority. According to those in the area, almost three-quarters of the city's Christian population have since left.

In April 2003, Palestinian militants took over Bethlehem's Church of the Nativity (the traditional birthplace of Jesus) at gunpoint, booby-trapped its entrance, and then terrorized 150 worshipers for 39 days. During this time they seized the priests' rooms (exiling them, and forcing the worshipers seeking refuge in the church to sleep on stone floors without provisions), devoured their food stores (6 months worth of food in 3 weeks), drank their liquor (contrary to Islamic law), stole church valuables such as gold crucifixes, and used pages from pew Bibles for toilet paper. At one point they also set fire to one of the church buildings and sought to blame it on the Israelis. When the militants were finally expelled, church officials found widespread destruction and desecration of the church property, and the church was littered with liquor bottles and thousands of cigarette butts. Yet, photos taken inside during the seige show these Muslim militants observing daily prayers in the church!

These accounts of the Palestinian Authority's intolerance, desecration, and destruction of the sacred sites of other religions in the Land have been described here to demonstrate that the agenda of militant Muslims is to replace competitive faiths. Thus they cannot honor agreements that require them to protect the sanctity of such sites—agreements that are usually part of the various negotiations for peace that have taken place in recent decades. In addition, these reports demonstrate that the destructive actions being taken by the Palestinian-controlled Islamic Waqf on the Temple Mount (see chapters 8 and 9) are consistent with the replacement goals of Islam and cannot help but inevitably lead to Israeli intervention designed to prevent the loss of not only the historical and religious character of the site, but also political control.

Another means by which Islam has sought to destroy opposing faiths is through historical revisionism. In the case of Jerusalem and the Temple Mount, the history of a Jewish identity for the city and site is being denied while an Islamic identity is being written in its place. To experience the gravity of the historical rape being committed against the Jewish people, let us look next at the revisionist claims of the Palestinian Muslims presently in charge of the Temple Mount.

Islamic Revisionist History and the Temple Mount

The Temple Mount was never there....There is not one bit of proof to establish that. We do not recognize that the Jews have any right to the [Wailing] Wall or to one inch of the sanctuary.

SHEIKH IKRIMA SABRI,
Palestinian mufti of Jerusalem

During the U.S.-led war with Iraq in 2003, reporters often highlighted the outrageous lies of the Iraqi Minister of Information known as " Baghdad Bob." When U.S. forces had bombed Baghdad and invaded the city, Baghdad Bob continued to release reports to the Arab world that American soldiers were far from the city and suffering serious casualties from the Iraqi army. Even when the media broadcast live the scene of Saddam Hussein's statue in the center of Baghdad being toppled, many throughout the Arab world refused to believe the images were real. They thought they were seeing elaborate computer simulations created by Hollywood, in part because the Arab press was still denying that Baghdad had fallen! This is not surprising in the context of the War on Terrorism, in which the Islamic world has taken pains to present the news coming from the West as propaganda designed to subvert the faith of Muslims. For example, much of the Islamic world still believes that Muslim

Arabs had nothing to do with the terrorist attack on the United States on September 11. Rather, they believe the event was deliberately staged by the U.S. administration as part of a Jewish and Christian crusade against Islam![1]

Truth is usually the first casualty of war, and as Ronald Hendel, professor of Hebrew Bible and Jewish Studies in the department of Near Eastern Studies at the University of California, Berkeley, has noted, "In the Middle East, lies in wartime often include lies about the past, since the past—or more precisely, public memory about the past—provides authority for claims about the present."[2] This has been particularly demonstrated in the war of words being waged by the Palestinian Authority in their recent revisionist history of the Temple Mount. At present, the official position of the Palestinian Authority may be summed up in their statement, "For Islam, there was never a Jewish temple at Al Quds [Jerusalem]."[3] The Islamic world has long been conditioned to receive such a statement as "truth" by their abhorrent view of Jewish history. This may be seen in the explanation of Saudi sheikh Abd Al-Rahman Al-Sudayyis, imam at the Al-Haram Mosque, the most important mosque in Mecca: "Read history and you will understand that the Jews of yesterday are the evil fathers of the Jews today, who are evil offspring, infidels, distorters of [others'] words, calf-worshippers, prophet-murderers, prophecy-deniers…the scum of the human race whom Allah cursed and turned into apes and pigs."[4]

Yet, would not the acceptance of such a statement about the Jewish Temple turn the Old and New Testaments into fraudulent documents, since they contain abundant details about the Jerusalem Temple? Surely Muslims have a greater respect for the holy books of Judaism and Christianity, from which their own religion borrows? The answer, as given by Dr. Ahmed Yousuf Abu Halabiah, Rector of Advanced Studies at Islamic University, is that

> the Bible today has no light and no teachings. Their Bible today is just a bunch of notes that were written down by

people who lie about God, his prophets and his Bible....
Those who do these kind of things are the descendants of
Abelis, meaning the descendants of the satans....They
fabricated a Jewish history book full of promises to
Abraham, Isaac and Jacob that he will give them the land
of Palestine.[5]

The Need to Understand Islam

The problem for westerners, in their pluralistic religious context, is that they have not been able to take such words seriously
as representing the Islamic worldview. During the 1979 U.S.-
Iranian crisis, *Newsweek* reporter Meg Greenfield called attention
to the West's ignorance of Islam: "We are heading into an expansion of the American relationship with that complex religion, culture and geography known as Islam. There are two things to be
said about this. One is that no other part of the world is more
important to our own well being at the moment—and probably
for the foreseeable future. The other is that no part of the world
is more hopelessly and systematically and stubbornly misunderstood by us."[6]

Subsequent decades have revealed to the West the seriousness
of our ignorance—especially through events such as 9/11 and the
U.S.-led war with Iraq, which have brought about an explosion
of information concerning the religion, beliefs, and intentions of
Islam's most militant adherents. Unfortunately, the predominantly Judeo-Christian West (particularly the United States) still
does not understand how irreverently Islam regards rival religions
and their historic holy sites. The western traits of religious pluralism and the disconnection of religion and politics has contributed to this lack of understanding, as professor Huston Smith
has noted: "The West's separation of church and state makes it
next to impossible for it to understand people who lodge religious belief not only at the center of their individual conduct, but
also at the center of their politics."[7] The East, by contrast, has

always lived with such beliefs, and for the past 1300 years has experienced firsthand Islamic enmity toward rival religions.

Historically, the attempt to accomplish Islamic religious and political objectives through military means in the Israeli-Arab conflict, and in its present focus, the Israeli-Palestinian conflict, has thus far failed. By contrast, the goal to revise history in order to affect the political process for religious ends has succeeded. Nowhere has Islamic revisionism been more prolific and pronounced than in matters related to the Temple Mount. In order for us to comprehend this, it is necessary to examine further Islam's theological concepts of other religions—which, in turn, control Islam's political response to the people and countries characterized by those religions.

How Islam Views the Jews and Jewish Religion

Islam views itself as the final and complete divine revelation, superceding and replacing all previous religions. Although Islam inherited its monotheistic character and values from the older religions of Judaism and Christianity, and based its origins and early history on key figures found in their sacred Scriptures, the Old and New Testaments, Islam rejects these religions as having strayed from the truth and their holy books as having been corrupted. As a result, Jews and Christians are treated as enemies of Islam and the subjects of *jihad:* "Fight against such of those who have been given the Scripture as believe not in Allah nor the Last Day..." (*Sura* 9:29).

The Jews, most commonly referred to as *Banu Isra'il* ("the Children of Israel"), are also referred to by the Qur'anic phrase *al-dhilla wa-al-maskana* ("humiliation and wretchedness"). This condition of the Jewish community in Muslim lands (a result of the imposition of inferior *dhimmi* status) was considered a proof of Allah's rejection of the Jewish people and the falsity of Judaism. Conversely, the prosperity of Muslims (a result of the conquest and absorption of non-Muslim cultures) was believed to be a demonstration of Allah's acceptance of Muslims and the veracity of Islam.

Concerning the Jewish Bible (Old Testament), Islam teaches,

> No copy of the original *Taurat* ["Torah"] granted by Allah to Musa is extant. As a matter of fact, during their long and chequered history, the Jews repeatedly lost their revealed books…the *Bani Isra'il* ["children of Israel"] failed to act up to the *Taurat*, they made it into (separate) sheets for show and concealed much of its contents…and they distorted and perverted Allah's word and changed its meaning (*Sura* 2:75, 213; 4:46; 5:14, 44; 6:91; 7:169; 10:93; 11:110; 16:124; 41:45; 45:17). The Old Testament in the Bible cannot, for these reasons, be regarded as the book revealed by Allah to Musa.[8]

Similarly, Islam declares concerning the New Testament:

> Allah took a covenant from those who call themselves Christians but they forgot a good part of the message that was sent to them" (*Sura* 5:15). "The *Injil* ['Gospel'] mentioned in the Holy Qur'an is not the New Testament or the four Gospels; but refers to the book revealed by Allah to His prophet, 'Isa, son of Maryam. By the time of Muhammad all of the books revealed up to that time had either been totally lost, or their original contents and the true message had been grossly perverted and distorted.[9]

Revision of Biblical Figures Related to the Temple Mount

Islam has recast accounts in the Jewish and Christian Bible with Arabic overtones while reinterpreting and revising the stories to conform to Muhammad's revelation. According to the Qur'an, the world's "first temple," the original *Ka'aba*, was erected by the first man, Adam, in Mecca (the hometown of the prophet Muhammad). This was later rebuilt by Abraham (Ibrahim), who, depicted as an Arabian sheikh in the Qur'an, was stated to be neither a Jew nor a Christian, but a submitted *hanif* ("adherent to perennial monotheism"), as well as his firstborn son Ishmael (Isma'il). Beside this mosque, Ishmael and his mother Hagar were later buried. While the biblical account of Abraham sets the stage for eventual selection of the Temple Mount in Jerusalem (Genesis 22:2,14; Exodus 15:17; Deuteronomy 12:5-6,10-11; 1 Samuel 24:16-25; 2 Samuel 7:10-13; 1 Kings 5:4-5; 8:15-20), the Qur'an ignores Jerusalem and establishes the priority and preeminence of Mecca and the Meccan shrine (the sacred mosque). Moreover, Muhammad is declared in Islam to be a descendent of Abraham through Ishmael, which sets him up as the final messenger and the superior over Jewish messengers and prophets who also shared this ancestry.

Although the Qur'an does not name the son whom Abraham was to offer as a sacrifice, Islamic commentators have traditionally argued that it was Ishmael, contending that Allah's reward for Abraham's obedience (with Ishmael) was a second son, Isaac. This revisionism strategically replaces the Old Testament's *person* of sacrifice and denies Isaac as the exclusive inheritor of the promises of the Abrahamic Covenant (Genesis 17:19,21). Moreover, Islamic tradition changes the *place* of sacrifice from the Old Testament's Mount Moriah in Jerusalem (Genesis 22:2) to the foot of a hill in Mina, three miles outside of Mecca. The Old Testament's record of Hagar and Ishmael being cast out by Abraham after the birth of Isaac and being saved by a well of water in the wilderness (Genesis 21:14-19) becomes, in the Qur'an, the miraculous creation of the sacred well of Zamzam in Mecca, said to have sprung from the foot of Ishmael. The present Palestinian-Muslim plan is to bring water from the well of Zamzam to the recently cleaned (of Jewish remains) cisterns of the Temple Mount, and by linkage to Mecca and the Ishmael tradition, to irreversibly transform the historic site of Jewish reverence to one of Muslim devotion.

Moses (Musa) is linked to Abraham as a founder of the monotheistic religion Islam claims to have restored, and his brother Aaron (Harun) appears alongside him as a prophet rather than a priest. However, since Moses is the most prominent figure in Judaism, Islam sought, in its elevation of Muhammad, to reduce Moses' status and significance. In the famous account of Muhammad's ascension to heaven during the Night Journey (*Sura* 17), we are told that when Moses met Muhammad he wept (in sorrow), because, thanks to Muhammad, more Muslims would now go to paradise than Jews. David (Da'ud) and Solomon (Sulayman), are also said to have been Muslims, a fact that, for Muslims, fits well with a denial that they would have built a *Jewish* Temple. Jesus ('Isa) is likewise a Muslim and a prophet of Islam, but is inferior to Muhammad, the final prophet.

Replacement of Judaism's Role on the Temple Mount

By turning the key founding figures and prophets of Judaism and Christianity into Muslims, Islam attempts to replace these religions while preserving their own time-honored reverence reflected throughout the Middle East. In creating the story of Muhammad's ascent to heaven there was an attempt to supercede similar stories concerning Moses and Jesus. When the Muslim ruler 'Abd al-Malik situated this event in Jerusalem and on the Temple Mount, holy places that had previously been revered only by Jews and Christians, he effectively usurped the site for Islam. As Emanuel Winston points out:

> By naming his new mosque "*al Aksa*," Malik's son tried to capitalize on the myth, bringing Muhammad to Jerusalem's al Aksa Mosque, where he then flew to heaven to receive the blessings of all the earlier prophets, Abraham, Isaac, Joseph, with the later addition of Jesus, et al. This would link or add the Jewish and Christian lineage to the Muslims in order to bring the strength of the Jews and Christians into Islam while eliminating the Jews' physical link to the Covenant. In Arafat's war against the Jews, he uses this myth by calling the Western Wall (a remnant of the Second Temple's retaining wall) the "*Buraq*" wall, furthering his spurious claim to the Jewish Temple Mount.[10]

Claims That the Temple Never Existed

As incredible as it may seem to those who are accustomed to reading the original literary sources (Bible, Dead Sea Scrolls, Josephus, Talmud, Roman and Greek historians) and are familiar with the archaeological evidence (Israelite monuments and artifacts, Hebrew inscriptions) in support of the Jewish past, the Palestinian Authority asserts as fact that such a history never existed. Most of their published statements are reactions to the traditional historical perspectives and appear in the form of caustic denunciations or angry threats. The Palestinian mufti of Jerusalem, Sheikh Ikrima Sabri, has declared:

> There is not the smallest indication of the existence of a Jewish Temple on this place in the past. In the whole city, there is not even a single stone indicating Jewish history.... The Temple Mount was never there....There is not one bit of proof to establish that. We do not recognize that the Jews have any right to the wall or to one inch of the sanctuary.... Jews are greedy to control our mosque....If they ever try to, it will be the end of Israel.[11]

In like manner, Hasan Tahboub, head of the PLO-backed Supreme Muslim Council, stated, "We expect the Israelis to give us back these holy places....We believe in freedom of religion, but Jews won't have rights there because these are our places."[12] And Yasir Abed-Rabbo, a senior aide to Yasser Arafat and one of the leaders of his team of negotiators with Israel, stated in an interview with the French newspaper *Le Monde* on September 25, 2000 (as reported in the Israeli daily *Ma'ariv*, September 26, 2000): "There never was a Jewish Temple in Jerusalem."

The Palestinian Authority ministry of information said in a December 10, 1997 press release that "there is no tangible evidence of any Jewish traces/remains in the old city of Jerusalem and its immediate vicinity." Palestinian Authority ministry of information official Walid Awad said, "Jerusalem is not a Jewish city, despite the biblical myth implanted in some minds....There is no tangible evidence of Jewish existence from the so-called 'Temple

Mount Era'….The location of the Temple Mount is in question…it might be in Jericho or somewhere else."[13]

In like manner, Palestinian Authority president Yasser Arafat has said, "I am sounding the alarm against the Jewish scheme, which aims to establish the Solomon Temple in the place of Al-Aqsa Mosque, after removing the mosque….Delivering holy Jerusalem from the monster represented by this continuous and advancing…threat of Judaization is a duty imposed upon all of us by Allah."[14] It is interesting to note, in these words accusing the Jews of Judaizing the Temple Mount, the very revisionism practiced by the Muslims in their attempts to Islamize the same site.

Photo by author

Arabic literature describing Jewish efforts to rebuild the Temple on the Temple Mount. Cover depicts Third Temple picture replacing Dome of the Rock, which was denounced by Ikrima Sabri.

Denial of Archaeological Evidence of Jewish History

Palestinians are also diligent to explain away, by the process of simple negation, any archaeological remains that Jews identify with the Temple. For example, Jeries Soudah, a Palestinian Authority leader who works with Yasser Arafat, says,

> It has not been proven that the Temple was ever located there [the Temple Mount]....Do the Jews have proof that this is the site of their holy place?...There are the arches and everything [beneath the Temple Mount], but are these things from a Jewish Temple being there? How do we know that these are not Muslim or Christian constructions?...Maybe there are certain pieces that prove that *something* Jewish was there. But there is no absolute proof that a Jewish Temple ever stood there.[15]

In my own conversations with Palestinians, every archaeological discovery is conveniently labeled either "Islamic" or "pre-Islamic," thereby avoiding any possible association of artifacts or structures with a particular pre-Islamic (Jewish) culture. Therefore, a Palestinian Authority information press release could state, as a fact,

> The archaeology of Jerusalem is diverse—excavations in the Old City and the areas surrounding it revealed Umayyad Islamic palaces, Roman ruins, Armenian ruins and others, but nothing Jewish. Outside of what is mentioned/written in the Old and New Testaments, there is no tangible evidence of any Jewish traces/remains in the Old City of Jerusalem and its immediate vicinity.[16]

Of course this information failed to mention that every archaeological artifact uncovered in Jerusalem, including the Islamic ones, was made by and identified by the same Jews who claim a wealth of Jewish discoveries!

Denial That the Western Wall Is Jewish

Palestinians likewise contend that the Western Wall is not Jewish but Muslim, and refer to it as Al-Buraq Wall because they

Photo by Ann Clark

Author with lentel stone inscribed with geometric design from the Second Temple. This artifact, discovered in the Mazar excavations at the southern wall, testifies to a Jewish presence on the Temple Mount in ancient times, contrary to Palestinian revisionist claims.

believe that the celestial steed of Muhammad (Al-Buraq) was once tied there at the time of the Night Journey from Mecca to Al-Aqsa, in *Sura* 17:1. Palestinian mufti Ikrima Sabri issued a religious decree on February 22, 2001 that stated the Western Wall of the Temple Mount is Islamic property and has no connection to Jewish history. "No stone of the Western Wall has any connection to Hebrew history,"[17] Sabri asserted. To Muslims, the Wall is the western wall of the Al-Aqsa Mosque (which Muslims call the entire Temple Mount platform). As such, Sabri said, it should not be called the Western Wall or the Wailing Wall but the Al Buraq Wall, after the name of Muhammad's horse.

The mufti's view of the Western Wall is not new. Yasser Arafat and his aides have made similar claims in the past. For example, Arafat once declared: "That is not the Western Wall at all, but a Moslem shrine,"[18] and Palestinian Authority religious affairs minister Hassan

Tahboob stated, "The Al-Buraq wall [the Western Wall] is Muslim property and it is part of the Al-Aqsa Mosque of course."[19]

Muslim history books teach that "Jews come to pray at Al-Buraq wall" which, in Islam, is only associated with Muhammad. For this reason the vigil of Jews at the Wall 24 hours a day must be confusing to Palestinians. One of those apparently confused is the spiritual leader of the Al-Aqsa Mosque, Sheik Muhammad Hussein. When a reporter friend of mine asked why Jews pray at the Western Wall if it isn't a retaining wall of the Temple Mount, as Muslims claim, he replied: "I don't know. Some people pray to the moon. Some people pray to Jupiter. I don't know why the Jews pray there!"[20]

Photo by author

The Western Wall, with Jewish worshipers, and the Dome of the Rock on the Temple Mount above. This wall is a remnant of one of the original outer retaining walls of the Temple Mount.

However, in the sixteenth century, the Ottoman Turkish sultan Suleiman the Magnificent, who rebuilt the present-day walls of the Old City, recognized the Western Wall as an official holy place to the Jews and had his court architect Sinan build them an oratory there. History records that Suleiman based his recognition on a longstanding pre-Islamic tradition concerning the Jews and the Wall. For example, the Babylonian Talmud (*Brachos* 32), codified around A.D. 600, teaches that when the Temple was destroyed, all the gates of heaven were closed, except for one. That is the Gate of Tears, or the Western Wall, which has also become known as the Wailing Wall because of all the tears Jews have shed there. One of the many pilgrim travelers to Jerusalem who observed this was Benjamin of Tudela. He noted in an account written in 1170 that the Wall was venerated by the Jews even then: "All the Jews, each and every one of them, write their names on the Wall." Likewise, the traveler Samuel Ben Shimshon of Lunee reported in his chronicle of 1210 that those beholding the Wall "tore their garments as is proper…and wept a great weeping."

Some scholars have questioned whether the wall mentioned in these pilgrim accounts was in fact the Western Wall, because after the Muslim conquest in 638, Jews were known to have prayed at the sites of the High Priest's Gate in the *eastern* wall and the Hulda Gates in the *southern* wall. The reason these walls were originally chosen was because during their periods of exile from the city, the Jews could view the Temple Mount only from the Mount of Olives, and these gates were within range. The change to the western wall is thought to have occurred after the fall of the Crusader kingdom, when the size of the city had been reduced, leaving the southern walls outside the city wall and thus outside of protection. The safer choice for pilgrims was the western wall within the city, a choice believed to have been made official in 1267 when Jewish settlement was renewed by Nahmanides. We also know that during the early Muslim period (A.D. 638–1099), one of the four gates in the Western Wall (from the Second Temple period), now known as Warren's Gate, served as a place of Jewish prayer. In fact, the internal space of the gate-passage (known as "the Cave"), in proximity to the ancient site of the Holy of Holies, was used as the main synagogue of the Jews. Therefore, there is no reason to doubt that the Western Wall itself had significance to the Jewish community from even before the Muslim conquest in 638.

Why the Denials?

The Palestinian Authority's denials of the Temple's past existence are based on religious belief and political expediency. Adnan Husseini, a senior Waqf official, argued from religious conviction when he once declared, "The mosques on the Temple Mount were built by the order of God (Allah]….Our sovereignty is not subject to compromise."[21] The religious basis for rejection of the Jewish claim to the Temple Mount is evident in the explanation of Palestinian mufti Ikrima Sabri: "The Temple could not have been built on the Temple Mount because the Al-Aqsa Mosque was built there. Allah would never have told them to build it if a Jewish Temple had been there."[22] This kind of religious reasoning, coupled with the notion that money is the only motive for Zionism, is mentioned in an argument against the Jewish Temple in an excerpt from a Hamas publication. Note here that the Hamas reasoning goes so far in its revisionism as to claim there was never even a historical Jewish presence in the *entire* country:

> Historians and archaeologists claim that the temple built by Solomon (peace upon him)—as the Jews claim—has no evidence of ever existing. The most likely of opinions is that the temple that the Jews are looking for is in fact the blessed Al-Aqsa Mosque. The Al-Aqsa Mosque in fact has a history predating the Prophet David (peace upon him). Imam Qurtuby said: "It is conceivable that it was built by the angels after finishing with the always attended house with the permission of their Lord Most High. The superficial meaning of the Hadith indicates this, and Allah knows best." The Hadith which has been narrated on the authority of Abu Zarr (r.a.a.) who said: "I said 'O Messenger of Allah, which mosque was placed on the earth first?' He (s.a.w.) said: 'The Sacred Mosque' (That is the Mosque where the Ka'ba is at Mecca. Tr.). Then I said: 'Then which?', he (s.a.w.) said: 'Al-Aqsa Mosque.' Then I said: 'How much is between them?' He (s.a.w.) said: 'Forty years.'" The idea of creating a nationalist nation for the Jews was a dream of many of the most influential Jews and Jewish thinkers. The suggestion of Palestine as this

nation springs from their religious belief—as they claim—that this is the promised land, and the Temple of God was in it. However, this belief is no more than a cover for the bringing together of the Jews. The new goal for choosing Palestine as a country for the Jews springs from a strategic and economic objective and not from a religious objective at all....Palestine forms the point of concentration of all the world powers, because it is the strategic centre for controlling money" (Reported in "Hamas, The Historical Roots and the Pact", p. 16).[23]

Palestinian propaganda to the Arab Muslim world promoting the revisionist myth that the Israeli government has captured the Dome of the Rock and is preventing Islamic pilgrimage to the Muslim holy places on the Temple Mount.

Palestinian Revisionism and Political Negotiation

This revisionism serves both a propagandistic purpose and a political one. This was dramatically demonstrated at the Camp David II Summit negotiations, to the chagrin of both Israeli prime minister Ehud Barak and U.S. president Bill Clinton. As time for the Oslo Accord's final status negotiations drew near, Yasser Arafat made it clear that the deciding factor in the negotiations would be the issue of sovereignty on the Temple Mount. Barak decided to make the ultimate concession and offer the Temple Mount to Arafat in terms he did not think could be refused. He offered the Palestinian Authority a practical sovereignty over everything on the Temple Mount, reserving only a symbolic sovereignty for the Jewish state over the remains of the Jewish Temple underground. Surprisingly, Arafat not only refused, but abruptly left the meeting. The official Palestinian Authority newspaper *Al-Hayat Al-Jadida* (August 12, 2000) reported the reason as Arafat explained it to President Clinton: "I will not allow it to be written of me that I confirmed the existence of the so-called temple underneath the mountain [the Temple Mount]." Arafat's revisionism cost him the prize he sought, but as Arafat stated later, to have acknowledged the existence of the Temple in any form would have cost him his life!

What Muslim History Really Reveals

Muslims claim that Mecca and Medina are the first and second holiest sites in Islam, and that Jerusalem and the *Haram al-Sharif* (Temple Mount) is the third holiest. However, if this is really the case, the history of the site should reveal evidence of care and concern over Jerusalem and its holy places. Yet just the opposite is revealed by a study of the site while it was under Muslim rule. As late as the 1850s, when Jerusalem was the largest city in the country, with a population of some 25,000, it was notorious for its filth and the worsening condition of its holy sites, especially the mosques and buildings on the Temple Mount. Jerusalem was without a sewage system, and had polluted water (which led to a severe plague that killed hundreds in 1864). A report in the 1860s mentions tourists' complaints of animal carcasses lying in the city's gates and streets. When the British Mandate began in 1917, British architects were asked to determine how to save the structures on the Temple Mount, which had been allowed to deteriorate during the 400 years of Muslim Turkish rule. Photos taken at this time show largely abandoned and dilapidated buildings, both the Dome of the Rock and Al-Aqsa Mosque in a ruined state, and the Temple Mount platform overgrown with weeds and strewn with rubble.

During the British Mandate, when European tourists came to see the Temple Mount, they were able to purchase *A Brief Guide to al-Haram al-Sharif,* an official guidebook to the site issued by the Supreme Muslim Council of Jerusalem. This body was appointed by the British government during the Mandate period to administer the Muslim affairs in Palestine, which included Waqf affairs. The guide focuses exclusively on the Muslim connection to the site, with the authors stating clearly: "...for the purposes of this Guide, which confines itself to the Moslem period, the starting point is the year 637 A.D."

In a copy of this guidebook published in 1935, we read this concerning the Temple Mount:

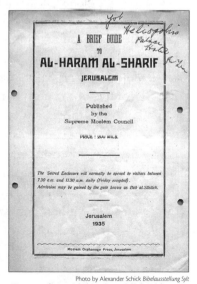

> The site is one of the oldest in the world. Its sanctity dates from the earliest times. Its identity with the site of Solomon's Temple is beyond dispute. This, too, is the spot, according to universal belief, on which David built there an altar

Photo by Alexander Schick *Bibelausstellung Sylt*
Cover of a guidebook published by the Moslem Supreme Council in 1935. The guidebook states that the site was that of the Jewish Temple.

unto the Lord, and offered burnt offerings and peace
offerings." A footnote then refers the reader to 2 Samuel
26:25.[24]

Judaism's unequivocal connection to the Temple Mount
comes up again on the last page of the booklet, which discusses
the "substructures" of the Dome of the Rock. While describing
the area of Solomon's Stables, the very area today's Islamic Waqf
officials have converted into a new mosque (see chapter 9), the
guide states: "...little is known for certain about the early history
of the chamber itself. It dates probably as far back as the construction of Solomon's Temple....According to Josephus, it was in
existence and was used as a place of refuge by the Jews at the time
of the conquest of Jerusalem by Titus in the year 70 A.D."[25]

The statements in this British Mandate guide reveal to us that
the same body that once *defended* the Jewish origin of the Temple
Mount today *denies* it. What is the difference between that day
and this? The difference is that an independent Jewish state exists
and is in control of Jerusalem and the Temple Mount. This
explains the historical revisionism, for Islamic religious law says
it is intolerable for Islam to be anything but a superior religion.
That is what motivates Palestinian revisionism and the battle for
exclusive control of the holy site.

In addition to these facts, a recently published article in the
Egyptian Ministry of Culture's weekly publication *Al-Qahira* has
undermined the traditional Islamic support for a claim to the
Temple Mount. Ahmad Muhammad 'Arafa, a regular columnist
for the publication, contended in the August 5, 2003 issue that the
interpretation of Muhammad's Night Journey "from Mecca to
Jerusalem" is the result of erroneous reading of the account in
Sura Al-Isra' (17:1).[26] Presenting a new analysis of the Qur'anic
text, this writer states:

> This text tells us that Allah took His Prophet from the Al-Haram
> Mosque [in Mecca] to the Al-Aqsa Mosque. Thus, two mosques
> are [referred to] here, the first of which is the Al-Haram Mosque,

and the second of which is the Al-Aqsa Mosque. "Al-Aqsa" is a form of superlative which means "the most distant." Therefore, the place to which the Prophet was taken must be a mosque, and not a place where a mosque was to be established later, nor a place where a mosque had once stood....But in Palestine during that time, there was no mosque at all that could have been the mosque "most distant" from the Al-Haram Mosque. During that time, there were no people in [Palestine] who believed in Muhammad and would gather to pray in a specific place that served as a mosque. Most of the inhabitants of Palestine were Christians, and there was among them a Jewish minority. Although the Koran refers respectfully to Jewish and Christian houses of worship, it does not call any of them a mosque, rather "churches and synagogues" (*Surat Al-Hajj* [22]:40). The construction of the mosque situated today in Jerusalem and known as the Al-Aqsa Mosque began only in the year 66 of the Hijra of the Prophet—that is, during the era of the Omayyad state, not during the time of the Prophet nor that of any of the Righteous Caliphs....the Night Journey (Isra') was not to Palestine; rather, it was to Medina. It began at the Al-Haram Mosque [in Mecca] after the Prophet had prayed there with his companion,(4) and both of them had left it, and the journey ended at the mosque of As'ad ibn Zurara, in front of the house of Abu Ayyub Al-Ansari, in Medina, where the Prophet built the mosque known as the Mosque of the Prophet.[27]

Moreover, in another article published two weeks later, the same writer argued that the change in Qibla (the direction which a Muslim faces in prayer) by Muhammad away from Jerusalem meant the city had lost its priority in Islam.[28] His arguments, though commonly made by non-Muslims, are extraordinary coming from a Muslim writing in an official publication of a Muslim country. His statements deserve careful consideration:

Palestine was conquered [by the Muslims] in the year 17 A.H. ["After the *Hijira*" = A.D. 638] in the time of 'Umar Ibn Al-Khattab, and in his day, the people [of Palestine] were [just] beginning to adopt Islam. Hence, how could there have existed in Palestine, at the time of the Prophet [i.e., before Palestine was conquered by Islam], a mosque, be it called "the most distant" [Arabic: al-aqsa] or not....Therefore, the mosque known today as the Al-Aqsa Mosque is not the one referred to by the Koranic words: "From the Al-Haram Mosque [in Mecca] to the most distant mosque (al-aqsa)." It is true that the Prophet did direct himself in prayer, according to Allah's instructions, toward *Iliya* [i.e., *Aelia*]—the name of Jerusalem in that period—for 17 months, and then, instructed by Allah, he redirected himself to the Al-Haram Mosque in Mecca. Aelia was the center of worship for the Jews, as it continues to be. This means that, for a while, the Prophet shared with them in their direction of prayer, and then he turned away from it toward another *qibla*....The change of *qibla* from Jerusalem to the Al-Haram Mosque [in Mecca] meant that Jerusalem was no longer the center of worship for the followers of Muhammad and that it no longer deserved to be respected by Muslims beyond what any historical city in their domain deserved. If this is not understood in this way [namely, that the change of *qibla* signifies that Jerusalem lost its previous religious status], then the change of *qibla* has no meaning....[29]

This Muslim writer further argued that the Al-Aqsa Mosque and the Dome of the Rock were not built as a result of Islamic reverence based on fact, but to promote a political agenda, and as a result, entered into an Islamic tradition of veneration. Although he argued on the basis of a now-disproved theory of diversion of Islamic pilgrimage because of the political rivalry between the caliphs 'Abd Al-Malik Ibn Marwan and Ibn Al-Zabayr (see chapter 6), the political basis for the erection of these structures has been historically documented. His comments, therefore, need to be considered:

The new mosque [in Jerusalem] was first called "the Mosque of Aelia," and prophetic traditions were invented mentioning this name [so as to invest it with Islamic significance]. Then the name 'Al-Aqsa was stolen for it [from the mosque in Medina], because it [i.e., the mosque of Aelia] was the most distant from Mecca and Medina. It was claimed that the Koranic expression "the most distant mosque" referred to it [i.e., the mosque of Aelia] because the mosque of the Prophet [in Medina] was neither "distant" nor "most distant" for the people of Medina....In sum... the religious connection of Muslims to Jerusalem ended with the change of the *qibla* from Jerusalem to Mecca. When 'Abd Al-Malik Ibn Marwan...began to build a large mosque in Aelia, religious traditions appeared glorifying this mosque and the Dome of the Rock....And what facilitated this [transfer of the name "Al-Aqsa"] is that the people of Medina did not call [their mosque] "distant" or "most distant," because it is a geographical term [which was not relevant to them]....We inherited these [traditions promoting the sanctity of Jerusalem] as if they were part of [the Islamic] religion.[30]

It has long been recognized by non-Muslim interpreters that the reason Muslims erected the Dome of the Rock and turned their attention toward Jerusalem was because of its prominence in the Jewish religion as the place of the Jewish Temples. Professor Ronald Hendel affirms this fact and contrasts it with the Palestinian denial of a Jerusalem Temple when he concludes:

> The very statement that "there was never a Jewish temple at Al Quds" is self-defeating. The Arabic term Al Quds, "The Holy (City)," is an abbreviation for the fuller term, Bayt al-Maqdis, which literally means "the Holy House." This fuller form was the normal Arabic name for Jerusalem before the tenth century c.e. It is clearly a translation of the Hebrew term Bet Ha-Miqdash, "the Holy Temple." In other words, the Arabic name for Jerusalem, Al Quds, has within it the memory that this was the city of the Jewish Temple.[31]

Therefore, the very name by which Palestinians and the Arab Muslim world call Jerusalem reflects the original Jewish sanctity toward Jerusalem because of the former presence of the Jewish Temples.

Yet despite historical evidence that denies a religious connection for Muslims to the city and the site—evidence that is accepted and advanced by some Muslim writers—Islamic revisionism and Palestinian propaganda have gained much ground through the media and Palestinian Muslims appear to be winning the battle for the Temple Mount at present. How is it that Israel lost the Temple Mount, and what does the future hold? That's what we will examine in the chapter to follow.

8

How Israel Lost
the Temple Mount

*We have lost the Temple Mount. Exactly 31
years after we heard, "The Temple Mount is
in our hands," the situation is that it is not in
our hands....We have simply allowed our sovereignty to disintegrate, and this is a terrible
disgrace for the Jewish people.*

GERSHON SALOMON

No battle was fought. No shots were even fired. Nevertheless, over the last decade, Israel lost the Temple Mount.
In a takeover peculiarly absent from newspaper headlines, control passed from the Jordanian custodians to the Palestinian Authority, who promptly scrapped the freedom of religious
access and status quo arrangement negotiated between Moshe
Dayan and the Jordanian-controlled Islamic Waqf in 1967. While
it is true that Dayan did not believe exercising sovereignty over the
Temple Mount was in the interest of Israel, he still believed that
retaining sovereignty over the site was a necessary part of maintaining the unified status of Jerusalem, which had just been won
in the war. And while he accepted the Waqf's restriction that no
non-Muslim expressions of worship be allowed on the Temple
Mount, he never anticipated a situation in which Israeli sovereignty over the site would be rejected, Jews would be banned from
the site, and new mosques and buildings would be constructed

without Israeli permits or archaeological supervision for the purpose of removing any trace of Jewish history from the site.

Dayan was a collector of biblical antiquities, but scarcely could he have imagined that one day, the priceless ancient remains at the site would be tossed into the municipal dumps. Nor could he have anticipated that the Israeli government would ignore the Muslim authorities' rejection of Israeli injunctions against mosque construction, as well as the Israeli Antiquities authorities' protests against archaeological destruction, and allow illegal acts to continue on Dayan's same grounds of "provocation." Despite Dayan's secular, pro-Arab reputation, I believe even he would have been dumbfounded!

In light of the Palestinian Authority's abuses on the Temple Mount, Israeli columnist Nadav Shragai has complained, "The ongoing destruction of the remnants of the Jewish past at a site that is the most important in the fabric of life of the Jewish people…combined with a situation that is straight out of the theater of the absurd, namely the prohibition on Jews to visit the site, which no one imagined could come to pass at the Temple Mount…is like a sword plunged into the heart of many Jews."[1] Rabbi Shalom Gold, too, has expressed the opinion of many who are disgusted about the exclusion of Jews from the focal point of their faith in the heart of their capital city. Speaking at the time the Waqf imposed its ban on Jewish visitation to the Temple Mount, he declared, "The lesson is that 'history is not made in the future but rather in the past.' History is *not* about telling our grandchildren what we did to prevent the continuing destruction. History is about our being responsible to our ancestors who set it up in the first place! We *had* a *Bais Hamikdash* (Temple) and *we let it go!* We had access to the Temple Mount and *we allowed access* to be denied to us, *this year!*"[2] This loss of access to the Temple Mount represents, in a practical sense, a loss of control of the Temple Mount. How did this situation come about? Who, in fact, really controls the Temple Mount? To find the answer, we must first understand the history of the control exercised over the site through the centuries, beginning with the Roman destruction of the Temple in A.D. 70.

Who Controls the Temple Mount?

After the Roman destruction, the ruined Temple Mount was governed by Roman authorities. When the Roman Empire adopted Christianity as its official state religion in the fourth century, the Temple Mount was placed under the control of Christian clerics and officials from Byzantium, the center of Eastern Orthodoxy. This continued until the Muslims invaded Jerusalem in A.D. 638 and assumed control of the city and site for the next 461 years. The successful conquest of Jerusalem by the Crusaders in A.D. 1099 ended the Islamic presence in the city and put the Temple Mount under Christian control for 88 years, after which the Muslim army of Saladin took control of the city. Although a Third Crusade against Jerusalem failed, it nearly reached the city, and fears of repeated attacks led in 1229 to a diplomatic agreement between the Egyptian ruler al-Malik al-Kamil and Frederick II, king of Germany and Holy Roman Emperor. This agreement divided the city between the Christians and the Muslims, with the Muslims receiving the Temple Mount.

In 1320 a development occurred that would affect the status of ownership at the sacred site for some time to come. That was the founding of the Abu Midyan Muslim trust *(waqf)*. Originally founded to help North African Muslim pilgrims go to Jerusalem, a *waqf* is property administered by the state or in private ownership (or both) for either a secular or religious purpose. The Western Wall and the Temple Mount became two of its property holdings in Jerusalem, a custodial claim that continues to the present day. Therefore, despite the succession of rules by the Mamluk and Ottoman kingdoms, the site continued to remain under the control of the Waqf.

British Control

When the British defeated the Ottoman Empire in 1917, Jerusalem came under British Mandate. Even so, mandatory government policy was careful to respect the religious claims by the various religious groups in the city—especially those of the Arabs, who had become an asset to the British military. The property owned by the Muslim religious trust *(waqf)* during the Ottoman period were centered in Jerusalem around the Al-Aqsa Mosque. These were considered protected endowments, and on this basis, Muslim authorities were left in charge of the Temple Mount, with the British Mandate government going so far as to even pay for repairs to the Al-Aqsa Mosque.

Under the improved conditions in Mandate Palestine, the Arab population was allowed to increase from 600,000 to 1,200,000, while Jewish immigration was restricted. The Palestine administration set up the Muslim Higher Council in 1921 to help manage religious affairs, run the mosques, and oversee the charitable trusts. A secular group, the council used religious issues to fuel a nationalist agenda, stirring up international Arab reaction by warning Muslims that the Jews were plotting to take over the Al-Aqsa Mosque. The infamous Hajj Amin al-Husseini, put into the office of grand mufti by the British in the same year, proclaimed this same warning in order to provoke the bloody riots against Jews praying at the Western Wall in Jerusalem and at the Tomb of the Patriarchs in Hebron.

Jordanian Control

When British Mandate administration ended in 1947, the war that ensued between the new Jewish state and the Arab forces from neighboring Muslim countries left the Jordanians with the eastern section of Jerusalem, which included the Temple Mount. A Jordanian mufti was placed in charge of the Waqf for the next 19 years. During those years, Jordan's King Hussein, despite signing a 1949 armistice agreement that permitted Jews to pray at the Western Wall, denied them access and declared Jordan as the exclusive custodian of the Muslim holy places on the Temple Mount. In keeping with this decision, in 1950 he annexed the city and the entire West Bank to Jordan, an act protested by many countries in the Arab League. When the Israelis captured the Temple Mount from Jordan in 1967, Israeli commander Moshe Dayan accepted Jordan's custodial status over the Muslim holy places and returned their jurisdiction to the Jordanian-administered Waqf. However, despite this peaceful gesture, King Hussein demanded the return to Jordan of all of the captured West Bank, including East Jerusalem, and frequently threatened war on Israel to enforce his claim.

Israeli Control

In the Six-Day War, Israel regained control of the Old City and the Temple Mount for the first time in 1897 years. However, despite the site coming under the sovereignty of the Jewish state, a sovereignty not even Moshe Dayan questioned, his ceding jurisdiction to the Waqf so that the Temple Mount remained a Muslim holy place was a historic decision that effectively removed sovereign control from Israel. The only concession Dayan had demanded from the Waqf was that the site be accessible to those of other religions who wanted to visit it. The Waqf made this concession, but sternly insisted that the holy places were exclusively Muslim and that no non-Muslim religious expression would be permitted in them. Consequently, Jews were forbidden to pray at the site, and Jewish police officers enforced the Waqf's dictates, frequently arresting and imprisoning Jews who defied the prohibition. In time, this reversal of roles obscured the fact that the Waqf maintained control only by permission of the State of Israel, and the Muslim authorities developed an exclusive control that would come to not only ignore but also challenge Jewish sovereignty. To see how this unfolded, we must look at the Palestinians who have, at present, assumed control of the site.

Palestinian Control

During the time Jordan occupied the West Bank and East Jerusalem, it never once considered this territory as belonging to the Palestinians. Yet Jordan allowed this territory to be used by Palestinian terrorists as a base of operations against Israel and some Jordanian army units even cooperated with the terrorists. However, with respect to the Palestinian population in Jordan, King Hussein actively resisted the ambitions of Palestinian nationalism (which included designs on his own kingdom). For example, Hussein put down Yasser Arafat's 1972 intifada (civil war) in Jordan in a massacre remembered by the Palestinians as "Black September."[3] However, a plan adopted by the Palestine National Committee and approved by the Arab League to create a Palestinian state within Israel in order to aid the Arab countries in eliminating the Jewish state required that the West Bank go to the Palestinians for this purpose. King Hussein reluctantly acquiesced to the demands of the Arab League to recognize the Palestinian Authority as the sole claimant to the lands captured by Israel during the Six-Day War. As the Palestinians escalated their conflict with Israel, they acted on this claim, declaring an ancient heritage in this territory and exclusive sovereignty over east Jerusalem and the Temple Mount, while denying any Jewish history at the site, and demanding Jerusalem as the capital of a Palestinian state. Moreover, since the collapse of the Oslo Peace Process and the resumption of the Palestinian intifada, ostensibly as a result of Ariel Sharon's visit to the site, the Palestinian Authority has barred Jews from entering the Temple Mount area and worked to convert the entire site into a strictly Muslim possession.

The Beginning of the Loss

Shortly after the conclusion of the Six-Day War and the removal of the Mograbi Quarter to create the Western Wall plaza and allow Jews greater access to the Wailing Wall, Moshe Dayan, the Israeli minister of defense, entered the Al-Aqsa Mosque and sat down in the Arab manner on the carpeted floor of the mosque to meet with Muslim officials of the Waqf. Now that the Israelis had control of Jerusalem, he wanted to demonstrate to the Muslim world that Jews had no intention of controlling the Muslim holy places in the same way the Muslims had when they formerly restricted Jewish access to them. This gesture was meant to diffuse Arab reaction to the Jewish capture of the Temple Mount and establish the Israelis as benevolent rulers whose conquest had not extended to the realm of religion. As a result of this meeting, the control of the Muslim mosques and shrines was handed over to the Waqf, though access to the Temple Mount was to be granted to the Jews. However, Dayan's demonstration of tolerance was interpreted as a show of weakness by the Arabs. And while Israel lived up to its end of this agreement, strictly enforcing Muslim rights, the Muslim officials did not honor the Israeli demand for shared access. As a result, Dayan has been judged with setting in motion the forces that caused the loss of the Temple Mount to the next generation. I do not wish to demonize Dayan, and in fairness must say that his own recollections of this meeting portray his actions as less compromising (though perhaps somewhat more naïve) than many historians have recorded. Consider his words on the matter:

> The government next had to deal with the status of the Jewish, Moslem, and Christian holy places in Jerusalem and its environs. I proposed that all the barriers and limitations of access to these shrines, which had been imposed by the Jordanian regime, be removed. We should now allow all Moslems and Christians, whether citizens of Israel or residents of the West Bank and the Gaza Strip, to visit and pray at their holy sites—the Dome of the Rock, the Mosque of El Aksa, and the Church of the Holy Sepulcher. For many years, the Arabs had barred the Jews from their most sacred site, the Western Wall of the Temple compound in Jerusalem and from the Cave of the Patriarchs in Hebron. Now that we were in control, it was up to us to grant what we had demanded of others and to allow members of all faiths absolute freedom to visit and worship at their holy places....It seemed to me that we had to find a way of removing the artificial barriers which the Moslem authorities and the British Mandatory administration had imposed on Jewish visitors who wanted to worship at their holy places without disturbing Moslem sensibilities. At the same time we had to ensure that so sensitive a matter would

not create a conflict that would inflame passions, ignite clashes and demonstrations, and cause an international uproar, particularly in Moslem countries....I asked them [the Mufti and Arab officials of the Waqf] to resume religious services in the mosque on the following Friday...[and] I added my hope that the Moslem religious leaders would not take advantage of such freedom by indulging in rabble-rousing sermons that would incite some of their followers. If they did, we would of course take appropriate action....We had no intention of controlling Moslem holy places or of interfering in their religious life. The one thing we would introduce was freedom of Jewish access to the compound of Haram esh-Sharif without limitation or payment. This compound, as my hosts well knew, was our Temple Mount. Here stood our Temple during ancient times, and it would be inconceivable for Jews not to be able freely to visit this holy place now that Jerusalem was under our rule. My hosts were not overjoyed at my final remarks, but they recognized that they would be unable to change my decision. They would have wished the entire area, not just the mosques, to remain under their exclusive control, with the continued ban on Jews.[4]

Based on Dayan's account, we are to believe that his task was to find a way for Jews "to worship at their holy places" (the Temple Mount) without offending the Muslims who occupied the site. According to Dayan, his proposal included Jews, as well as Muslims and Christians, having "free" and "absolute" access to the entire Temple Mount compound, "to visit and pray at their holy sites—the Dome of the Rock, the Mosque of El Aksa, and the Church of the Holy Sepulcher." And any Muslim action against this freedom of access, including provocative sermons in the Al-Aqsa Mosque, would be met with appropriate government reaction (this was meant as a threat). However, despite the unambiguous language of Dayan requiring prayer on the Temple Mount, permission for the Jews to *pray* on the Temple Mount was in fact *not* negotiated at the meeting, as Dayan soon revealed.

On August 16, 1967 came the first test of the status quo initiated by Dayan and the Muslim officials. As such, it evidenced what had actually been conceded by Dayan at his historic meeting. The date coincided with the most solemn of the Jewish holy days, *Tisha B'Av*, the traditional day of remembrance of the destruction of the Jewish Temples. But, this *Tisha B'Av* marked a distinct departure from those commemorated over the past 2000 years, for it was the first celebration to take place after the liberation of the Temple Mount, and therefore it was to symbolize an end to the Jews' mourning. Leading the commemoration on this special day was the chief army chaplain, Rabbi Shlomo Goren, who had also been the first rabbi, since the destruction of the Temple, to recite prayers at the Western Wall after it came under Jewish sovereignty. Rabbi Goren and more than 30 Jewish men (organized as several *minyanim* or religious quorums), went to the Temple Mount to pray. Afterward, the Israeli government received complaints about the matter from the Waqf. According to Dayan, "Although, understandably, no minister wished to take a formal position stating baldly that Jews were forbidden to pray on the Temple Mount, it was decided to 'maintain current policy,' which, in fact, banned them from doing so."[5]

Reading between the lines of Dayan's statement, it is interesting to note that if "current policy"—that is, status quo—had been decided by the government with Dayan as its agent, then none of the government ministers would admit to such. Why would the Knesset be ashamed of its own decision? Moreover, if this was indeed "current policy," why did Rabbi Goren and his *minyan* assume they had the right to pray, and further, why were they not forbidden to pray at the site? And why was a government meeting needed to "consider" the matter if it were already "current policy"? Perhaps, as Rabbi Goren later told me, the reason was that Dayan had acted without the approval of the government when he met with the Waqf, and his decision had become an obligation that forced the government to comply even though most of its members were in disagreement. Whether or not this was the case, Dayan makes clear in his autobiography the reason he accepted a ban on Jewish prayer:

> It was evident that if we did not prevent Jews from praying
> in what was now a mosque compound, matters would get
> out of hand and lead to a religious clash....We should cer-
> tainly respect the Temple Mount as an historic site of our
> ancient past, but we should not disturb the Arabs who were
> using it for what it was now—a place of Moslem worship. [6]

The justification that Dayan here describes set a precedent for dealing with the Waqf and the attitude toward the holy places that has continued to be adopted by successive governments ever since. It is simply this: At present, the Temple Mount is not a place of Jewish worship; therefore, there is no reason to provoke the Arab world by making the Temple Mount a religious issue. But since 1967, the Temple Mount has been *the* religious issue, provoking Arab wars with Israel, riots within Israel, and wrecking every peace plan as soon as it reaches the negotiating table. Today the site does not enjoy the status quo envisioned by Dayan under the "current policy"; rather, his compromise with the Waqf has led to a significant change in the status quo.

What Has Happened to the Status Quo of the Temple Mount?

When the Israeli government began to enforce Dayan's status quo, non-Muslims were allowed to enter the Temple Mount compound as tourists but forbidden to engage in any kind of religious expression, because that would violate Islamic law. For the next 33 years, the Israeli police assigned to the Temple Mount—as well as the Israeli courts—rigorously protected the Muslims' concerns. Every attempt by Jewish individuals or groups to pray on the Temple Mount was met with arrests and usually resulted in permanent expulsion from the site. Nevertheless, the Muslim authorities, and many others in the Arab world, have repeatedly asserted that the Israeli government is plotting to take over the site, destroy the mosques, and rebuild the Temple.

Responding to these accusations, Israeli foreign minister Shlomo Ben-Ami has rhetorically asked, "Does anybody think that there is a sane person in this country, this government, who wants to harm the sacredness of Islam, who wants to harm Al-Aqsa? We have had sovereignty over the Temple Mount for 30 years, and we have never changed the status quo."[7] Israel, to be sure, had produced the religious freedom it had promised: Jews had free access to the Western Wall, Christians could freely carry crosses down the Via Dolorosa and pray at the Church of the Holy Sepulchre, and Muslims could freely worship at their mosques on the Temple Mount. In fact, religious access under Israeli rule was something of which Israel could boast, as Prime Minister Ariel Sharon did recently: "Only under the sovereignty of Israel has Jerusalem been open to all faiths. Jerusalem and the Temple Mount, the holiest site to the Jewish people, is something you should stand up and speak out about."[8]

For Jews, however, that freedom was restricted to the Western Wall, a structure technically not part of the ancient Temple, but only of the outer retaining wall of the compound on which it once stood. True, Jews for centuries had revered the Western Wall

Photo by Alexander Schick *Bibleausstellung Sylt*

A Jewish gathering at the Western Wall. Jews today have the freedom to worship at the Wall, yet at times have been endangered by Palestinians who throw stones and other objects from the Temple Mount above.

and sought access to it for prayer. That, however, was because the Temple Mount was inaccessible to Jews and the Western Wall was the closest they could come. It was the Temple Mount toward which Jews prayed three times daily, not the Western Wall, a fact apparently overlooked by those who gave up access in 1967 despite the reality that the Temple Mount was finally once again under Israeli sovereignty. Because the Western Wall had been "enough" for the Jewish people for centuries, those who yielded the control of the Mount's holy places back to the Waqf thought the Western Wall was all that the Jews needed.

Another aspect of the status quo was that Muslim authorities were to recognize and respect the Israeli government's political sovereignty over the Temple Mount. Legally, this meant the Waqf had to make official requests of the Israeli government for anything that might affect the site's status quo, such as construction repairs that might jeopardize existing archaeological structures. Yet the Israeli government has rarely exercised its sovereignty in such matters. For example, in March 1994, the government closed the Western Wall after the Hebron mosque shooting, when angry Arabs stoned Israelis at the foot of the wall. It was the Israeli government on this occasion that changed the status quo and restricted its own citizens from enjoying the rights won in the Six-Day War. Many wondered why the Jewish site below the Temple Mount was closed and not the place above, from where the violence originated. The answer was that such an action would "disturb" the Arabs. Rabbi Benny Elon, presently the Israeli government's minister of tourism, well explained the situation: "We [Israel] do not impose sovereignty over the Temple Mount, and as a result, we are afraid of rocks thrown over to the Western Wall. We have already conceded the Temple Mount [to the Palestinians] so the Western Wall also must be evacuated because it is dangerous."[9]

Since the negotiations that took place during the Oslo Peace Process, even greater violations of the status quo have taken place. Dr. Aaron Lerner, director of Independent Media Review & Analysis, recalls how Israel comported itself when it captured the

Rabbi Benny Elon (left) with author.

Temple Mount and contrasts this with the Palestinian occupation of the site:

> During the period of Jordanian occupation from 1948 to 1967, all Jews were barred entry into the entire Old City. When the Arabs failed to destroy the Jewish state in 1967 and instead found themselves facing an Israel with lines extending to the Jordan River, the representatives of the Waqf on the Temple Mount prepared for the worst. But Israel didn't pay the Arabs in kind. The city was not cleared of Arabs and, Mordechai Gur's memorable "The Temple Mount is in our hands" notwithstanding, Moshe Dayan made it clear to the Waqf that the mount remained firmly in its hands. Today Arafat's appointees incite the masses against Israel in their Friday sermons broadcast by the Palestinian media from the Temple Mount, in gross violation of the Oslo Accords.[10]

In fact, it may be said that every condition that Dayan required of the officials of the Waqf in 1967 has been ignored or abandoned by the Palestinians in charge today. From the beginning, Jews (as well as all non-Muslim visitors) had to pay exorbitantly to enter the holy places. Then, at the whim of the Palestinian Authority, they were denied access to them altogether. Perhaps even more startling is that the Palestinians began denying what Dayan had stated in 1967 was undeniable to Muslim officials—namely, that "this compound…was our Temple Mount [and] here stood our Temple during ancient times."

The Changing of the Guards

One of the most significant historical changes to the status quo on the Temple Mount, and one that has most contributed to the loss of control of the site to the Israelis, is the change in the Waqf from a Jordanian-controlled Islamic Trust to a Palestinian-controlled one. The original status quo was negotiated with the Jordanian-controlled Waqf and was sustained without change until Jordan made a peace treaty with Israel. In the 1994 peace treaty, Israel recognized Jordan as the sole protector of the Islamic holy sites in Jerusalem—that is, on the Temple Mount. Even though Jordan had officially recognized the right of the PLO to represent the Palestinians of the West Bank in 1988, this did not include any role in the religious guardianship of Jerusalem's holy places. Moreover, not until 1998 did King Hussein of Jordan "officially announce" that he supported the Palestinian cause to establish a Palestinian State in the West Bank.

Following Israel's recognition of Jordan's status as caretaker of Islam's holy places on the Temple Mount, Jordan installed a Jordanian mufti in Jerusalem and undertook the structural restoration of the Dome of the Rock. However, the next year Arafat installed his own Palestinian mufti, Ikrima Sabri (who is virulently anti-Semitic and anti-American). Sabri usurped the authority of the Jordanian mufti, ordered the Palestinians to ignore the Jordanian mufti's religious dictates, and demanded that the Palestinians observe religious events on different days than those determined by the Jordanian mufti's calendar.

These actions were not done as a result of any agreement by the two parties or with Israeli approval. Rather, the Palestinians took over the rights conferred to the Jordanians in 1967 and reaffirmed in 1994. The Palestinian Authority was clearly upset over Jordan's peace treaty with Israel and may have feared that this new arrangement between Israel and "the custodian of the Islamic holy places in Jerusalem" could lead to Jews having greater access to and privileges at the Temple Mount. More importantly, Jordan's peace treaty meant that politically and religiously, the Palestinian Authority would take a back seat on the question of sovereignty exercised over the site—a position they desperately wanted to change because after the signing of their Declaration of Principles in 1993, they had asserted that the flag of their new state "would be raised over the walls, mosques, and churches of Jerusalem." The PLO had demanded that East Jerusalem serve as the capital for its proposed state and insisted upon control over the Temple Mount. However, the Oslo Accord had postponed negotiations on the status of Jerusalem and its holy places until the final phase of the peace process because of the impasse that existed between Israel and Palestinians at the time—an impasse that could have derailed the peace process. For this reason, the Accord stipulated that the Palestinian Authority should not assert itself politically in the city or over the holy sites until these negotiations were completed.

Yet the Palestinian Authority violated this stipulation by opening a diplomatic headquarters in the Orient Hotel in East Jerusalem and installing Faisal Husseini as the Jerusalem administrator for the Palestinian Authority. Soon after, leaders from foreign countries sympathetic to the Palestinian cause were being welcomed at the Orient House—which signified their official recognition of the Palestinian sovereignty over Jerusalem, since such receptions are the privilege of heads of state. In keeping with this illegal assertion of political sovereignty over the city, the installation of the Palestinian mufti was an illegal assertion of religious sovereignty over the Temple Mount.

The sanctity of the site was also usurped when Faisal Husseini died and was buried on the Temple Mount. While it is traditional for heroes and leaders of the Arab people to be buried in places revered by Muslims, this was an intentional and flagrant violation of the Jewish laws of ritual purity. Yasser Arafat, too, has announced he will be buried on the Temple Mount. The reason behind these interments, of course, is to prevent Jews from ever building the Temple on the Mount, since they cannot enter a cemetery, which the site has now become.

What Caused the Change in the Status Quo of the Temple Mount?

The initial cause of a change in status quo on the Temple Mount happened unexpectedly as Jerusalem began the celebration of its 3000th year as Israel's capital. After midnight on September 27, 1996, officials in the Ministry for Religious Affairs were relieved to have finally completed an exit for the Western Wall Tunnel, a main tourist attraction that was literally booked 24 hours a day due to its being able to accommodate only 30 people at a time. This limit was imposed for insurance and safety reasons because the lack of an exit in the tunnel required visitors to turn around and go out the same way they had come in. "At last," the officials said, "people will be able to go through safely and without restrictions. Even the Palestinians will be pleased because all the tourists will exit right into their shops in the Muslim Quarter!"

Little did the officials realize that in the morning, the Palestinians would incite a violent riot that forced a closure of the tunnel and the Temple Mount and resulted in the death of 80 people throughout Jerusalem and the West Bank territories. The rioting Palestinians heaved stones from atop the Temple Mount toward Israelis below at prayer at the Western Wall, while loudspeakers on the Mount called for Arabs to come and defend the holy places. Yasser Arafat also addressed the international media and claimed that the newly carved tunnel exit threatened the Muslim mosques on the Temple Mount, even though he knew full well that the exit was at the opposite far end of a 2000-year-old tunnel and an even older Hasmonean water tunnel, some 1500 feet to the north of the Al-Aqsa Mosque and almost 1000 feet away from the Dome of the Rock. Even so, he called the tunnel "a crime against our religious and holy places...completely against the peace process."

Undoubtedly, Arafat's unfounded accusations were nothing more than political propaganda intended to attack the new Benyamin Netanyahu government in front of the Arab world. The truth, as Jerusalem mayor Ehud Olmert stated at the time, was that "the tunnel has no connection to the mosques—it is far away—this is about who will control Jerusalem." This became apparent when the Waqf used the event as an excuse to call for an official rejection of Israeli sovereignty over the Temple Mount to initiate an illegal construction project at the southwestern corner of the compound. While the Rabin government had given approval for a limited renovation project in this area, it had done so in exchange for the Waqf's agreement that the exit tunnel could be opened for the tourists! Eventually the Waqf went on to make extensive renovations and to dump numerous archaeological artifacts in the course of doing so. This brought on a blatant reversal of the status quo, returning the Temple Mount to pre-1967 conditions.

The second, and most recent, cause of a change in the status quo was Ariel Sharon's visit to the Temple Mount on September 28, 2000. We must remember that Sharon's action was an entirely proper, authorized, and legal activity under the status quo agreement of 1967. As to the facts, Yasser Arafat and his mufti had warned Sharon not to enter the Temple Mount, a challenge to Israeli sovereignty that could not go unanswered. As a government official, Sharon had unrestricted right of access to any place under Israeli sovereignty, and especially to his own religion's most sacred site in his nation's capital city! His visit was an official inspection tour because of alleged violations of the status quo by the Palestinians, and he was accompanied by a group of 1000 people, including security guards, Arab Knesset members, and officials of the Waqf. His route bypassed the mosques and went directly to the construction area in the southwestern corner and the inspection went without incident.

As we know, a major riot occurred the next day. The riot was orchestrated to provide the Palestinians with a political basis for resuming the intifada against Israel. While most of the world has believed that Sharon provoked the Palestinians to renew their intifada by his entrance to the Temple Mount area, the truth is that the Palestinians used Sharon's visit to further counter Israeli sovereignty while calling for Palestinian sovereignty over the site.

Has the Temple Mount Been Regained?

In mid-September 2003, three years after the closure of the Temple Mount, and despite the public protests of Yasser Arafat and denials of cooperation with the Israelis by the Waqf,[11] the Israeli government re-opened the site, stating it had "normalized" access. As if to signal a return to the status quo that had begun with the site's capture by Israeli forces during the Six-Day War, at the re-opening, an Israeli security guard checking bags at the entrance to the Western Wall Plaza recited the famous announcement from that battle: "The Temple Mount is in our hands!"[12] On the ramp leading from the plaza to the Mughrabi Gate, the single non-Muslim entrance to the Temple Mount, the police officer stationed there asserted, "It's open, go wherever you want!"[13] Even Jews formerly exiled from the site—such as Orthodox rabbi Yehuda Etzion, the founder of the *Chai VeKayam* movement (who was convicted of attempting to blow up the Dome of the Rock in 1984 and permanently banned from entering the site thereafter) and hassidic rabbi Yossef Elboim of the Movement for the Establishment of the Temple (who used to regularly lead Orthodox Jews to walk in prescribed areas of the Temple Mount before the closure) toured the site unhindered![14]

Likewise, Rabbi Chaim Richman of The Temple Institute, who in the past could only view the Temple compound from the institute's rooftop, led a group of Orthodox Jewish visitors around the site, pointing out Temple-related structures while a photographer freely snapped pictures of piles of the Waqf's mosque construction materials as well as of its destructive activities on the Mount. Given these developments it appears as if the Israeli government has finally begun to assert its sovereignty over the site and return conditions to the status quo.

Photo by author

An Israeli Knesset member is halted by Israeli police as he attempts to force entry onto the closed Temple Mount in a demonstration of "freedom of access under the law."

However, there are still some severe restrictions. The site is open, but only for a few hours of the morning on select days. Visitors cannot go into or near any Muslim structure, including the Dome of the Rock and the Al-Aqsa Mosque. These areas and buildings, formerly open to visitation under the status quo agreement, remain closed by order of the Waqf.[15] Yes, the radical rabbis were allowed to enter the site, but they were also soon ejected as soon as they attempted to pray. As one Waqf official explained to a tourist: "This entire site is a mosque. This is a holy place for

Muslims. Jews cannot pray here. This should all be under the authority of the Islamic Waqf, not of the occupying forces."[16] In response, when asked their feelings about visiting Judaism's holiest site under the auspices of the Waqf, some religious Jews leaving the site replied, "It feels like the Diaspora."[17]

Indeed, it seems that perception and reality are very different with respect to the Temple Mount being back in Israel's hands. The perception is that the Temple Mount is again open, but in reality it remains closed to what matters most. Moreover, the new arrangement that gives the appearance of restoring the status quo in fact marks another concession to the Waqf by the Israeli government: entrance to the Temple Mount plaza but no further, and permission for all non-Muslims to enter, but no non-Muslim expressions of faith are allowed.

This change of affairs should not be underestimated. In 1967 the original status quo allowed people of all religions to enter all of the religious sites, including the Dome of the Rock and the Al-Aqsa Mosque. Although the Israeli government conceded to the Waqf's prohibition against non-Muslim prayer, the Waqf later modified this prohibition to cover everything from a tourist carrying a Bible onto the site to tour guides showing a picture of the ancient Temple when giving an explanation of the site's history. Politically, the Israeli government's failure to insist on a return to the original status quo is nothing less than a *de facto* surrender of Israeli sovereignty and a declaration of Palestinian sovereignty. Religiously, it amounts to a strategic usurpation of the historic reality of the Temple Mount as a place shared by the three great monotheistic religions, severing Judaism and Christianity's historical links with the Temple and replacing it with an exclusively Islamic claim. Practically, it is an Islamic conquest imposed on Israel without compromise or negotiation by the same entity that has used homicide bombers to kill some thousand Israelis since the declaration of the Al-Aqsa war in 2000.

Israel has indeed lost the Temple Mount. Yet, in a sense, it never actually possessed it. A cover story in *The Jerusalem Report* entitled "The Heart of the Matter: Why Israel Agonizes over the Temple Mount It Doesn't Quite Own" says: "For 33 years Israel has enjoyed the ambiguity of claiming the Temple Mount is 'in our hands' without wanting to exercise that claim."[18] But even if Israel can be said to have lost the Temple Mount, it must be recognized that there is still more to lose. Those who now control the Temple Mount are not ambiguous about what they want to do. They are presently attempting to change the Temple Mount itself in order to destroy any evidence of Jewish connection with the site. What is being done on the Mount is one of the most shocking and largely unreported stories of our time, and we will learn more about it in the next chapter. Read on!

Jewish and Arab Actions on the Temple Mount

People	Secular Jews	Orthodox Jews	Arabs
Status	non-religious	religious	Muslim
Political Perspective	cause political problems	cause religious problems	increase political/religious power
Relative to Peace Process	impediment to peace process	no peace without God's presence	imperative to peace process
Relative to Resident Population	will increase fanaticism at site	will secure Jewish future in Jerusalem	will secure Islamic future in Jerusalem
How Viewpoint Is Demonstrated Politically	allow Waqf to control site, overlook violations of status quo	protest Jewish religious exclusion by activist demonstrations	exercise exclusive religious control, ban on non-Muslim entrance to site, mosque construction
Ultimate Goal	abandon site to Muslims as concession to peace	gain control of site for rebuilding of Jewish Temple	transform site into unified mosque to rival mosques in Mecca and Medina

9

Welcome to the Al-Aqsa Mosque!

The Temple Mount is completely Islamic.
MK ABDEL MALIK DEHAMSHE
of the United Arab List

*The adversary has stretched out his hand over
all her precious things, for she has seen the
nations enter her sanctuary...*

LAMENTATIONS 1:10

The Islamic conquest of the Temple Mount has made unprecedented strides over the past decade under the direction of the Palestinian Authority. The strategy of the Palestinian Authority has been to use the religious exclusivity inherent in Islam to usurp the political sovereignty won by Israel's conquest of the site in the Six-Day War. I did not realize the extent of this usurpation until July 2000, only two months before the closure of the site, when I was walking around the platform and looking at the visible evidences of construction. While there, I noticed workmen descending, by ladder, into an opening in front of the Dome of the Rock. Looking into the opening I saw a shaft some 50 feet deep that intersected with a tunnel below, where workmen were moving about. Impetuously I started down. However, I didn't get far, for an ascending Arab workman met me on the ladder, forcing me to return to the top. Upon reaching the top he smiled and said, "Welcome to Al-Aqsa!" Although I knew the whole compound was known by that name in Arabic, based on the reference in *Sura* 17:1, we were speaking in English and Arabs usually use the term with tourists to refer to the Al-Aqsa Mosque located in the southern end of the compound. However, at that moment we were standing in front of the Dome of the Rock. I sensed then as never before, what this Muslim, and every Muslim believes: The entire 35 acres on which I stood was a mosque exclusive to Islam. To understand this perspective, which is at the center of the Islamic destruction of the old (Jewish) and the construction of the new (Muslim), we need to examine the goal that is driving the Palestinian Waqf's fervent activity.

The Temple Mount in Islamic Revisionism

Historically, Arab leaders—and even the Muslim Supreme Council itself—have said that Jewish Temples existed on the Temple Mount. These statements, however, are from a time before the Arab world became obsessed with removing the State of Israel from the map of the Middle East. This obsession has been particularly obvious since 1967, when Israel gained sovereignty over the Temple Mount with its Muslim mosques. Since then, Islamic clerics in Jerusalem have called upon the Muslim *Umma* (Muslim Brotherhood) to remove the Jewish "threat" to their holy places. Even though in 1967 the Israeli Knesset passed the Safeguarding of the Holy Places law, which has been repeatedly upheld by the decisions of the Israeli High Court of Justice,[1] Muslims have continued to believe the Israeli government has been plotting to destroy the mosques and rebuild the Jewish Temple in their place.

After the Oslo Peace Process began in 1993—with one of the aims being negotiations to resolve the status of Jerusalem and the holy places—the Palestinian Authority initiated a campaign of revising the history of the Temple Mount in the hopes this would help them to secure exclusive sovereignty over Jerusalem and the Temple Mount by the time they reached the final stage of negotiations. This revisionist effort consists of an overt denial that

Jerusalem ever belonged to the Jews and that the Temples ever existed. Despite the obvious absurdity of this claim to anyone living in or visiting the city, this attempt at revisionism was introduced to the textbooks used in the Palestinian schools, preached by the Jerusalem mufti and imams at the mosques in the areas under Palestinian autonomy, and disseminated widely and consistently to the international media. Surprisingly, Palestinian Muslims, even those who live in East Jerusalem and daily see the archaeological evidence of the Second Temple period, have come to accept the arguments as valid and champion the concept that the Jews are trying to steal the Palestinians' history. And, the Palestinian-controlled Waqf has an even bigger objective in view as it continues revising the history of the Temple Mount.

What Is the Goal of the Waqf's Construction?

At the same time that the destruction of Jewish remains is designed to remove any historical connection at the site with Israel, so is the Islamic construction activity designed to give the Temple Mount an Islamic identity. This is nothing more or less than what the first Islamic caliphs attempted to achieve when they first came to the Temple Mount as conquerors 1300 years ago and replaced Jewish and Christian holy structures with Islamic ones. In the course of all this revisionist activity, the Waqf has adopted three goals: 1) to de-Judaize the Temple Mount; 2) to Islamize it by turning it into a new supermosque; and 3) to provoke Israel to restore the status quo and then justify violence against it for its actions.

De-Judaizing the Temple Mount

Since its inception, Islam has endeavored to replace Jewish history with Islamic traditions in order to advance Islam's claim of superiority. Likewise, wherever the followers of Islam have encountered a rival religion in the countries they conquered, they have either destroyed all traces of that religion or sought to eclipse it by building greater Muslim structures. The building of mosques to secure this dominance was promised a special reward in the

Hadith: "Whoever built a mosque (intending Allah's pleasure), Allah would build for him a similar place in Paradise" (*Sahih Bukhari*, Volume 1). The act of asserting religious dominance has been seen as especially necessary in Jerusalem, where both Judaism and Christianity are prominent. For this reason, throughout the centuries, Muslims have built mosques, shrines, cupolas, Islamic prayer platforms, offices, and other kinds of structures on every part of the Temple Mount. With the same purpose they also closed the Golden Gate and built a cemetery in front of it, and they turned the inside of this gate into an Islamic center and library.

Such acts are part of a long history of destructive attempts to obliterate any trace of Jewish history and thereby de-Judaize the Temple Mount. In the 1980s, the Waqf dug a large trench near the Dome of the Rock to relocate utility equipment and ended up exposing more than 16 feet of a six-foot-thick wall believed to be from one of the courts of the Second Temple. Rather than allow Israeli archaeologists to study the wall, the Waqf destroyed it and covered the trench. In 1993 the Israeli Supreme Court found that the Waqf was guilty of 35 violations of Israeli antiquities laws—violations that involved irreversible destruction of ancient features on the Temple Mount. Among these were the deliberate removal of a row of stone steps near the Dome of the Rock, the planting over with gardens of evidences of the Temple's location in the northeastern corner of the Temple Mount, and the plowing up and paving over of a long row of exposed stones in the eastern area.

Such work continues to be done today in order to create a new historical reality for the Palestinians and support their claim that they, not the Jews, have been the sole sovereigns of the sacred site. By removing all the visible remains of the First and Second Temples, they will be able to validate their claim that there is no evidence of a former Jewish presence on the Temple Mount. Emanuel Winston, a Middle East analyst at the Freeman Center, made this observation:

Over a period of time, the Wakf began to Arabize the Temple Mount by excavating beneath its surface....They needed a history where none existed before. They are trying to co-opt the Jew's history as others have done before—as well as their geography and holy sites....This de-Judaization of the Temple Mount was intended to be the ultimate proof of Muslim dominance over Judaism and title to the entire Temple Mount area including, by extension, all of Jerusalem.[2]

Islamizing the Temple Mount as a Unified Mosque

Another goal of the Muslim authorities is to Islamize the Temple Mount and turn the whole of the Haram into a unified Islamic supermosque. An early illegal step in this direction was the burial of Palestinian Authority leader Faisal Husseini, the nephew of Haj Amin al-Husseini, the grand mufti who worked with Adolph Hitler on "the Jewish Problem." Faisal Husseini was the administrator for governmental affairs for the Palestinian Authority in Jerusalem and one of the most outspoken individuals against Jewish access to the Temple Mount. Husseini's burial on the Temple Mount has served three purposes: One, it has provided further justification for the Palestinian Authority's claim to the site. Two, it has served to desecrate a site claimed as holy to the Jews. And three, it has disrupted Jewish plans to rebuild a Temple since Jewish law forbids Jews from moving graves.

Ultimately, the Waqf's goal is to completely transform the entire Temple Mount and make it an exclusively Muslim mosque. Professor Eilat Mazar observes that this agenda has been openly announced by the Palestinian Authority:

> It has come to be very clear and it was declared by the Islamic authorities—they didn't hide it—of course, they hide the destruction—but they didn't hide their intention to convert the entire Temple Mount into a mosque. They declare it [has been] a mosque ever since the time of Adam and Eve...[but regard] non-Islamic people's religious or

cultural interests as provocative. They don't really care about showing that there was no First or Second Temple; [they say] it wasn't there—and that's it, period! There's not even a level of academic argument.[3]

Yasser Arafat has politicized the illegal construction by ordering that the underground halls under the Temple Mount be unified into a single fortified space that would become the largest mosque ever built on the Mount. This was confirmed in June 2000 when Nadav Shragai, a correspondent for Israeli newspaper *Ha'aretz*, revealed that the Waqf's master plan, which had also been given to Israeli prime minister Ehud Barak before the Camp David II Summit, included turning the entire Temple Mount into a rival of the Great Ka'aba Mosque in Mecca.

Islam teaches that the foundations of the Ka'aba in Mecca were laid by Adam and Eve, and to make such a claim for the Haram in Jerusalem is to turn it into a rival, in Islamic tradition, to Mecca. However, there are no traditional Islamic sources that say Adam and Eve had anything to do with Mount Moriah in Jerusalem. The only mention of Adam in connection with Jerusalem in Islamic literature is a late Muslim legend concerning the collection of dust for the creation of man. In this tale, because the earth would not willingly give some of its dust to Allah's angels, the angel of death forcibly took dust from earth's "surface" (Arabic *Adim*, thus the name for man, *Adam*). The dust was red, white, and black in color, which explains, for the Muslim, the origin of the different races. Significant here is that the dust used to create Adam's head came from Mecca, the dust for his chest from the sanctuary in Jerusalem, the dust for his loins from Yemen, the dust for his feet from Hejaz, and the dust for his hands from the east (right) and west (left). However, what possible sanctuary could have existed in Jerusalem *before* the creation of man? It couldn't have been one founded by Adam and Eve, since neither of them had yet been created! Even so, as we have seen with the Muslim denial of the historicity of the Jewish Temples, an Islamic claim does not require anything more than itself. Eilat

Mazar reflects the frustration archaeological authorities express toward such religious dogma:

> Whatever they want to say, they say. [They say] the whole area was built from the time of Adam and Eve as a mosque. [How] can you argue with it? The problem with the fundamentalists is that it's black and [white] and you cannot argue with [these] colors. [How can] you have arguments with people who think this way and [whose] evidence [comes out of the] dark. You cannot argue with the dark.[4]

Another means by which the Palestinian-controlled Waqf intended to create a rival to Mecca in Saudi Arabia was to bring sacred water from this site to the Temple Mount and thereby create an elevated sanctity for the whole of the Haram as a mosque. In order to accomplish this, the Waqf planned to drain the 37 known subterranean cisterns under the Temple Mount and refill them with sacred water transported from the well Zamzam in Mecca. Students of the Qur'an will remember that it was in this very well that the heart of Muhammad was washed after the angel Gabriel cut him open from his chest to his navel and removed it for this purpose. Professor Mazar explains this novel scheme of the Palestinian Authority:

> The [Muslim authorities] were even saying so themselves in their papers. It was quite clear and based on evidence that they planned to clear the underground cisterns of the Temple, which are huge, and to bring holy water from Mecca, upgrading the holiness of the site. The holiness of Mecca [derives mainly from] the holy stone of Mecca, the Ka'aba, but also together with the sacred water from Zam Zam, a well nearby. If you bring this sacred water to Jerusalem there is no need to go to Mecca....Of course, this was just one idea of many [on] how to convert the whole site into an Islamic, and only Islamic, mosque.[5]

The attempt to convert the ancient Jewish cisterns into Islamic sacred pools was instigated by Sheikh Rayadh Salah, head of the

Israeli Islamic movement, who has directed the other Temple Mount renovation activities for the Waqf. Using donations raised throughout the Arab world and with the help of Israeli-Arab volunteers, he began removing tons of ancient debris in ten of the cisterns. These cisterns are actually underground spaces, many containing huge halls, with some encompassing 100 square meters. Although many were designed to serve as water reservoirs, others took this function in secondary usage. As a result, the fill that has accumulated within these underground structures, mostly from the Second Temple period, undoubtedly contains a rich collection of archaeological material. When the Israeli chief of police of the Temple Mount station learned of this activity, he ordered the cleanup operations halted after only one or two cisterns had been so cleaned, but his orders were ignored. None of my sources know exactly what further progress has been made by the Waqf in cleaning these cisterns, but it is known that the Saudis objected vigorously to the Palestinian plan to upgrade the sanctity of the Temple Mount in this way. They apparently feared that the creation of such a rival mosque would divert pilgrims from Mecca, especially pilgrims from "Palestine," who would not see the need to travel so far to the east when the sacred Zamzam waters were in their own country.

Provoking Israel and Justifying Violence

A final goal of the flagrantly defiant acts on the Temple Mount is to incite Israelis (whether Temple activists or elements within the government) to enforce their sovereignty and justify a retaliatory reaction. The Palestinian Authority and the Waqf have already publicly warned that any such attempt would be interpreted as a Jewish attack on their holy mosques and would result in violence from Muslims the world over. Thus, the Waqf's provocative actions are a thinly veiled guise to intensify the intifada or provoke an all-out war between Israel and the Arab states. There is certainly a precedent for this, for the Palestinian Authority has used a number of "excuses" to instigate fighting.

For example, each demonstration by the Temple Mount Faithful has been greeted with threats, and violent riots occurred in response to the opening of an exit for tourists in the Western Wall Tunnel. Likewise, Sharon's visit to the Temple Mount was used by the Palestinians to begin the Al-Aqsa intifada, even though Sharon never entered or came near a mosque. In the same way, the Temple Mount Faithful have never been allowed onto the compound, and the exit tunnel never breached the Temple Mount but went underground in the opposite direction of the mosques. Tragically, each one of these restrained acts, all legally sanctioned, still incited the Muslim authorities to call for *jihad* to defend the mosques, request the United Nations to condemn Israel, and create in the world press an image of Israel as an aggressor. If the Palestinians, working in concert with a greater Islamic agenda, seek to bring about a major confrontation between Israel and the Arab world, then there seems to be no better way for them to achieve this end than through the Temple Mount.

Photo courtesy of Israel Government Press Office

Palestinians demonstrate for Palestinian sovereignty over Jerusalem and the Temple Mount (note T-shirt with English word *Jerusalem*).

How Did the Situation Get So Bad?

When the Temple Mount came under Israeli control in 1967, Israeli archaeologists wanted to carry out scientific explorations of the ruins on the Mount, but the Israeli government refused to give them access because it feared a backlash of violence from the Arab world. To preserve the peaceful arrangement negotiated with the Muslim Waqf, the government strictly enforced the status quo, arresting Orthodox Jews who sought to pray at the site and closing the single entrance gate for non-Muslims. The key word here is *provocation,* a term used frequently by the Palestinian Authority and the Waqf to justify threats of violence and riots by Muslims at the Temple Mount. Professor Mazar again explains:

> *Provocation* is a word that can be used very wrongly. If you are teaching your child how to rightly behave, are you making a provocation? If you tell him don't eat candy, it's not good for your health, are you being provocative? [However, some will say] if the child is behaving badly and won't be quiet, "Go ahead and eat as much candy as you want!" It's the same [with] provocation on the Israeli side, [which is] to maintain the law conducted inside the Temple Mount in order to preserve people's lives and the place. This is a provocation? If this is a provocation [and we let them have their way], then we are approaching a very bad end to it.[6]

At the same time, for the Israeli government to preserve the status quo meant the Waqf could not carry out any work at the site that might violate this archaeological ban. Israeli law required the Waqf to submit detailed plans of any repair work or construction activity planned on the Temple Mount as well as any changes in the use of the structures at the site.

In compliance with this Israeli law, in 1993, the Rabin government was approached by the Waqf with a request for permission to use the Solomon's Stable area for prayers by overflow crowds at the yearly celebration of Ramadan. In recent years, Muslim crowds from the Gaza Strip and West Bank have numbered above 350,000. To relieve the congestion, the Waqf sought to create a prayer area within the Solomon's Stables' ancient subterranean halls. The Rabin government saw an opportunity with this request to make one of their own to the Waqf. Since the 1991 opening of the Western Wall Tunnel—a 1000-foot-long passageway parallel to the lower levels of the western retaining wall of the Temple Mount—there had been a need to create an exit for the tourists visiting the site. Because of insurance restrictions, tourists were only able to enter in small groups that had to go back out the same way. The only way all the tour groups could be accommodated at this popular site was to schedule visits around the clock, 24 hours a day. Creating an exit would alleviate this problem. The Rabin government proposed cutting an exit that would take tourists into the Muslim Quarter, increasing the traffic for the Arab merchants in this area. The Waqf accepted the deal and the next October, used the Solomon's Stables area for their prayers.

Unfortunately, in 1994, Yitzhak Rabin was assassinated, and Benyamin Netanyahu eventually succeeded him as prime minister. For the next year and a half, Netanyahu's government was occupied with keeping the Oslo Peace Process on track while dealing with a growing number of terrorist attacks. Concurrently, Yasser Arafat and his Palestinian Authority were out of the headlines for some time.

Then on September 25, 1996, Arafat saw his chance to return the "Palestinian plight" to the news headlines. This date marked the opening of the long-awaited exit to the Western Wall Tunnel. With Rabin's death and the change in government, the project had been delayed. However, because the Waqf had approved the project, Netanyahu went ahead and ordered the exit to be built to accommodate the surge of tourism expected during the Jewish high holidays. But as soon as the exit was completed, the Muslim authorities instigated a riot and Yasser Arafat declared to the international media that the Israeli government was attacking the mosques in an attempt to destroy them and rebuild the Temple. Even after Mayor Ehud Olmert of Jerusalem stated to the international media that this was "nonsense," and archaeologists demonstrated that it was impossible for the exit to endanger the mosques, the rioting continued for a week, with more than 70 Palestinians and 17 Israeli police officers killed.

Muslims today continue to believe that the opening of the exit was an attempt by the Israeli government to take over the Temple Mount. One Islamic website at the time showed an archaeological illustration in which the Western Wall Tunnel of the Second Temple was depicted for comparison with the modern remains. Misunderstanding that the picture was of the site 2000 years ago (which was destroyed over 620 years before any mosque existed on the Temple Mount), it declared: "In that picture there is no record of any Islamic holy sites, and that includes the Al-Aqsa Mosque, clearly reflecting the actual plans to destroy the Al-Aqsa Mosque and to build the 'Temple' in its place."[7]

Work that continues today within the Western Wall and Hasmonean tunnels is also interpreted by the Muslim authorities to be attempts by the Israeli government to weaken the substructure of the Haram and cause Arab buildings to collapse. In the summer of 2003, a dig carried out by Wyatt Archaeological Research under permit from the Israeli Antiquities Authority (within the Herodian period quarry mislabeled as "Solomon's Quarry" and also thought to be the site of "Zedekiah's cave") elicited a negative response from East Jerusalem Muslims. One moneychanger, when he learned I was an archaeologist, declared that Israel was trying with this work to again destroy the Muslim holy places. Nothing I could say could change this conviction nor his belief that the Jews had never discovered anything that proved their Temples had existed!

Adding to the fears of the Waqf and the Muslims in East Jerusalem, as well as the Muslim world, is the expectation that Jewish nationalist groups who want to see the Jewish Temple rebuilt will eventually assault the mosques on the Mount. Of these groups, the Temple Mount Faithful is dreaded the most. This organization, which receives permission from the government to hold symbolic demonstrations annually outside the gates of the Old City and near to the Temple Mount, openly denounces the Muslim presence on the Temple Mount and proclaims the soon rebuilding of

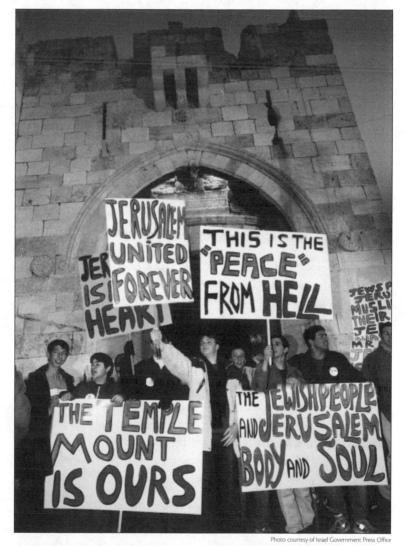

Photo courtesy of Israel Government Press Office

Jewish activists outside Jaffa Gate in Jerusalem protesting Islamic claims to the Temple Mount during the Oslo peace talks.

the Temple on the site. When I interviewed Palestinian mufti Ikrima Sabri about an Associated Press news release in which Yasser Arafat was shown holding a photo with the Dome of the Rock removed and the Temple in its place, the mufti replied that he had given Arafat the picture to show the world that the Jews had an agenda against the Islamic mosques. He went on to explain that since no Temple ever existed there, the Jewish obsession over the Temple Mount is merely an attempt to legitimize the Zionist occupation of Jerusalem. He also said that if groups like the Temple Mount Faithful attempt to harm the mosques, they will face a billion Muslims from all over the world who will come to defend the site to the last drop of blood!

As a result of these suspicions, all non-Muslim visitors to the Dome of the Rock and the Al-Aqsa Mosque have been subjected to increasing harassment. Professor Eilat Mazar explains:

> You couldn't carry a Bible inside; you were stopped at the entrance of the place and searched for a Bible. You cannot carry a Bible inside the Temple Mount. Why? Because it is provocation. You cannot carry the New Testament inside the Temple Mount. Why? Because it is provocation. You might read in it and get close to whatever is dear to you—which would be a religious attitude—and this [is not allowed because religious expressions] are just for the Muslims—nobody else. [However] it's not just the Bible—it's also explanations about the First or Second Temples, etc. This is provocation. You cannot show a sketch of the Second Temple period [while] standing in the corridor of the place—it's a provocation. In the full 145 dunums [of the Temple Mount] you cannot stand and try to explain or show [a picture of the] Second Temple restoration—forget about it. It's provocation![8]

Continually complaining to the Israeli authorities, and especially the foreign media, that Jews and other tourists were offending Muslim sensibilities and causing "provocation," the next step in the Waqf's plan was to remove the non-Muslim presence from the site. Tourists, and especially religious Jews, some of whom had been ascending the Temple Mount despite the rabbinical ban against entering the holy site, were to be excluded so the Haram could be purely Muslim.

The opportunity to enforce this ban occurred when Ariel Sharon, a Knesset member and then-leader of the Likud party, visited the Temple Mount in order to investigate reports that the Waqf's underground construction work had destroyed archaeological remains. A security force of some 1000 Israeli police escorted Sharon and his six-member delegation, a precaution made necessary by the growing conflict with the Palestinians over administration of the site and the protests issued by the Palestinian mufti Ikrima Sabri and officials of the Waqf, who were against the visit (for more details, see pages 114-17). The Sharon team, which was accompanied by Arab Knesset members and Waqf representatives, did not attempt to enter any of the mosques, but only surveyed the construction work at the area known as Solomon's Stables. The visit ended peacefully.

However, later that day, Palestinian radio and television broadcasts inaccurately accused Sharon and the Israeli delegation of "defiling" the mosques. And on the *Voice of Palestine* radio program, Yasser Arafat declared the Sharon visit to be "a serious step against the Muslim holy places," and called all Arabs and Muslims throughout the world to unite and fight such "aggressions."

The next day, the mufti delivered a sermon at the Al-Aqsa Mosque focused on the "desecration" of the mosque by the Israeli government and called for *jihad* "to eliminate the Jews from Palestine." Spurred into action by the mufti's war call, the congregation numbering in the hundreds rushed onto the Temple Mount to apply the sermon. Some wrestled with police guarding the Mughrabi Gate, which leads to the Western Wall, while others hurled stones down upon the Jews at prayer at the Wall.

The Palestinian Authority also declared the Oslo Peace Process had ended and that the intifada, supposedly suspended with the signing of the Declaration of Principles in 1993, was being renewed because of Sharon's "provocation" on the Al-Aqsa compound. Within a week the violence begun at the Temple Mount had spread throughout the country and Muslims destroyed a Jewish holy site—Joseph's Tomb in Nablus (biblical Shechem). Television cameras also recorded the death of young Mohammed al-Dura during a firefight between Israelis and Palestinians. His death, which was used by the Palestinian Authority to create international sympathy for their "occupation" and prove Israeli aggression, stirred an increase in rioting, eventually escalating the intifada into a small-scale war. An official inquiry later revealed the boy could not have been killed by Israeli fire. Recently, the boy's death itself has been suspicioned as staged for the cameras and an investigation is underway to examine controversial new footage that supports this claim.

Immediately after the riot at the Temple Mount, the Waqf announced that all Jews were banned from the site. Citing security concerns, the Israeli government then closed the site to all non-Muslims, an act that many have said was a grave mistake for Israeli sovereignty, since the Palestinian Authority used the closure as a cloak for further destruction of antiquities and as a means to secure its own sovereignty over the site. This display of Islamic sovereignty even extended to the exclusively Jewish Western Wall, which the mufti declared was not Jewish, but Islamic, based on a tradition that says Muhammad had tethered his celestial horse Al-Burak at the site during his ascension to heaven from the sacred Rock at the center of the Haram. Adding to this, the mufti also attempted to resurrect old British Mandate legislation that had restricted Jewish prayers at the Western Wall "from disturbing Muslims."

The Al-Aqsa intifada situation has also caused problems for many Christians. I experienced this firsthand when I went to Israel a month after the Al-Aqsa intifada had begun. I was working on part of a film project on the life of Jesus, and along with some crew members at the Church of the Nativity in Bethlehem, was arrested by the Palestinian police. When asked why we, as Christians, were being detained, one policeman replied, "Because Christians are Zionists!" Fortunately, a while later we were released, but the growing mob of angry Palestinians in Manger Square, near the police station, could have made the story turn out differently. Only the week before, two young Israeli soldiers who were not in uniform had attempted to report to their army unit and were confronted by a Palestinian mob. Frightened, they fled to the Palestinian police station in Ramallah. Rather than protect them (as the Oslo Accord required), the police turned them over to the mob, who lynched them in the police station and threw their bloody bodies out of the police station window in full view of an international television audience. We had escaped such a scene, but we were still trapped in the city because we had to wait for a gun battle between the next-door Arab town of Beit Jala and the Israeli settlement of Gilo to subside.

Despite the control the Waqf currently enjoys over the Temple Mount and the absence of any non-Muslims at the site, Palestinian authorities continually assert that any attempt to alter this situation—even through Israeli demonstrations outside the site—will be considered provocation and lead to a violent reaction. This threat was tested on July 29, 2001, when the Temple Mount Faithful were permitted to bring a cornerstone for the Third Temple to an outer gate of the Old City in a *Tisha B'Av* ceremony (a national commemoration of the destruction of the First and Second Temples). Palestinian leaders had warned the Israeli government that the act would provoke clashes similar to those that erupted after Ariel Sharon's visit to the Al-Aqsa Mosque. The Waqf called on their faithful to come to the shrine to protect the mosque compound "with their bodies" if the cornerstone was brought in (which the Israeli authorities had assured would not happen). Nevertheless, on the day of the event, the Muslim mufti used the loudspeakers on the Temple Mount to proclaim, "God is Great!" This incited the Palestinians at the site to throw rocks from the Temple Mount onto Jews praying at the Western Wall below. Demonstrations also spread across the West Bank, with hundreds in the town of Nablus burning effigies of Sharon and the Temple. It was, in part, this reaction to the Temple Mount Faithful that led to security concerns and a reclosure of the Temple Mount by the Israeli government during *Tisha B'Av* in 2003.

Over the next three years at the site (2000–2003), the destruction of antiquities and the construction of new mosques continued without any interference from Israel, although not without some objection by Israeli authorities. "All of this has been done," reported Israeli journalist Nadav Shragai, "despite protests from the Israeli government, the city municipality, and the Antiquities Authority."[9] Every request from reporters, archaeologists, and inspectors who wanted to visit the site was flatly refused. As Palestinian mufti Ikrima Sabri asserted: "We don't wait for permission from anybody." At the beginning of the Waqf's activity, former Jerusalem mayor Ehud Olmert and the Israeli Antiquities Authorities called for a stop to these illegal acts by the Waqf, and more than 140 Israelis across the political spectrum, including 82 Knesset members, signed petitions against the illegal constructions. However, the then-Barak government refused to interfere while the sensitive political negotiations over the site continued, and Attorney General Elyakim Rubinstein refused to impede the Waqf in any way.

What Is Being Done to Stop the Destruction?

If the State of Israel has sovereignty over the site, if the Israeli Antiquities Authority is required to supervise all excavations in the country, if the Municipality of Jerusalem must approve all construction permits, and if the Israeli police unit assigned to the Temple Mount are to enforce the law requiring the preservation of all holy places, then how is it that the Palestinian destruction has continued this long? Why is it that Jewish lobbyists, who are so active in other Jewish causes, have not been successful in getting someone in Washington to issue a bill condemning the Muslims' change in the status quo and demanding an open investigation? Reporter Nadav Shragai wondered at the government's indifference, saying, "Imagine...if a Jewish group stormed the Al-Aqsa Mosque and began dynamiting it or ramming it with heavy construction equipment. How long would that be tolerated by the Arab world?"[10]

Professor Eilat Mazar explains the problem of inaction and denial by the Israeli authorities:

> After 9/11, with the Americans concerned with their own problems, the [Israeli] government found themselves alone in confronting the [Temple Mount] problem, [but] that's no excuse for not doing anything about it. They preferred in many cases to let them destroy an enormous amount of antiquities...and kept quiet in order to keep everything quiet....Amir Drori, the director of the Antiquities Authority, was there [on the Temple Mount]. He... saw the Antiquities Authority as a government institution, so he [also] kept quiet. Letters were being written inside the system saying it was not right, [and] the [antiquities] law was not being fulfilled, but they didn't say a word about what was going on at the Temple Mount. It took us some time to understand that they don't fulfill their job because they can't....Drori [was pressured] to say that there is nothing [wrong going on (at) the Temple Mount]. [However] he was cornered by a Knesset member, and this was much too much for him at a certain point, and he said, "That's enough! We all know what's going on there!" It's hard for the authorities from the inside to really declare the truth. That's why we built this committee...in order to cry out to the world and to confront the government so they can't say they didn't know.[11]

The committee to which Professor Mazar refers, and which she heads, is the Committee for the Prevention of the Destruction of Antiquities on the Temple Mount. This is a nonpolitical, volunteer organization made up of well-known Israeli public figures, archaeologists, writers, lawyers, justices, and members of the Security Services that was formed in 2000. Here, she describes one of the investigative functions of the committee with respect to the Muslim activities on the Temple Mount:

> We take aerial photographs...that show tractors, back-hoes, and trucks loading tons of fill, and dumping it out-side the area. [From a series of these photos] we can see tractors going in and hitting ancient structures and clearing them out. So when [the authorities] say there are no tractors or backhoes working on the Temple Mount, we show that there are several, and when they say that no destruction has taken place, we can show large amounts of highly disturbing destruction.[12]

The committee has confronted Israeli government officials with this information and has made the following demands: 1) To stop the destruction taking place on the Temple Mount; 2) to open the Temple Mount to Israeli and international media; 3) to enable the Antiquities Authority to fulfill its duties and guard the antiq-uities of the State of Israel; and 4) to see that the status quo on the Temple Mount is kept and ensure that all changes are done in a way that would not destroy ancient remains.[13] Although a number of Israeli leaders listened to the pleas of the committee and promised to address the situation, they have been stymied by a growing number of Palestinian terrorist attacks and by warn-ings from the Palestinian mufti Ikrima Sabri that there would be bloodshed if Israel attempted to interfere with the Muslim admin-istration of the site.

Then, in June 2003, after 33 months of closure to non-Muslims, the Israeli authorities, upon hearing a unanimous report from security officials that Israel was setting a dangerous precedent by keeping the compound closed to non-Muslims for so long, reopened the Temple Mount to restricted visits (Sunday through Thursday from 9:00 to 11:00 A.M.) by approved tour groups under police escort.[14] Even so, the status quo was not restored, as these groups were only permitted to enter the Temple Mount platform and not the Dome of the Rock or Al-Aqsa Mosque—in violation of the 1967 law of religious access. In August 2003, entrance to the site was abruptly suspended by the police, in response to a classified report that warned of violence if provocation occurred at the annual commemoration of *Tisha B'Av* as well as a public threat by Yasser Arafat of "grave consequences" if the visits continued.

One week later the site was again reopened after covert meetings between the Israeli authorities and the Islamic Waqf, in which a temporary accord was reached. However, the same restrictions were implemented once again, and the status quo was not renewed. Nevertheless, the Committee for the Prevention of the Destruction of Antiquities on the Temple Mount hopes that the reopening of the site to even restricted tour visits by non-Muslims may aid in curtailing the Muslim destruction of ancient remains and illegal construction activity. Even though tourists aren't allowed to come near to the places where illegal activity has taken place, the hope is that the presence of tour groups may cause the work to be suspended in order to avoid public awareness of what's happening.

This first step at restoring Israeli sovereignty at the site may, of course, lead to others that will surely move the Muslims toward confrontation. Israel has stated that, at any rate, it will not take a step backward again. Internal Security minister Tzahi Hanegbi declared this when he announced with the reopening that "Palestinians will no longer be permitted from barring non-Muslim visits to the site holy to all religions."[15] In response, the Palestinian mufti and other Islamic clerics have denounced the Israeli action in their Friday sermons. Previously when Israel had threatened to reopen the Temple Mount to Jews, the Palestinian mufti and Yasser Arafat were alone in issuing threats. For example, the grand mufti of Lebanon's Sunni Muslims, Sheikh Muhammad Rashid Kabbani, proclaimed the "beginning of the end for the State of Israel." The former Iraqi foreign ministry urged the start of a holy war to liberate the Islamic site. Such threats hearken back to the days before the State of Israel, when the Temple Mount was under Muslim rule and any entrance by non-Muslims into the area was punishable by death. With the political situation between the Israelis and Palestinians continuing to disintegrate, we may soon see both parties moving toward a more significant battle for the Temple Mount.

The basis for the next battle may well involve the destruction of Jewish remains—and construction of new Islamic structures mentioned in this chapter. However, to comprehend the extent of these acts we must expose the details, which have largely been veiled in secrecy. Join us as we look behind the veil in the next chapter.

10

The Battle of the Bulge

Our holy and beautiful house, where our fathers praised Thee, has been burned with fire; and all our precious things have become a ruin.

ISAIAH 64:11

The southern wall is beginning to buckle because of the destruction carried out by the Waqf. These walls were not built to support tractors and loaded trucks. The path of the rainwater has also been changed in the process, and water is trickling down the walls and eating away at them...it is about to fall and once a catastrophe happens, Israel will be blamed.[1]

PROFESSOR EILAT MAZAR

Suppose one evening you are at home watching television, when suddenly a gang of thugs break in, tie you up, and steal all your belongings. As they load your property in their trucks they tell you not to worry, for these things were never yours in the first place, that the stuff had always belonged to them, and furthermore, you've never even lived in that house![2] Insane, you say? Yes it is! But that is the same line the Palestinian Authority has been giving to the world for years as they banned Jews from the Temple Mount, and more recently, wantonly destroyed ancient Jewish artifacts while bulldozing and carting away tons of historically rich debris and removing priceless Jewish antiquities to sell on the archaeological black market to the highest bidder. The Palestinian pitch goes like this: The site has never had any historical connection with the Jewish people, and nowhere in the city of Jerusalem is there evidence that the Jews existed

Photo by Alexander Schick *Bibelausstellung Sylt*

The subterranean area known as Solomon's Stables located at the southern end of the Temple Mount. The photos show before and after the mosque was built within these ancient chambers.

Photo by author

there in the past, and there have never been any Jewish Temples on the Temple Mount because it has only and always been an Islamic holy place.

However, the Palestinians have recently run into a serious complication. Like a slow, hidden leak that eventually floods your basement, the destructive activities carried out by the Muslims on the Temple Mount have caught up with them—in the form of a bulge. At first it was a small protrusion about 35 feet wide on the outer surface of the southern wall of the Temple Mount, but over time the bulge has grown, threatening to collapse not only the ancient enclosure wall, but to bring down with it the newly constructed al-Marawani Mosque with hundreds of Muslim worshipers.

Closed for Renovations

The structures at the southern end of the Temple Mount, Solomon's Stables and the Eastern Huldah (Double Gate) passageway, are archaeological remnants related to the ancient Temple complex. Solomon's Stables is an underground Herodian

Photo courtesy of the Israel Exploration Society, Jerusalem

Muslim Waqf construction activity at the Solomon's Stables area of the Temple Mount. As can be seen in the photo, a massive excavation (removing 18,000 square feet of archaeologically rich soil) cut into the ancient structures completely disregards the fragile state of the structures.

substructure at the southeastern corner of the Temple Mount that consists of a row of subterranean halls. It received its name during the Crusader period when the Knights Templar turned it into a stable for their horses. There is a mysterious structure beneath this one (opposite the Single Gate) which has never been explored. The Eastern Huldah passageway is the only intact Herodian structure remaining on the Temple Mount and has never been opened to the general public. The ceiling of this passageway was domed and decorated with geometric and floral relief designs (which included the seven species of fruits in the Holy Land), and it is known that a beautiful marble pillar supports the middle of the tunnel. This unique remnant had been used during the Second Temple era as the main southern entrance to the Temple Mount. Today a monumental staircase at this site, excavated in the late 1970s, ends at a sealed gate in the southern wall. But behind this wall is the concealed passageway, long in need of archaeological preservation.

Beginning in 1996, Sheikh Rayadh Salah, an Israeli-Arab citizen who is head of the Israeli Islamic Movement, began directing activities with the Waqf to renovate these structures in order to accommodate 10,000 Muslim worshipers. Working without any

Photo by Angie Alvarez

Professor Eilat Mazar

archaeological supervision, Waqf workmen made whatever alterations they desired to this delicate site. It also seems they were especially instructed to get rid of anything that appeared pre-Islamic. This followed what has been a persistent pattern of Waqf activity for two decades on the Temple Mount, in which ancient remains are concealed or destroyed so they can't be used as evidence of prior Jewish possession of the site. An investigation of such destruction

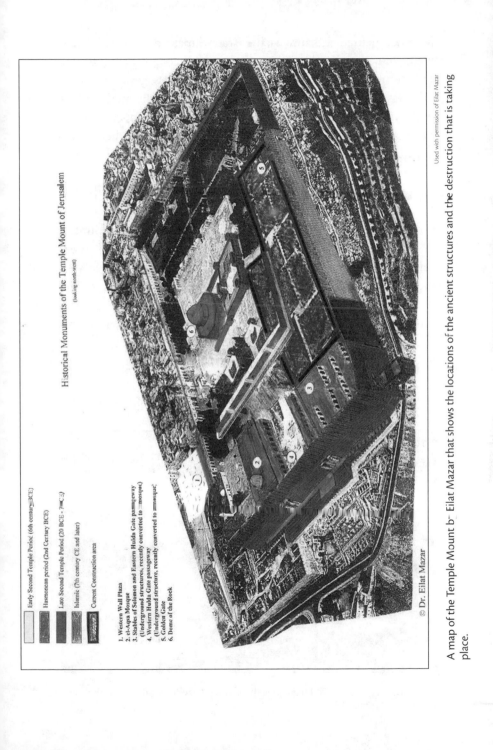

Historical Monuments of the Temple Mount of Jerusalem

(looking north-west)

Early Second Temple Period (6th century BCE)

Hasmonean period (2nd Century BCE)

Late Second Temple Period (20 BCE - 70 CE)

Islamic (7th century CE and later)

Current Construction area

1. Western Wall Plaza
2. el-Aqsa Mosque
3. Stables of Solomon and Eastern Hulda Gate passageway
   (Underground structures, recently converted to a mosque)
4. Western Hulda Gate passageway
   (Underground structure, recently converted to a mosque)
5. Golden Gate
6. Dome of the Rock

© Dr. Eilat Mazar

Used with permission of Eilat Mazar

A map of the Temple Mount by Eilat Mazar that shows the locations of the ancient structures and the destruction that is taking place.

was documented and, in 1993, the Israeli Supreme Court ruled that the Waqf had violated Israeli antiquities laws no less than 35 times.[3] This destruction includes the Eastern Huldah passageway, in which priceless ancient decorations were destroyed and the marble pillar in the tunnel was covered over by cement.[4] This happened when the Waqf created the al-Marawani Mosque, now the largest mosque in Israel. It covers about 1.5 acres and is able to hold at least 10,000 people. The next year, in 1997, the Waqf converted the Western Huldah Gate passageway, another Second Temple period site, into a second new mosque, thereby completing the destruction of these ancient southern entrances to the Temple Mount.

In November 1999 the workmen began to make an "emergency exit" for the new mosques, a project that further violated the original construction agreement. Over a period of three days and nights bulldozers and backhoes dug constantly, cutting through the ancient Temple Mount wall, resulting in a gaping pit 18,000 square feet in size and 36 feet deep. In January, another hole, 1250 square meters in area and 12 meters deep, appeared north of Solomon's Stables. Eilat Mazar, an archaeologist at the Hebrew University's Institute of Archaeology, the granddaughter

Photo courtesy of Eilat Mazar

Construction supplies piled high near the Golden Gate for work on another new mosque in this area.

of the late Benjamin Mazar (whose records of the famous excavations at the foot of the Temple Mount she is preparing for publication), and author of *The Complete Guide to the Temple Mount
Excavations*, has kept a detailed record of what the Waqf has been
doing at the site. Concerning the construction of the emergency
exit she notes, "An enormous amount of ancient fill—20,000
tons—was dumped out. What was in there? I don't even want to
start thinking. You can imagine what is happening when you
excavate with backhoes—everything that could have been there
surely was! So it was robbed or dumped into the garbage!"[5]

Later the same year the Waqf also constructed buildings
within the boundaries of the Temple Mount, adjacent to the
northern wall, between the Gate of Forgiveness and the Afel Gate.
According to Rabbi Chaim Richman of The Temple Institute, who
has been monitoring the Waqf's activities, "Several structures that
had been preserved underground in their entirety for nearly two
millennia had been unearthed, including a water aqueduct from
the Holy Temple. These were then completely demolished by the
Moslems with exacting precision."[6] Adding his voice to the protest,
Jerusalem archaeologist Ronny Reich, who directed the most
recent excavations at the southwestern wall of the Temple Mount,
said, "Information that could have contributed to the current
debate over whether Jerusalem was a strategic city in King David's
time has also been lost forever with the removal of so much material from the Waqf's excavation."[7] And one Israeli group, trying
to convince the Israeli Knesset to stop the illegal proceedings,
stated, "There is a full-scale destruction of antiquities underway
on the site!"

Still, the destruction and construction continued. In February
and March of 2001, the Palestinian Authority ordered the razing
of an ancient arched structure that had been built against the
eastern wall of the Temple Mount. The purpose of this destruction was to further enlarge the emergency gate of the new mosque
at Solomon's Stables. What's more, this "simple" exit had become
a broad, double-arched opening with landings of monumental
proportions (18,000 square feet).

In 2002–2003, the pavement that started at the southeastern corner of the Temple platform was extended to the eastern wall, and the inside of the Golden Gate has seen construction and the landing outside it has been paved. Reports have also been made in U.S. newspapers of an underground tunnel dug between the Dome of the Rock and the Al-Aqsa Mosque. None of the archaeological authorities I spoke with in Israel could confirm such a tunnel, and Jon Seligman, district archaeologist of Jerusalem with the Israeli Antiquities Authority, claimed that it was nonsense. Perhaps, but it is possible. In July 2000 I observed (and filmed) an entrance to just such an east-west tunnel during construction work near the Dome of the Rock (see chapter 9).

Sawing the Sanctuary

One of the most serious accusations against the Waqf's destructive actions on the Temple Mount has been the report of their illegal use of an industrial saw in their construction work. Professor Mazar explains the nature of this problem:

> They brought inside the Temple Mount enclosure an industrial saw and [with it] started to turn ancient stones into building material for [their] construction. We have photographs showing clearly how it was done. There is a pile of ancient stones on one side, [and on the other] the saw and dust from the saw and bright shining new stones to pave areas....You wouldn't think such a thing could happen! [However] the authorities in Israel were afraid to admit it and said [to us]: "There is no such saw. You are just making provocation. There is [only] a small saw that cuts small stones, to do small building projects." It took us some time in order to prove there was such a saw cutting ancient stone there. This is the problem when this area is closed, everything is hard to prove.[8]

The additional tragedy of the use of an industrial saw is the kind of ancient stones reported to have been used by the stonecutters. According to workers at the site, any stones with decorations or inscriptions were re-cut so that their markings were

Photo courtesy of Eilat Mazar

An industrial saw belonging to Palestinian construction workers on the Temple Mount, and used to reshape ancient stones, including those with markings on them, into blocks for modern use.

obliterated. The stones were then fashioned into new building material for the mosque's construction. Can it be imagined what priceless historical relics might have been destroyed in this way? The classic Latin phrase translated "I came, I saw, I conquered" has been memorized by generations of history students concerning the exploits of Julius Caesar. Playing upon these words, it might be said with respect to the mechanical stonecutting activity of the Muslim authorities that they "came, *sawed*, and conquered" with respect to the Jewish history of the Temple Mount!

Treasures in the Trash

In the course of the construction work, hundreds of truckloads of archaeologically rich debris were dumped by cover of night in the el-Azariya municipal dump and mixed with garbage so as to obscure the historical relics within. That this was purposefully done was revealed when the manager of the dump was informed that the trucks contained earth with archaeological value. He redirected the trucks to a clean area, but after four truckloads were dumped in this area, the trucks stopped coming

Photo courtesy of Eilat Mazar

Ancient stones excavated from the Temple Mount by the Palestinian construction workers and dumped along a path near the Dome of the Rock.

to this dump. The next evening, around midnight, the trucks began dumping tons of debris at a new site in the Kidron Valley. This site was open and exposed the archaeological remains to weather and pillaging by locals. In addition, the Work Department of the Municipality of Jerusalem carelessly dumped rubble from their own nearby excavation of drainage sewers over the lower slopes of Temple Mount debris at this site, further complicating the recovery of ancient remains.

Despite these difficulties, and despite limited access to these dumps by certain authorities, archaeologists and their students have been able to search through the garbage in el-Azariya and in the Kidron dumps and have uncovered significant artifacts that have provided clues as to how the ground was stratified at the Waqf's construction site and what historical periods are represented by the finds. Archaeologist Zachi Zweig has released an analysis of artifacts recovered from the dump sites and dated by Drs. Gabriel Barkai, Aren Maeir, and Dan Bahat.[9] The artifacts include stoneware, pottery, ceramic, and glassware items, although for analysis purposes, only 72 pottery rims (the easiest

Photo courtesy of Binyamin Lalizou

Piles of ancient fill and construction debris taken from the Temple Mount dumped near the Dome of the Rock.

artifacts to date) were considered. The following chart shows the breakdown of these pottery fragments and the percentage representing each historical (archaeological) period:

Period	Number	(Percentage)
First Temple (Iron II)	10	(14%)
Second Temple (Hellenistic, Early Roman)	14	(19%)
Late Roman	4	(6%)
Byzantine	11	(15%)
Early Muslim and Medieval	12	(17%)
Unidentified (probably Ottoman)	21	(29%)

In addition, hundreds of monumental artifacts have been recovered from the dump sites or photographed on the Temple Mount. These include broken columns, cut building stones, and large ornamented stones. Clusters of massive masonry stones that were discovered by the Waqf workmen and then demolished have been uncovered in the Kidron dumps. Numerous other rubble

Photo courtesy of Eilat Mazar

Broken pillars and stones uncovered by Palestinian construction workers, but inaccessible for study by archaeologists.

piles of ancient masonry stones, ashlar blocks, and pillars cover parts of the Temple Mount compound. Policemen on the Mount also reported seeing a water channel with arches dismantled, and stones in the shape of an arch were discovered in one of the Kidron dumps. Worse, according to a Waqf worker, stones with decorations and inscriptions were found during the construction work. He reported seeing writing on the stones in ancient Hebrew as well as seeing a five-pointed star symbol (a symbol common during the Hasmonean period).[10] One of my sources told me that some of these inscribed stones were smuggled out by workers to be sold on the antiquities black market.

One such stone, in the form of a sandstone tablet and reputedly from the Eastern Wall excavations, surfaced in 2003 in the possession of Israeli antiquities collector Oded Golan and caused a media sensation. It was dubbed "The Joash Inscription" because it was inscribed with 15 lines of dedicatory text in ancient Hebrew recording how the Judean King Joash (835–793 B.C.) attempted to repair and preserve the century-old First Temple. More remarkably, the wording of the inscription closely paralleled the biblical text of 2 Kings 12:1-6,11-17. Archaeologists proclaimed the inscription one of the greatest discoveries of all time—if it proved to be genuine. One of the problems connected with the smuggling of artifacts from the Waqf's construction site is that once an artifact is removed from its archaeological context, it loses its value for archaeological identification purposes and makes its authentication more difficult. In the summer of 2003, the Israeli Antiquities Authority, as well as competent epigraphists who examined the text, rendered the verdict that "The Joash Inscription" was a forgery. Even so, the brief excitement over the possibility that the inscription might be genuine cannot help but make us wonder what genuine artifacts might have been discovered and concealed or destroyed by the Waqf's excavation efforts and construction work.

Political Consequences of the Waqf's Construction

The most serious political consequence of the Waqf's destructive work is the change in the status quo on the Temple Mount,

Photo courtesy of Eilat Mazar

An ancient lintel stone uncovered in the construction is probably from the Second Temple.

which formerly was thought to have provided stability at the site. According to a senior Israeli security official, "Status quo is more powerful than law here, and more important than law. When you get political issues in a holy place, it's not good for all sides."[11] Since 2000 the status quo has been changed, and with the resumption of visits to the Temple Mount by Israeli order in 2003, it has still not been restored as before. Many believe it will never be restored because the Waqf has made so many changes to the site—in violation of the original construction agreement. Adnan Husseini, director of the Waqf, has said he believes Israel does not want to restore the status quo, but intended, with the reopening of the Mount, to let Jewish activists onto the site to pray (also a supposed violation of the status quo). However, non-Muslim individuals are restricted by the Waqf from entering any mosque, and must stay on the outside plaza, while Muslim workers continue to do their construction activity covertly. Which group, then, is more in violation of the status quo?

Will the lack of status quo at the Temple Mount lead to the next great conflict at the site and spread to other Muslim states in the Middle East? Gerald M. Steinberg, analyzing the situation for the *Jerusalem Post*, thinks so:

> Jerusalem remains a source of major instability, as Muslim and Palestinian officials keep the Temple Mount closed, and construction continues in secret, fueling reports of gross destruction of Jewish sites. Every action in Jerusalem eventually has an equal and opposite reaction, and the current situation is extremely explosive. Yesterday's events may have been contained, but as long as the situation remains unchanged, the tension will grow.[12]

Or as one commentator suggested, "Perhaps Israel is waiting for what some view as the inevitability of renewed war in the Middle East before asserting its military authority over the most sacred ground in Jerusalem."[13] And, a recent controversy over a bulge in a section of the southern wall of the Temple Mount has had the potential to drive Israelis and Palestinians toward that inevitable confrontation. Let us now consider this "battle of the bulge."

The Bulge in the Temple Mount Wall

As the Holy Land observed the change to a new millennium in 2000, people began to notice that a damp bulge had appeared in the southern retaining wall of the Temple Mount, close to where it joins with the eastern wall. At this time the bulge was about 10 meters (33 feet) in diameter, but a year later it had grown to a length of 30 meters (98 feet). Before work began on the Temple Mount in 2002, the bulge had nearly doubled in size to 190 meters (623 feet) long and protruded outward as much as 70 centimeters (2.25 feet) in some areas. Because the bulge is in a popular tourist area and also visible from the main road that passes near the wall, it is open to scrutiny and has therefore drawn extraordinary media attention. As Professor Mazar points out:

> We were shouting about destruction inside the Temple Mount compound but television [cameras] couldn't go in[side] so nothing was published and people didn't know about it. [However, since] the bulge in the southern wall is on the outside it couldn't be hidden by the authorities. Although the Islamic authorities, the Waqf, said there is nothing to it...they couldn't [deny] it for long because... the televisions could stand on the outside and [show] what we were talking about. Everybody could see there is a problem, so they had to face the problematic issue.[14]

Observing the southern wall from below, it can be seen that the base of the wall was built of neatly arranged layers of Herodian stone. This section of the wall has endured without any problems for 2000 years. However, the upper part, where the bulge has appeared, is visibly different, revealing that portion of the wall to have been previously destroyed and rebuilt. Most of these repairs were done over the centuries, most recently by the Ottomans. According to Dr. Dan Bahat, the former district archaeologist for

Photo used with permission from Alxander Schick *Bibelausstellung Sylt*

The bulge at the southern wall grows. The first photo shows the beginning of the bulge in 2000, and the second photo shows the last stage of the bulge in 2003 before repairs.

Photo by author

Jerusalem, "The problems begin in the eleventh century. In 1033, a terrible earthquake struck Jerusalem. All the southern wall of the old city was destroyed—the wall built by Herod the Great when he added to the Second Temple. Later that wall was repaired by the Moslems, for about 30 years, it took from 1034 to 1064."[15] Bahat also says the repair job 1000 years ago was poorly done. The original Herodian wall was constructed from massive, closely fitted blocks of stone, and the Muslims used smaller, poorly fitted stones.

Despite this past history of the wall, a report drafted by Israel's Antiquities Authority cited the cause of the bulge as coming from the unauthorized construction work by the Waqf on the new mosque in Solomon's Stables. The new floor put in the ancient structure, the bulldozing of a new entrance, and the accompanying massive construction directly behind the wall were said to have contributed to the bulge. Also, stress from the construction of the Marawani Mosque caused cracks in the stone, and rainwater was diverted from its natural drainage path and ended up seeping through the mosque and into the wall. Other archaeologists were less restrained in their criticism, stating that the Palestinian construction was the only cause of the damage. Adnan Husseini, the director of the Waqf, blamed natural erosion for the swelling in the ancient mortar in the wall. He minimized the danger of the bulge and told Israeli archaeologists that the bulge was a result of Israeli excavations.

A quite different opinion concerning the timing and cause of the bulge was offered by the activist organization the Temple Mount Faithful in their official newsletter, *Voice of the Temple Mount Faithful*. After reporting the international response to one of the organization's demonstrations (during which they carried their "Third Temple cornerstone" (see chapter 11) on a flatbed truck outside the southern wall on *Tisha B'Av* 2001, they stated,

> On the day after the event a large bulge was noticed on the
> southern wall of the Temple Mount....The bulge was not

caused by the hands of any man. Everyone understands that it was caused by G-d Himself who did it on the same wall in front of and not far from the location of the cornerstone.[16]

In other words, it was not the Waqf nor the Israeli government that had caused the bulge, but it was an act of God designed to demonstrate His desire to rebuild the Temple!

Clearly, the decay in the wall had to be fixed to prevent the condition from worsening. Yet while the bulge is an engineering problem, repairing it is a political one. The Waqf began repairs in April 2002, but was stopped by Israeli authorities, who believed the imminent possibility of a collapse of the wall required their assuming responsibility for repairs, since the bulge was on their side of the wall. Husseini contended the Israelis were deliberately exaggerating the severity of the problem in order to justify their intervention.

In 2003 the Jordanians were brought into the picture. Raef Nijem, vice president of the state-run Jordanian Construction Committee, also minimized the threat of collapse, stating that the Jordanian team that examined the site found only a few gaps in the wall caused by rain that had entered cracks over the last several hundred years, and that several eroded stones that might fall would only fall outward, away from worshipers.[17] Still, Israeli authorities insisted that not only the southern wall, but other parts of the southern compound, were in danger of collapse.

The Potential for Future Disaster

Israeli authorities have stated that the change in status quo on the Temple Mount by the Muslim authorities requires a resolution. However, given the destructive actions of the Waqf in de-Judaizing the site and Islamizing it, it will be impossible to return to the same conditions that existed in the past. The new conditions created by the Waqf which have resulted in unintended problems—such as the bulge in the southern wall—may also have created the potential for future disaster at the Temple Mount. For example, Professor Mazar explains her concern for the unsupervised activities of the Waqf, which have shown no knowledge of nor regard for the structural integrity of the Temple Mount compound:

> The whole compound of the Temple Mount is an ancient compound. It is 2000 years of construction in a very poor state of preservation. When the Islamic authorities were converting the Solomon's Stable into the largest mosque in Israel containing 10,000 people, without any supervision by the archaeological authorities, they did it fast, unprofessional, and the result was all kinds of destructions, [for example the] bulge on the southern wall. So, if somebody is really ruining the place, it's them—they are irrigating all kinds of gardens without any kinds of supervision, causing bulging in the surrounding walls. They [also] let tractors and trucks go inside. But we need to remember that the whole surface of the Temple Mount is very, very thin—King Herod did not plan it to carry tractors and so many people together with their backhoes [and other heavy equipment] driving about it. We know that the preservation is very poor underground, so it's just a matter of time, where, and on what scale, that it is going to crash and be destroyed. I think the destruction of the Temple [Mount] is going to occur by the illegal activities of the Islamic authorities.[18]

While such a statement may seem sensational to many, Professor Mazar is not alone in warning of an imminent collapse. No less an authority than Shuka Dorfman, director of the Israeli Antiquities Authority, has stated, "Although I cannot predict the exact time frame, I am convinced that if hundreds of thousands of Moslems gather on the Temple Mount, the southern wall next to the Al-Aqsa Mosque would collapse."[19] Gabriel Barkai, a recipient of the Israeli prize in archaeology, has also cautioned, "I'm not a prophet. I can't say exactly when, but there is no question that it will collapse! All you need is a big group to congregate up there for the equilibrium to start shifting. It's a matter of time."[20]

Both the Israeli and Muslim authorities have been well aware of this potential disaster, but neither side has permitted the other to do anything about it. In the case of the bulge in the southern wall, the Muslim authorities claim to have fixed some 60 percent of the wall under the supervision of UNISCOW. But, according to Israeli officials, this amounted to nothing more than patching the minor damage that had already occurred. These officials contend that the Waqf does not have the knowledge or ability to stop the fast-eroding bulge itself. They argued that because the bulge was on Israel's side of the wall, and because they had the experience and equipment to correct the problem, they should be allowed to fix it. Muslim authorities responded with their usual objection that the Israelis were not really interested in repairing the wall, but simply looking for an excuse to bring down the mosque and rebuild the Temple. As Sheikh Abdul Azzim Salhab, general manager of the Islamic Waqf, stated, "Israel was trying to

Photo by Angie Alvarez

Bulge at southern wall, with scaffolding from Jordanian repair workers.

stir a problem from the issue of the wall renovation to gain control of the Mosque."[21]

Late in 2002, Jordan, which is supposedly the official custodian of the Muslim holy places on the Temple Mount, sent a team from the Royal Scientific Society to Jerusalem to study the situation. In the spring of 2003, Jordanian workmen erected scaffolding for the renovation of the wall (see photo on previous page). By fall 2003, the scaffolding still remained and the work was far from completed. And even this repair work may not solve the greater problem that now exists, as Professor Mazar explains:

> The Jordanians are doing their best, no one thinks otherwise. The problem is they are not supervised by anyone. [What] if they do something wrong, [what if] after they fix it [it still] falls? Who are they going to blame—the Jordanians or Ariel Sharon? He is the one that is really responsible for the preservation of the Temple Mount. This is inside of Israel and it is Israel's responsibility. It is a crime that it has not been done this way.[22]

If future problems occur as a result of this work or from the renovations made by the Waqf in their mosque constructions, chances are high that Israel would be blamed—resulting in the very situation Israel has been attempting to avoid by exercising restraint over the matter with the Muslim authorities.

A Preview of What Could Happen

The world did not have to wait long for a preliminary "situation" to erupt in Israel. On Tuesday, September 23, 2003, one of the Temple Mount walls collapsed. However, it was not the bulge in the southern wall that succumbed, but a 430-square-foot (40-square-meter) section of a modern wall of the Islamic Museum adjacent to the Al-Aqsa Mosque. Visible to Jewish worshipers at the Western Wall, the collapse of the surface stones exposed the substructure of dirt and fill (see photo on next page). It also exposed the fear that this was just the beginning of the inevitable disaster predicted by archaeologists such as Eilat Mazar, who observed, "This collapse might cause a terrific series of collapses."[23] As though responding to the violence around it, the collapse took place in the same area that had been the scene of riots earlier in the month between Muslims and Israelis who battled over renewed Jewish access to the Temple Mount. The Waqf contended that the collapse was unrelated to their construction activity near the site and blamed the tragedy on Israeli authorities. Director Adnan al-Husseini stated the wall's collapse resulted from "the Israeli intervention in our work and preventing us from maintaining it after we stated it was in urgent need for a rapid action to prevent its collapse."[24] In light of the Waqf's unsupervised activities elsewhere on the Temple Mount, it is hard to believe they were prevented by the Israelis from repairing the wall. In addition, no wall has ever collapsed before, and this took place after the Waqf began their destructive work in the area. We can see in the Waqf's accusation the hint of a greater charge that will come in the future should other walls and structures fall: that the Israeli government deliberately

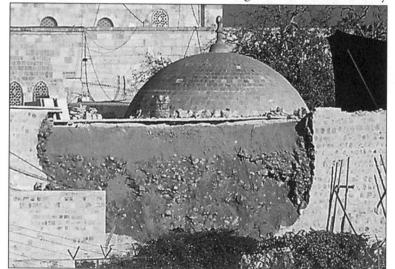

Photo courtesy of Ann Clark

Collapsed portion of wall of the Islamic Museum next to the Al-Aqsa Mosque on the Temple Mount (September 2003).

caused or allowed the catastrophe in the hope the mosques would be destroyed.

In relation to the collapsed wall, Professor Mazar warned, "It is frightening to think of this collapse, and what could happen in the future....This collapse should be a warning bell. If a catastrophe occurs, the whole world will blame Israel."[25] Whether the cause is one of the earthquakes that frequent the area or the cumulative effect of abuse to the ancient structures on the Temple Mount, it does not take much to imagine a scenario that could develop in the future. Let's visualize such a hypothetical situation for a moment.

It is the Muslim celebration of Ramadan, and hundreds of thousands of Muslim worshipers have crowded onto the Temple Mount, with 10,000 more in the al-Marawani Mosque. Suddenly, without cause, the southern wall buckles and then breaks. Without the outer southern retaining wall for support, the inner walls of the al-Marawani Mosque burst apart, crushing the thousands of worshipers within. In a chain reaction, the vaulted substructure of Solomon's Stables that contains the mosque caves in, bringing down the Al-Aqsa Mosque located above it along with thousands of worshipers as well as the vast stone platform at the southern end of the Temple Mount compound.

No one knows how far such a disaster could spread and how many Islamic and Israeli structures and lives would be affected, but one Israeli official with the Ministry of Internal Security described such a scenario as "the Third World War."[26]

Daniel Pipes, director of Middle East Forum, is more explicit in his opinion of the outcome: "This disaster would lead to at least wide-scale fighting in Jerusalem and a heated international crisis. If things really went wrong, it could precipitate a wave of violence in Europe and a full-blown Arab-Israeli war [or] it could unleash an end-of-days messianism in the three monotheistic religions, with unforeseeable consequences."[27] It is no wonder that *Newsweek* magazine in its report on the bulge termed this "Jerusalem's Armageddon Wall."[28]

The possibility and danger of such a scenario playing itself out is very real, given the Waqf's response to the collapse of the Islamic Museum wall. And it is clear from the political controversy over the bulging southern wall, which has reached international proportions, that the site is ready for a major confrontation. To be sure, the Muslim alterations of the structures on the Temple Mount have brought about this change in the status quo.

Yet, while the Waqf and the Palestinian Authority are racing to complete their constructions in order to obscure a Jewish presence at the site, Jewish activists are busy preparing for a construction of their own that will one day remove the Muslim presence. These preparations are for the rebuilding of the Temple and constitute one of the most volatile acts that are advancing the battle for the last days' Temple. Come and see what is happening today in this battle to rebuild.

11

The Battle to Rebuild

The first nail in the Temple should start World War III.... [to rebuild the Temple] you have to have the political background, you have to have the capability; but this could happen tomorrow![1]

Rabbi Nachman Kahane

I t was the evening of *Tisha B'Av*, the most solemn day on the Jewish calendar. I had joined a crowd of some 10,000 people packed into Safra Square in Jerusalem for a reading in unison of *Eicah* ("Alas!"), the Hebrew title for Jeremiah the prophet's mournful book of Lamentations. As the reading progressed, more Israelis assembled on the street adjacent to the square. By the time the service had concluded, 100,000-plus people had arrived at the starting point of the annual walk around the walls of the Old City. Newspaper advertisements had stated the purpose of the march: "We will assemble to proclaim our eternal bond to the Temple Mount, where our First and Second Temples stood, and where *the Third Temple will be built, speedily in our days*" (emphasis added).

As I watched the crowd, I could see in the sea of faces people filled with determination, others ecstatic with the moment, and still others weeping tears. Many carried Israeli flags, while others carried handmade signs proclaiming their loyalty to Jerusalem and especially to Jerusalem's future Temple.

These people were not fringe-group fanatics, but everyday Israeli citizens—Ashkenazi, Sephardi, Russian, and Ethiopian Jews, young and old, singles and families—mingled with international Christian groups who had also joined the throng to show their solidarity for the cause. These were walkers, not warriors, but even so, they were joined in force by those in the country who are waging a special battle for the Temple—a battle to rebuild.

In this chapter, we will look at two of the organizations within the so-called Temple movement that are the most prominent in terms of their political and religious preparations for the building of the Third Temple, and which are most often cited by the Palestinian Authority and Arab press as the greatest threats to the Islamic holy places.

The Proponents of the Plan to Rebuild

The Temple Institute

Since 1986 a group of rabbinical scholars, researchers, designers, artisans, and craftsmen under the direction of Rabbi Yisrael Ariel have been involved in raising the awareness of and educating the Jewish public about the significance the past Temples play in Jewish heritage and the hope for the building of the Third Temple. In the Jewish Quarter of the Old City of Jerusalem, this group has created what they call a "Temple-in-waiting"[2] in order to fulfill the biblical commandment of Exodus 25:8, within the limits possible today, to "construct [God] a sanctuary [Temple]." Known as The Temple Institute (Hebrew, *Machon HaMikdash*), this organization, located within view of the Temple Mount itself, has been at the forefront of the publication of Third Temple research. Rabbi Ariel and those connected with The Temple Institute believe there is a direct correlation between the problems Israel has faced and the lack of a Temple. In fact, they contend that the problems the world is suffering results as well from the Temple's absence. The purpose of The Temple Institute, then, is to hasten the building of the Third Temple day and the coming of the Messiah.

Model of the Third Temple displayed by the Temple Mount Faithful during their *Tisha B'Av* march to the Temple Mount, August 2003.

Creating the Vessels of the Temple

The most highly profiled work of The Temple Institute—and the one for which it has gained notoriety[3]—is its authentic recreation of the 103 sacred Temple vessels necessary for resumption of the Temple services as well as computerized visualizations and blueprints for building the Third Temple. One of the first items created was a special computerized loom to manufacture the priestly garments, which must be woven as a single piece in a complex "garment of six" pattern (in which each individual thread consists of six separate threads spun into one). Among the items that have been or will be created are the eight garments of the high priest—four of woven white flax (inner robe, belt, turban, pants) and four of various materials (golden crown with words "Holy to the Lord," the remembrance stones and jeweled breastplate bearing the names of the tribes of Israel, the woven ephod (to which these items are joined), and the outer robe decorated with bells and pomegranates—the silver trumpets (for

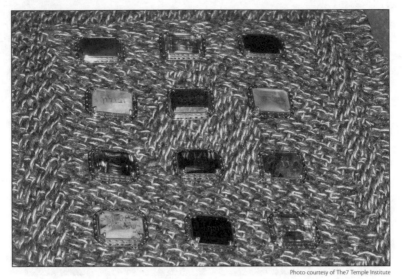

Photo courtesy of The7 Temple Institute

The high priest's jeweled breastplate and woven ephod. This is one of many items made by The Temple Institute in Jerusalem in anticipation of a rebuilt Temple.

calling the Israelites to assemble for worship at the Temple), the blue-purple dye (*tchelet*) for the *Tzitzit*, ritual and sacrificial items such as the barley altar, the 11 sacrificial incense spices, urns, ewers, incense pans, forks, shovels, carts (for burnt offerings), the gold and silver *mizraqot* (vessels used to catch and dispense the sacrificial blood on the altar), a copper laver or basin (for priestly purification), copper flasks, measuring cups (used in the libation offerings), vessels for the meal offerings, the lottery boxes (for the Day of Atonement), the mortar and pestle and stone vessels (*kelal*) for grinding and holding the purifying ashes of the red heifer, a six-foot-tall gold menorah (candelabra),[4] the cleaning instruments, oil pitchers, the golden Altar of Incense, and the Table of Showbread.

Constructing a Temple Training Model

In the mid-1990s, The Temple Institute constructed a full-scale altar for priests to practice the performance of the sacrificial service, but it was dismantled a year later when a change in management occurred at the Dead Sea Works plant where it had been constructed. In 2003, in this same Dead Sea region, at the Jewish community of Mitzpe Yericho (between Jerusalem and Jericho), a more ambitious project was undertaken by The Temple Institute: a full-scale model of the Temple. Covering an area of 25,000 square meters (269,000 square feet), this model, erected according to the Institute's blueprint for the Third Temple, will function as a training site to prepare priests for future service once the new Temple can be built.

The Temple Institute has for many years conducted a secondary school for educating students about the Temple, including its music, design, and sacred duties. The Temple training model will provide advanced training to many of these students, some of whom come from a priestly heritage and have sought to pursue priestly training. Besides giving The Temple Institute's architects the opportunity to perfect practical elements of their research designs, this model will, for the first time, permit those training for the priesthood to become knowledgeable about aspects of the Temple ritual only possible through performance in an accurately scaled structure.

Searching for a Red Heifer

According to Numbers 19, the ashes of a red heifer are necessary for the ritual purification of the Levitical priests and Temple vessels, as well as the construction workers who will be involved in building the Third Temple. Therefore, the acquisition of the ashes of a halachically kosher red heifer is a prerequisite for the rebuilding of the Temple. The Temple Institute's rabbi Chaim Richman wrote a book *The Mystery of the Red Heifer*, to explain the biblical and rabbinic regulations concerning the ritual ceremony conducted with this animal.

Because the birth of a pure red heifer is extremely rare, and none have been born in Israel over the past 2000 years, The Temple Institute has searched for ways to import a strain of red cows to Israel in the hopes of producing a halachically kosher heifer. For a number of years Rabbi Richman represented The Temple Institute in negotiations with Mississippi rancher Clyde Lott, a Pentecostal preacher and breeder of red Angus cattle. He had hoped not only to provide herds for breeding a ritually qualified red heifer, but also to stimulate the Israeli cattle industry. However, after some time, The Temple Institute separated itself from Lott, citing religious problems and certain misrepresentations.

Then in March 2002, a red heifer was born at Kibbutz Kfar Hassidim near the port city of Haifa, and raised hopes that an Israeli-born red heifer had miraculously arrived. Many Orthodox Jews, such as Yehuda Etzion, leader of the Temple activist organization *Chai VeKayam,* viewed the birth of this heifer as heralding the imminent rebuilding of the Temple. Etzion stated, "We have been waiting 2000 years for a sign from G-d, and now He has provided us with a heifer!"[5] Jewish tradition has long maintained that the ashes of only nine red heifers were used from the time of Moses to the fall of the Second Temple, and the ancient rabbis predicted that when the tenth red heifer was born, the messianic age would occur. This, of course, made many people even more excited.

One month after the birth, Rabbi Richman and other rabbis went to inspect the heifer to see if it was qualified. According to

Photo courtesy of The Temple Mount Faithful

The red heifer named Tzlil that was being raised in Haifa but is now disqualified.

biblical and rabbinical law, a qualified red heifer cannot have a blemish and must never have worn a yoke. This means it cannot have or acquire any physical injury, scar, or other impairment, such as hairs of a color other than red. Such defilement would disqualify it as a candidate for the ceremony of the red heifer, which takes place once the heifer reaches three years of age.

However, in November 2002, authorities at The Temple Institute, who had been monitoring the red heifer's progress, were forced to pronounce it disqualified. Thus, the production of a pure and unblemished red heifer remains an ongoing project of The Temple Institute in preparation for the rebuilding of the Temple.

Battling for the Temple Mount

The Palestinian and Muslim authorities are quite aware of the activities of The Temple Institute. When I met with Palestinian mufti Ikrima Sabri in 1998, he revealed he was familiar with their work and spoke vehemently about a picture of the rebuilt Temple, distributed by The Temple Institute, which Yasser Arafat had shown him. Publications in Arabic and English sold in certain shops in the Old City, as well as in bookstores in East Jerusalem, include descriptions and pictures of the red heifer and the ritual vessels made by The Temple Institute and warn of the threat this poses to the mosques, which would be replaced by the Jewish Temple. These publications, as well as the Arab press, also highlight the activist (they call them "terrorist") history of The Temple Institute's founder and director, Rabbi Yisrael Ariel.

After serving with the paratroop unit that liberated the Old City and the Temple Mount in 1967, Rabbi Ariel organized an activist group known as *Tzfia*, whose stated objective was to regain control of the Temple Mount. In March of 1983, Rabbi Ariel, with 38 of his yeshiva students and a group of Israel Defense Forces soldiers from Kiryat Arba and Jerusalem, organized a plan to tunnel beneath the Al-Aqsa Mosque for the purpose of holding Passover prayers.[6] But before the group could reach the Temple Mount, they were intercepted and turned back. In April of 1989, Rabbi Ariel and Joel Lerner, director of the Sanhedrin Institute, were successful in gaining entrance to the Temple Mount. This time they intended to offer a Passover sacrifice on the Temple Mount, an act they believed would begin the process of redeeming the site for the rebuilding of the Temple. On this occasion, too, Rabbi Ariel and his group were prevented from completing their plan. Their actions were highly publicized by the Arab media, and the next year (October 1990), when the Temple Mount Faithful group announced its intention to lay a cornerstone for the Third Temple on the Temple Mount, the Arab riot which ensued and left 17 Palestinians dead cited Rabbi Ariel's plan as a cause.

Although Rabbi Ariel's work is primarily confined to the scholarly realm, in the battle for the Temple Mount, his Muslim opponents consider him a ringleader among those dedicated to the destruction of the Temple Mount, or "the third holiest site in Islam."

The Temple Mount Faithful

The most visible activist organization today is the Temple Mount and Land of Israel Faithful Movement, or simply the Temple Mount Faithful (Hebrew, *Ne-Emanei Har Habayit*). The central goal of this organization is "to liberate again the Temple Mount from Arab occupation, and then to rebuild again the Third Temple in its right place, on the Rock in the center of the Temple Mount, a Temple that will be again a center of religious, national, spiritual and moral life for Israel."[7] More than any other activist organization, it has developed an outreach among not only Israelis and Jews outside the Land, but also a supportive network among Christians, who further its outreach through a newsletter, Web site, and lecture tours. Rather than complement the work of The Temple Institute, the Temple Mount Faithful are competing with The Temple Institute in its efforts to spearhead the rebuilding of the Temple. This can be seen in the movement's own development of architectural plans for the Third Temple and a Temple model, creation of priestly apparel and Temple vessels, raising of a red heifer, and training future priests.[8]

The Founder

The founder and leader of the Temple Mount Faithful is Gershon Salomon, an Orientalist and lecturer in Middle Eastern studies, who specialized in the history of the Kurdish people. Salomon, a tenth-generation Jerusalemite, is a descendant of Rabbi Avraham Solomon Zalman Zoref, who settled in Jerusalem in 1811. Zoref was one of the first Jewish pioneers in Jerusalem to start the redemptive process of preparing the people and the Land for the coming of the Messiah on the Temple Mount, and he was stabbed to death by Arabs in the Old City who were trying to prevent Jewish expansion.

Salomon, who is still an officer in the Israel Defense Force, has witnessed or fought in most of Israel's wars and once led a company in the Golan Heights. In 1958, during a battle with the Syrian army, he was injured when he was run over by a tank. According to Salomon, he was miraculously rescued from death by angelic intervention. It was at this time that Salomon says he also heard the voice of God speaking to him and telling him that He was not yet finished with him. He understood this as a divine call to consecrate himself to the work of the Temple Mount. He felt this was confirmed when, during his service in the Six-Day War, he was among the soldiers who participated in the liberation of the Temple Mount.

Salomon believes that when Israel captured the Temple Mount in 1967, the exile that began with the destruction of the Temple in A.D. 70 ended and the period of restoration began. According to Salomon, the Israeli return of control of the Temple Mount to the Muslims and his government's lack of courage to do what God had commanded in the Torah is preventing the present generation from experiencing the biblical prophecies of restoration. He believes he is called to help reverse the secular government's hesitations. According to his published statement of purpose, "he has dedicated himself to the vision of consecrating the Temple

Mount to the Name of G-d, to removing the Moslem shrines placed there as a symbol of Moslem conquest, to the soon rebuilding of the Third Temple there, and the G-dly redemption of the people and the Land of Israel."[9]

Salomon credits Rabbi Zvi Yehuda Kook, the son of Rabbi Avraham Kook (the first chief rabbi of Israel in the early part of the century and spiritual father of the religious Zionist redemption movement of Israel), as his inspiration for liberating the Temple Mount. In keeping with this philosophy of religious Zionism, Salomon interprets current events in Israel and the world in the light of what he understands as prophetic fulfillment in process. Although the secular Israeli government has prevented the rebuilding of the Temple since 1967, Salomon and his followers believe that the present generation is the one that will finally realize the prophetic dreams of their Jewish forefathers.

The Preparations

The Temple Mount Faithful use demonstrations, the media, and publications to increase public awareness of their political and spiritual goals. They have established a center in which is displayed models of the Tabernacle and Temple, created by Russian immigrant Michael Osnis, as well as ritual vessels, priestly garments, an altar of incense, and various copperware for the sacrificial service. Plans are in the works for the construction of a six-foot-tall gold menorah, and members and friends of the movement have sent offerings of gold, silver, and jewelry to help fund the project (cf. Exodus 25:1-9,31,39). The group also commissioned Jerusalem architect Gideon Harlap to prepare architectural plans for the Third Temple and intend to present these to the planning committees of the Municipality of Jerusalem and the Israeli government.

The Third Temple Cornerstones

In 2001, the Temple Mount Faithful created two cornerstones for the Third Temple, which they use not only to draw attention to the cause of rebuilding the Temple, but which they hope will be used in the actual construction of the new Temple. Back in 1989 the group made their first cornerstone, which was consecrated in a ceremony at the Pool of Siloam located deep in the Kidron Valley below the Temple Mount. For a time, this stone was displayed in a major traffic circle in eastern Jerusalem not far from the Damascus Gate of the Temple Mount and near to both the American Consulate and the Protestant Garden Tomb, a placement intended to demonstrate the movement's political and religious agenda to these representative bodies. Eventually, this first stone was stolen by an unknown opponent of the Temple Mount Faithful.

The two replacement cornerstones, like the original cornerstone, came from Mitzpe Ramon, a famous crater in the Negev that bears marble stone that closely resembles the stones used in the construction of the First and Second Temples. This location also has a symbolic significance, for it is geographically close to the area of Mt. Sinai where Israel received the Torah and instructions to build the Temple. Diamond cutters were employed to shape these new cornerstones, each weighing 6.5 tons and being

Photo by author

Temple Mount Faithful founder Gershon Salomon with the two cornerstones prepared for use in the construction of the Third Temple.

considerably larger than the original cornerstone, which had not been cut but left in its natural state. After Succot 2001, the two replacement stones were placed on a hilltop overlooking the site of the Holy of Holies on the Temple Mount.

The plan of the Temple Mount Faithful is to lay these cornerstones on the southeast and northeast corners of the original location of the Temple and, in this way, inaugurate the rebuilding of the Third Temple. However, as expected, the Israeli courts and authorities have repeatedly denied the organization's appeals for permission to lay the cornerstones. Each year, the Temple Mount Faithful renew their appeals and parade the cornerstones throughout Jerusalem and around the walls of the Old City on a flatbed truck that is bedecked with Israeli flags and a banner in Hebrew and English. In this way the stones testify to the Israeli public as well as the Arab residents of eastern Jerusalem of the nearness of the rebuilding of the Temple and the coming of Messiah Ben-David (the ruling king or Messiah). According to Salomon, these stones (and the first cornerstone, which he believes will one day be returned to them just as the Philistines returned the Ark—see 1 Samuel 6–7—are "godly stones [that] will

Photo by author

Gershon Salomon and Temple Mount Faithful members during a march around the walls of the Old City.

Israeli police officers guard the Mughrabi Gate entrance to the Temple Mount.

begin the accomplishment of the end times in which we are living right now."[10] Furthermore, Salomon believes that the preparation of the two new cornerstones has initiated the process of creating the rest of the stones for the rebuilding of the Third Temple.

The Confrontations

The outspoken opposition to the Arab and Palestinian nationalism in the biblical Land of Israel, coupled with overt public demonstrations aimed at removing Muslim domination of the Temple Mount, have made Gershon Salomon and the Temple Mount Faithful enemy number one. From the very first demonstration of the movement in 1989 (at which I was present), fierce reaction has come from the Palestinians in Jerusalem and spread to other cities throughout the West Bank. On the morning of October 8, 1990, the first major confrontation occurred as a result of the group's announced intention to lay a cornerstone on the Temple Mount. Although Israeli police had assured Muslim authorities that the group would be prevented from entering the Old City, rumors were circulated by the Arab press and in sermons at the Al-Aqsa Mosque that the group was coming to pray on the

Temple Mount and desecrate the Islamic holy places. So, when more than 20,000 Jews assembled for Kol Ha-Moed Succot services at the Western Wall, more than 3000 Palestinian Arabs began to pelt the crowd with stones from the Temple Mount above. This was later found by official inquiry to have been an event orchestrated by Faisal Husseini, a relative of Yasser Arafat, who, under the Oslo Accord, served as the administrator for the Palestinian Authority in Jerusalem.[11] As loudspeakers on the Temple Mount sounded a call for Muslims to kill the Jews who were coming to take their holy places, the Israeli police first fired tear gas to dispel the rioters, then rubber bullets, and finally, live ammunition. When the fighting was over, some 17 Arabs lay dead.[12]

Members of the United Nations, including the United States, voted to condemn Israel for the incident. Saddam Hussein, who only months before had invaded Kuwait and was being threatened by an Arab League alliance with the United States against him, used the Temple Mount incident to divide this alliance, calling for a universal Muslim *jihad* against Israel and firing Scud missiles at Israeli targets in Tel Aviv. But for the restraint of Israel in retaliating against these attacks, brought in part by intense pressure and assurances from the United States, Israel's response might have engaged the entire region in the Gulf War. Subsequent demonstrations have provoked similar riots, threats of war from the Arab world, and international condemnation.

The Opposition to the Plan to Rebuild

While some believe the rebuilding of the Temple will strengthen the Israeli government's claim to East Jerusalem (in much the same way the erection of Islamic mosques at the site has given greater control to the Arabs), there are others who contend that building the Temple would be destructive to the secular Israeli form of government, and therefore, the government has opposed the Temple movement as a matter of self-preservation. Emanuel Winston, Middle East analyst for the Freeman Center, believes that the Israeli government has supported the Waqf's management of the site over the past three decades in order to prevent religious Jews from gaining control and affecting a change in the secular political status quo:

> The concern of the non-observant is that, if the prophesied Third Temple of the Jews were re-established along with ancient Temple ritual and law, a secular government would be made less important. Therefore, having the Arabs claim the whole Jewish Temple Mount and core out its center is acceptable, even desirable to the secular Israeli governments who have been mostly ideologically Left with some violently anti- or non-observant. Clearly, successive Israeli governments have been ready to issue a "quit claim" deed to the Arab Muslims, offering the illusion that they had no choice. If one tracks Oslo in terms of abandoning most Jewish holy sites, you would find that it all leads up to the disposal of Solomon's Temple—with a secular society to follow.[13]

Evidence of this was seen at the beginning of the Oslo Peace Process when leftish Labor party prime minister Yitzhak Rabin was assassinated by an Orthodox Jew representing those who believed the Oslo Accord was betraying the Jewish nation by giving their land to the enemy and abandoning the Temple Mount to pagans. Immediately after, acting prime minister Shimon Perez, who had been politically left of Rabin, banned "Messianic Jewish" (nationalistic Orthodox Jews) leaders and organizations as being subversive and a threat to the government. The justification for this was that these Messianists were looking for a Messiah who was to replace the government with messianic rule, and hence, the Messianists were plotting the overthrow of the government. Overnight, some Temple activists closed down their offices and went underground (such as the Temple Mount Yeshiva and Chai VeKayam), fearing arrest at the hands of a secular government that had no regard for their religious beliefs. In fact, many of these activists had already been arrested through the years for precipitating or engaging in activities that violated Islamic law by asserting Jewish religious rights over the Temple Mount.

Prime Minister Ehud Barak, who offered to Yasser Arafat and the Palestinians at the Camp David II Summit sovereignty over the Temple Mount, demonstrated additional evidence that affirms the contention that the Israeli government supports the Waqf's control of the Temple Mount. Barak contended that since the Palestinian demand on the holy places was non-negotiable, and because the Clinton administration was pressuring him to comply with those demands, it was necessary for Israel to make a historic compromise for the sake of peace. Had he not been forced to ask for the Palestinian concession of a "symbolic sovereignty" for Israel (in accord with the United States's proposed negotiation plan for Jerusalem), in which the archaeological remains of the Jewish Temples would be recognized to exist beneath the site, the Palestinian Authority might have sealed the deal. However, because Palestinian policy requires a denial of the Temple's existence, Arafat had to reject the offer, stating, "I will not have it said of me that I recognized the existence of a so-called temple." Even so, it was apparent by this unprecedented offer that the Israeli government was indeed willing to issue a "quit claim" deed to the Arab Muslims.

Now, this doesn't reflect the sentiments of all Israeli government officials. There are Knesset members who have lobbied for Temple activists and even joined them in some of their activities. Too, every prime minister elected in the past decade has supported a united Jerusalem with sovereignty over the Temple Mount. Although Barak attempted to hold on to both with his compromise, the Palestinian Authority's rejection has made it difficult, if not impossible, for another prime minister to make a similar offer. Moreover, in recent years, the Temple movement in Israel has become more visible and developed significantly in terms of public approval. As this popular support for the rebuilding of the Temple continues to grow, there are some in the Temple movement who have come to feel that the tide is about to change in their favor.

Is the Day Growing Near?

Shortly after the national commemoration of *Tisha B'Av* in the Jewish year 5763 (August 7, 2003), during which the police had closed the only gate that provides Jews with access to the Temple Mount (including members of the Temple Mount Faithful), the same authorities opened the gate wide so members of the group could enter unhindered. Gershon Salomon, who had been restricted (even at times when the gate was open) from entering the Temple Mount, and whose very presence near the site had provoked Muslim riots, described what he witnessed on that day and shared his belief that the change will eventually allow the Temple movement to accomplish its goals:

> The Minister of Internal Security stated that the Temple Mount would never again be closed to Israelis and non-Moslems. Moslems who tried to prevent Israelis from going up on the Temple Mount were arrested by the police, and the police station on the Temple Mount again started to act intensively to prevent Arab riots, to keep the gates open and to protect Israeli sovereignty on the hill of the G-d of Israel. This was a historical decision and an opening for the other stages that will follow and which will lead to the rebuilding of the Temple.[14]

Now possessing the right as Israeli Jews to enter the Temple Mount area, the Temple Mount Faithful, on October 13, 2003, again made a pilgrimage to the Temple Mount and attempted to lay their cornerstones at the site during the annual celebration of Succot. However, despite the positive changes that had recently occurred, much still remained unchanged, especially the prohibition against non-Muslim religious expression at the site as well as activities that might endanger national security. The attempt to lay cornerstones for the Third Temple made the Temple Mount Faithful guilty on both counts, so again, the group was turned away.

Given that Israeli sovereignty has been re-asserted over the site and it's been promised that the gate to the Temple Mount will never again be closed to Israelis and non-Muslims, will these Temple movement groups press onward with even greater earnest to achieve their goals? How long will the Israeli authorities tolerate Palestinian Authority control over the Temple Mount—especially in light of the current conflict with Palestinian terrorists, who have offered no possible resolution other than all-out war? A first stage in the liberation of the Temple Mount seems to have been taken, as Salomon has observed. Will it lead to other stages that will, in turn, conclude with the rebuilding of the Temple?

If so, then these are exciting times in which to live, for we may very well witness the happenings that will climax in this momentous event.

Part III:

THE FUTURE BATTLES

12

Setting the Stage for the Last Days' Temple

This is the duty not only of the people of Palestine, but also anyone who believes that there is no god but Allah....The Aksa Mosque is being assaulted every day....The mosque is being subject to programmed and organized demolition. The occupation is destroying the blessed Aksa Mosque....O, Muslims! They [Israelis] are working towards destroying the mosque under pretext of searching for the purported Temple. They are destroying it. They are desecrating the sanctity of the blessed mosque.... The Aksa Mosque is crying out to you, O, Muslims, O, believers, save it....Isn't there an Omar [Ibn al-Khattab] amongst you? Isn't there a Saladin amongst you? Doesn't the Aksa Mosque deserve that we sacrifice all what is dear and precious to us in order to liberate it and defend its dignity?[1]

I t is universally conceded that there is no more volatile acreage on earth than the Temple Mount. If the Temple Mount is dynamite, and if the present struggle for the site has lit the fuse, how long will it be before it explodes? What current controversies may be propelling this already-fiery conflict toward war? In order to understand the political problems and the potential they hold for erupting into the next battle for the Temple Mount, let us consider the various minor battles being waged that are contributing the sparks necessary to set the conflict ablaze.

The Present State of the Conflict

The reaction of militant Islam toward the battle for the Temple Mount is characteristically one of violence and threat of war. Sheik Ahmed Yassin, the Islamic spiritual leader of the Palestinian terrorist organization Hamas, has declared that any attempt by Jews to seize control of the Temple Mount or to destroy Islamic shrines would lead to a bloodbath: "They will start a fire in which they shall perish."[2] We have also seen that Temple activism has raised the tension in the battle for the Temple Mount to a height never before realized in the past 1360-plus years, and Islamic reaction has followed suit. Whenever these Jewish groups act, they are regarded by the Muslims as agents of the Israeli government seeking to destroy their holy places. Although the Israeli government repeatedly denies any association, Adnan Husseini, director of the Waqf, still contends: "We consider the government and these two groups as one body. The government leaves these persons working...we are blaming the government...."[3]

Husseini also accuses the Sharon government of changing the status quo by his visit to the Temple Mount, prevention of travel of Palestinians age 40 and younger from the West Bank to the site, and closing the site to tourists. The Sharon government's current erection of a security fence—especially around contested boundaries in Jerusalem—is interpreted by Palestinians as a further attempt by Israelis to isolate Muslims from their holy places and control the Temple Mount, with the ultimate goal of rebuilding the Temple. This view appeared justified when the Israeli government allowed Jews and others to visit the Temple Mount despite Yasser Arafat's protests. Even though it was the Palestinian Authority that violated the status quo by barring Jews from the site in 2000, and even though Israel's restoration of visiting rights continues to respect the Muslim ban on entrance to Islamic holy sites on the Temple Mount, Adnan Husseini contends that it is the

Israeli government who does not want to restore the status quo. He argues that re-opening the Temple Mount to let Jewish activists pray at the site is, in fact, the first step toward restoring Jewish religious rights to their holy place. This would lead, the Waqf fears, to the final step: the rebuilding of the Temple.

In like manner, when two Israelis were detained in 1998 for allegedly plotting to throw a pig's head onto the Temple compound, Palestinian leader Yasser Arafat said, "We have always warned of this; many times, we have warned of the attempts of Israeli extremists to defile Al-Aqsa and destroy it." By contrast, as the Islamic Waqf destroys ancient remains of the Temple in their unauthorized mosque construction projects,[4] the Waqf authorities warn, "There will be massacres if there is any attempt to stop the opening of the mosque."[5] And when Knesset member Rabbi Benny Elon and Rabbi Yisrael Ariel, head of The Temple Institute, proposed for a synagogue to be built on the Temple Mount (based on evidence from archaeologists and historians that such a synagogue once occupied the site[6]), the Waqf violently opposed the proposal as an attempt to subvert Palestinian sovereignty over the site. However, in hearing these accusations it must be remembered that the Temple Mount is still under Israeli sovereignty, and Israel can do whatever needs to be done at this site when necessary. This was demonstrated in 1998 when Palestinian terrorists, who escaped from the Israeli security forces in Jerusalem, ran to the Temple Mount and received refuge from members of the Waqf, who tried to prevent the Israeli police from catching them. However, Islamic jurisdiction did not stop the Israeli police officers from entering the site and arresting the terrorists. This demonstrated Israel's ability to assert its sovereignty on the Temple Mount. However, entering the sacred site to catch terrorists is a very different matter from entering the site to pray. And while the Israeli government has demonstrated the resolve to do the former, it has fought against every attempt by those who want to do the latter.

For this reason, many in the peace camp in Israel have come to believe their government may eventually abandon the Temple Mount, and have set their hopes on the possibility for renewed negotiations between the Israelis and the Palestinians with the hope of sharing or, if necessary, surrendering the Temple Mount.

Can the Temple Mount Be Negotiated?

University of Glasgow professor of history and author Bernard Wasserstein once wrote that in Jerusalem, "the violence reflects the lack of consensual polity. The 'eternally unified capital' of the state of Israel is the most deeply divided capital city in the world."[7] At this stage, the violence in Jerusalem has created an atmosphere of despair, and peace plans and accords have been considered fruitless. The present Road Map to Peace is largely viewed as nothing more than a restatement of past failed proposals that call for a return to the indefensible pre-1967 borders that did not prevent Israel from being attacked by the surrounding Arab countries in the first place. However, more to the point, none of these proposals have succeeded in presenting a workable plan for sharing Jerusalem and the Temple Mount. In light of the absence of potential peace partners and the urgency of both the Israelis and Palestinians to change what they perceive as an altered status quo on the Temple Mount, any negotiation appears to be an impossibility. However, even if willing and acceptable partners existed (as they supposedly did in the Oslo Peace Process), and even if negotiations were resumed, they are still doomed to failure. The reason for this is that the dispute is religious, not political. If Israel were to withdraw from all the disputed "occupied territory" it captured in the 1967 Six-Day War, peace could still not be secured with the Palestinians because, according to its charter, the PLO was founded to liberate the lands occupied by the Jews *before* 1947!

What's more, even if Israel were to abandon all the territory it occupied as a result of the war in 1948 and returned to the territory allocated to it by United Nations Resolution 181 (section 2), there would still be no peace because the Arab League rejected that original partitioning of Palestine and went to war in 1948 for the sole purpose of eradicating the very existence of a Jewish state in their midst. In every case, the decisions of the Arabs were based on the inflexible dictates of their religion. Nothing has changed nor can change in the Islamic agenda because the Qur'an has commanded the faithful to wage *jihad* with the world of non-Muslims, and once any land has been conquered by Islam, it is considered to be forever the possession of Islam, even if it is lost again to non-Muslims. Islamic law requires such land be returned to Muslim rule and forbids a permanent peace with those who possess it. The only peace possible with Jews, then, is if they accept the status of *dhimmi*, which would require the dismantling of the Jewish state and the suppression of the Jewish people as severely deprived second-class citizens under Muslim rule. It is for these reasons that the Temple Mount, all of Jerusalem, and all of Israel will remain on the Islamic agenda for *jihad* and why peace can never come to the region—short of the Islamic threat being removed.

With respect to the Temple Mount, since 1967, it has been impossible to negotiate the right for Jews to utter even a single prayer *on* the Temple Mount, despite the fact that Orthodox Jews just a few yards away at the Western Wall pray *toward* it day and night. That access for prayer will never be permitted to the Jews is clear from Adnan Husseini, chairman of the Islamic Endowment in Jerusalem, who threatens to use violence against Jews if they attempt to pray on the Temple Mount. In like manner, the sheik of the Al-Aqsa Mosque, when told that Jewish rabbis had planned to pray on the Temple Mount, declared, "We will not stand idly by....the rabbis will not enter the Al-Aqsa Mosque, not over our dead bodies and shrouds."[8]

If it is impossible to negotiate a Jewish prayer on the Temple Mount, how would it ever be possible to negotiate sovereignty over the site? Further complicating this issue is the deep division among the Israeli authorities themselves over how to deal with the Temple Mount—a division that reflects a similar schism in Israeli society. Let us first examine the battle that is being waged by Israeli bureaucrats, then let's survey the battle of belief among the religious segment of Israeli society, and finally, let's look at whether or not the secular sector would support its government's decisions related to the Temple Mount.

The Battle of the Bureaucrats

Yisrael Medad, writing in the *Jerusalem Post,* has observed, "For over a century Zionism has been singularly unsuccessful in coming to terms with what to do about the Temple Mount— whether as the site of the destroyed two Temples, as the future platform upon which the expected Third Temple will be built, as an archaeological treasure, or as a cultural and historical reference point."[9] This observation betrays the political problem of having a secular movement—even though based on spiritual principles—that tries to deal decisively with an issue as profoundly political yet resolutely religious as the Temple Mount.

The Zionist founders of the Jewish state were secular, nonobservant, Jews, and many were even antireligious. Nevertheless, coming out of the Diaspora and into the historic Land of the Bible revived the traditional belief in Jerusalem's sanctity and of its vital significance for the Jewish people. For this reason, David Ben-Gurion, Israel's first prime minister, fought to make Jerusalem again the capital of the independent Jewish state. For this reason, too, in 1967, when the Israel Defense Force recaptured the Temple Mount, both soldier and statesman hurried to the newly won Western Wall to weep with joy like lost children who had found their way home. And, despite their professed secularism, they offered their prayers at the wall alongside the most deeply religious Jews.

It is here that a great contradiction appears in Zionism's relationship with the Temple Mount. From the day Zionist leaders recovered this historical treasure sought and fought for by Jews through the millennia, they have acted as though its return to Israeli sovereignty is more a frustrating problem than a fulfilled prophecy. Over the past three decades of possession, the governments of

Israel, whether Labor or Likud, have allowed the Muslims who control the Temple Mount to abuse the rights accorded them by their predecessors, and have tolerated and even ignored the calls from the Al-Aqsa Mosque to kill Jews and instigate riots, stone Israeli citizens at the Western Wall, reject Israeli sovereignty, and attack Israeli police officers. The Israeli government has absorbed accusations against the government of plots against Muslims, the illegal construction of buildings on the site and the wanton destruction of the archaeological remains of the Temple and other evidences of Israeli heritage, the banning of Jews from access to the Temple Mount (in violation of the status quo agreement), and the unconcealed attempt to transform the site into an exclusively Muslim property.

These activities against the Jewish state have occurred in spite of the appeals and protests of Knesset members, city mayors (of Jerusalem), archaeologists, university professors, and hundreds of public demonstrations to deal with the abuses and illegal acts of the Muslim Waqf. Surprisingly, these abuses have increased and been allowed to occur on an even more massive scale during the administrations of the most hawkish prime ministers Israel has ever elected. The Arab riots and reactions against the Western Wall Tunnel exit, the Palestinian occupation of the Temple Mount, and the illegal construction on the Temple Mount all began under the administration of Benyamin Netanyahu. Under Ehud Barak the Waqf increased its rejection of Israeli authority, and despite Barak's offer to grant sovereignty of the site to the Palestinian Authority, reserving only a symbolic underground sovereignty over ancient remains for Israel, Yasser Arafat refused his offer and ended the Oslo Peace Process. Worse still, under Ariel Sharon, the Waqf banned Jews from the Temple Mount, elevated their denials of the existence of ancient Temples and of a Jewish connection to Jerusalem, continued to incite Muslims to stone Jews at the Western Wall, and furthered the archaeological destruction taking place on the Mount. In spite of the courage shown by these men against Arab attacks while they were in the Israeli military, they have shown little resistance to the Arab challenges to Israeli authority but have continued the policy introduced by Moshe Dayan to not "disturb" the Muslims.

Why have these Zionist leaders appeared to work against the religious Jews' hope of reclaiming the Temple Mount and rebuilding the Temple? Why have they appeared to concede more to the Muslims who call for the destruction of the Jewish state than to nationalist Jews who have fought and died for their country? Berel Wein attempts an answer with regard to the secular/spiritual divide in contemporary Zionism:

> The current spate of intellectual, post-Zionist, estranged-from-Judaism thinkers and writers who claim the right to dominate Israeli culture and politics have no clue as to the existence of the heavenly Jerusalem. It has become increasingly clear that those who no longer have a vision of the heavenly Jerusalem have also loosened their ties to earthly Jerusalem. It is no wonder that they have only a peripheral attachment to the earthly Jerusalem.[10]

However, even among those who have such a vision, there is a significant schism that, like that evident among the secular Zionists, has prevented a consensus to form in regard to the Temple Mount.

The Differences in Perspective

The battle for the Temple Mount involves a battle of belief not only between Jews and Muslims, but also between Jews and Jews. The opposing viewpoints between Jews and Muslims are well known, having been widely publicized as the focal point of the conflict today. We have already examined these positions and it is certain that the groups that represent them will remain intransigent, with each side making greater claims and/or threats in the future while calling for support from their respective communities to help protect or reclaim their sacred sites.

Back in 1867, Sir Moses Montefiore had himself carried onto the Temple Mount in a litter. He was of the mistaken notion that if his feet did not come into contact with the ground he would not be guilty of violating Jewish law (*halacha*), which forbade entrance to this site that was holy to the Jews. Despite his best efforts, he was almost excommunicated by Jerusalem's rabbis.

Such opposing viewpoints within Judaism affect the political response of the Israeli government, and are, in fact, often present among government officials themselves. The secularists say that if Israel has lost the Temple Mount, then it is better that it remain lost. It is better, this group contends, that Muslims occupy the site than Jews. We can expect this perspective to come from secularists and liberals who view religious tradition (fundamentalism) as a threat to Israel's peaceful development as a modern nation in a world of religious pluralism and as an impediment to international recognition.

Then there are nationalist and religious Jews who, for quite different reasons, see the Temple Mount issue as a dangerous diversion for the State of Israel, and for the Jewish people in general, in their present struggle for political and spiritual survival. For nationalist Jews, the overriding concern is to hold on to what the Jewish state has accomplished over the past half-century without encouraging the cycle of violence that has characterized that history. To such Israelis, who have known little peace and seen a great deal of bloodshed, the prospect of holding on to, much less seeking greater access to, property that has been in the possession of Muslims for 1300 years, and which has caused the collapse of every attempted peace process, is unconscionable. They reason, "We have gotten along well enough without the Temple Mount; why do we need something that prevents us from obtaining peace?" According to this mindset, it is the religious extremists (*datit*) who historically brought Judaism into ruin and are doing so again by their refusal to let go of the past. Representing the public sector with this viewpoint, Richard D. Rogovin has written, "If the Moslems want it, and we don't need it, let us swap whatever right of worship we claim there for peace. Let us put an end to talk of a Third Temple. If the absence of peace could destroy the first two, the third will never be secure."[11] With the same conviction, *Jerusalem Post* columnist Hillel Halkin has declared, "Even the most fiercely nationalist corner of my incorrigible Jewish soul, though it might not want to yield an inch elsewhere, would gladly get rid of the Temple Mount. I'd consider threatening the Arabs with war if they didn't permanently take it off our hands."[12]

The second group that vehemently opposes Jewish access to the Temple Mount does so on religious, not political, grounds. This group consists of ultra-Orthodox Jews or *Haredim*, whose objection stems from their belief that Zionism, as a secular movement, cannot achieve the spiritual ends necessary to fulfill the prophesied restoration of the Jewish nation. From their perspective, even though some six million Jews have left the physical Diaspora, they remain, as does all of Judaism at present, in the spiritual Diaspora. Consequently, they disagree with the Orthodox Jews in the Temple movement who, following the nationalistic and spiritual teachings of Rabbi Kook, believe the modern State of Israel has ushered in the messianic era. The basics of their argument are that the majority of Israelis have no spiritual connection to Judaism and therefore have not fulfilled the prophecies of spiritual return, the Messiah has not yet arrived to provide the proper political structure for the nation (a theocracy, based on the Torah), and therefore, all of the traditional *halachic* prohibitions related to the Temple Mount remain in force.

Many of these ultra-Orthodox Jews also believe that the fully built Third Temple will descend in fire from heaven after a worldwide spiritual revival takes place in which all of mankind (including the Arabs) will convert to Judaism. For this reason, the thought that any Jew (all of whom are in ritual impurity) would dare to enter the sacred space formerly occupied by the Holy of Holies, even for prayer, is a violation of the highest order at this time in Jewish history. A prominent spokesman for this group, Uri Lupolianski, has attained the influential political position of mayor of Jerusalem (the first *Haredi* in this office). While his predecessor, Ehud Olmert, a secular Jew, was an outspoken champion of Jewish rights on the Temple Mount, Mayor Lupolianski adopts a diametrically opposite stance. When recently faced with the controversy over the closure of the Temple Mount to Jews, he brusquely stated, "Jews who wish to pray on the Temple Mount are as inappropriate as someone urinating outside a downtown department store."[13]

At present there is a growing divide between secular and religious Jews over how the government should respond to the demands of the Palestinian Authority, which includes an uncompromising demand for possession of the Temple Mount. Undoubtedly, the next battle for the Temple Mount, though dictated by political concerns, will include a battle of belief within the Israeli community and Judaism. Nevertheless, there need not be a consensus or even agreement between these parties in order for the Jews to regain religious access to the Temple Mount or even to rebuild the Temple. Such a consensus did not exist in the time of the Second Temple, with the secularists (such as Hellenistic Jews) and the ultra-Orthodox (such as the *Yahad,* the Jewish community at Qumran) remaining separate from the Temple establishment. Still, the chief rabbinate of Israel has continued in its position that Jews are forbidden to enter the Temple Mount area, despite opinions such as those of former Askensazi chief rabbi Shlomo Goren, who claims that permitted areas could be distinguished from nonpermitted areas. But for now, it seems that until one of these Orthodox religious groups can gain a dominant influence and leadership in the political system in Israel, a stalemate will continue.

The Secular Jews and the Temple Mount

The majority of Israel's population is secular. How will they respond to any decisions their government makes regarding the Temple Mount? Secular Zionists might cringe at the thought, but the very word *Zion,* from which their political movement took its name, is a reference to biblical Mount Zion, whose exalted position is defined by the Temple's presence.[14] However, as far as most secular Zionists are concerned, the Temple Mount is an obstacle to the cessation of violence that has plagued the modern generation for most of its existence. Carrie Hart, an experienced news commentator and Israeli living in Jerusalem, is among those who believe that the present passion for peace has so consumed the secular Israeli society that they will make any concession to secure it:

> There are some Israelis living here who will not be content until they go through the completed process of the peace accords. They will not be satisfied until they have tried every human effort to keep their sons from fighting and being killed on the battlefield. They will not be quiet, or hold their voices, until they see the outcome of their demands for two lands, two peoples, two flags, two anthems, peace within their borders, peace with their Arab neighbors. Even if it takes an internationalization of Jerusalem, they will not stop pushing their concept of peace...at all costs.[15]

On the other hand, there is evidence that more secularists than ever before are leaning toward the Israeli government asserting its rights on the Temple Mount and taking control of the site despite the threats of the Muslim authorities or the Islamic world. Polls conducted by both Temple Mount activists and independent agencies have shown there is a marked change in Jewish society's attitude toward even the idea of rebuilding the Temple. As noted earlier, whereas only 18 percent of Israelis polled in 1989 (considered a high number then) were in favor of rebuilding the Temple, the number, in some polls, had increased to 58 percent by the year 2000 and as high as 80 percent in one poll by 2003. Certainly a war-weary public could as easily decide to quit making concessions to the enemy and look toward the Temple Mount as a symbol of national solidarity and the expression of an independence long denied to the Zionist movement. If the prime-ministerial elections over the last decade offer a clue, then the

Israeli public has increasingly elected candidates who take a strong stance on Israeli sovereignty in Jerusalem and the Temple Mount.

Even then, there is still a division in Israeli secular society—between the right, left, and moderates—that remains as deep as that which exists between the secular and religious factions. So how will the Israeli electorate vote in a future election that includes debate over the Temple Mount issue? Perhaps the trend toward electing prime ministers who pledge to retain Jewish sovereignty over the Temple Mount will continue. Or, if pressured by foreign powers and a waning domestic economy, Israelis may once again, as in the past, trust international guarantees and give peace a chance—at the expense of Israeli sovereignty over the Temple Mount.

Whatever the future may bring, Israel's current leadership has opted to secure itself from Palestinian militants by separating itself from regions now under Palestinian autonomy—a move that has the potential, especially in Jerusalem, to give Temple Mount activists a new sense of security about exercising their ambitions on the holy site, and to spur Palestinians to say that the Temple Mount will continue to be an impediment to peace until they are given full possession and control over it.

Fencing Off Jerusalem

As a result of the seemingly unstoppable homicide attacks instigated by Palestinian militants, the Israeli government erected a ten-foot-high perimeter fence along the Israel West Bank border. The "peace fence," as the Israelis call it, follows the largely successful model of a defensive fence built in the Gaza Strip years ago. Israeli officials note that during this second intifada, almost no attacks have originated in the Gaza Strip. The hope is that the new West Bank barrier, some 370 miles long, will help deter future homicide bombings by completely separating Palestinian areas in the West Bank from those in Israel.

Jerusalem, which has been the special focus of Palestinian homicide attacks during the second intifada (21 attacks, killing 113 and maiming hundreds) is also included within the fenced area. This, of course, includes so-called East Jerusalem with the Temple Mount. The barrier is intended to help prevent violence, and can be removed if the Palestinian Authority proves itself capable of securing and maintaining peace for Israel on its borders. Palestinians contend that the barrier "will be the cause of the next war."[16]

In Jerusalem, Jewish neighborhoods form a ring around the minority Palestinian population of East Jerusalem (of some 200,000 people). It is this area that the Palestinian Authority claims as the capital of its Palestinian state. The Israeli government rejects this claim, having officially annexed the area as part of the united city back in 1980. The fence now surrounding this area brings the reality of this fact to the Palestinians and demonstrates the Israeli government's commitment to never again divide Jerusalem.

The greatest provocation of this fence, according to Palestinian spokesmen, aside from separating Palestinians in Jerusalem from their relatives in the West Bank, is that it cuts off Palestinian Muslims from access to the Haram and the Al-Aqsa Mosque. Israelis, since the beginning of the Al-Aqsa intifada, have restricted access to the holy site for Muslim men outside Jerusalem who are under the age of 40, as this was considered part of the profile of a potential homicide bomber. Palestinians believe the fence will be permanent and permanently restrict such Muslim access—an access Islamic leaders have promised them will be unlimited and exclusive to Muslims in a Jerusalem under the sovereignty of the Palestinian Authority.

The nations that have sought to implement the proposed Road Map to Peace in the Middle East have stated that the fence creates a barrier to talks between Israelis and Palestinians and should be removed. The Israelis, for whom the issue of security is paramount, argue the opposite, stating that once Israel's population feels safe from homicide attacks, it will support talks with the Palestinians.

While the fence around Jerusalem is yet another source of disagreement, there is now another conflict brewing—one that is not around Jerusalem, but beneath it!

The Battle Beneath Al-Aqsa

In January 2004, the Palestinian press reported a secret Israeli plot—financed by an American Jewish millionaire—to tunnel beneath the Temple Mount from within the Western Wall Tunnel. The Western Wall Tunnel represents a lower course of the stone masonry of the northern extent of the western Temple Mount retaining wall (of which the Western Wall is a part). Over successive eras other structures were built alongside and on top of the

Photo by Alexander Schick

Inside the Western Wall Tunnel. It is this tunnel which caused Muslim officials to contend that the archaeological work being conducted within it was a government plot to destroy the mosques above it on the Temple Mount.

first-century remains, creating the modern appearance of an underground tunnel. When the tunnel was rediscovered and excavated in the 1980s, a stir was caused when it was realized that an ancient gate found in the wall was the closest entrance to the site of the ancient Holy of Holies within the destroyed Temple. A further sensation was caused when it was revealed that two Israeli rabbis had conducted a clandestine excavation within the gate in search of the lost Ark of the Covenant, which, according to Jewish tradition, is hidden in a secret chamber beneath the Holy of Holies. The rabbis' work was halted short of their goal when the Muslim authorities learned of the dig and stormed the group's hastily hollowed-out tunnel. The ancient entrance gate was then sealed by order of the Israeli government to prevent further incursion beneath the Temple Mount and avoid provocation of the Muslim authorities, who claimed the Israeli government was supporting the dig in an attempt to collapse the Arab buildings situated above. In 1996, a northern exit cut in this tunnel by order of the Netanyahu government renewed the Muslims' charges and resulted in riots in Jerusalem and throughout the territories. Despite the Muslim threats, archaeological work inside the Western Wall Tunnel has continued unabated to the present day.

The latest proposed project, an underground tunnel to be constructed by the Western Jerusalem Development Company at a cost of $8 million, is planned to connect the Western Wall Tunnel to an extension tunnel reported to snake under the Temple Mount compound and exit to the south in a Palestinian-occupied area in the Kidron Valley known as Silwan. The purpose of the tunnel is to protect Jewish worshipers at the Western Wall in case of attack, a danger that has grown more likely during the second intifada, and to help increase tourism to the area, which has dropped drastically since the violence was renewed. According to Rabbi Samuel Rubenbach of the Wailing Wall Legacy Fund, the tunnel will also allow Jews to carry out excavations from the Western Wall. Excavations, and even surveys of the Temple Mount area, have always been forbidden by the Muslim authorities, but archaeologists have long dreamed of having the opportunity to explore beneath the site, where it is believed there are remains of the two ancient Jewish Temples.

Even though no architectural plans have been drawn nor licenses issued for the work, Muslim officials at the Waqf, and especially the Palestinian mufti Ikrima Sabri, have issued stern warnings against the work, declaring, "This is a dangerous situation and I call upon Muslim governments and people to heed this dangerous situation."[17] Could such a project, if it materializes, be the catalyst for the next battle for the Temple Mount? It is certainly possible as the present Al-Aqsa intifada continues to escalate and the Palestinian Authority fails to achieve its goals through either terrorism or diplomacy.

War over the Temple Mount appears inevitable. When will it occur, and what will be its outcome? Having seen the current climate that is preparing for war in the Middle East, let us look to Scripture, which contains prophecies about these last days of distress that are coming to the Temple Mount.

13

The Future Battles for the Temple

As we watch the events in Israel, the Middle East, and all over the world, it strengthens the feeling that the next step is the great end-time war. [1]

Earlier in this book we considered the historical pattern of attack on the Temple Mount, which represents the place of God's presence on planet earth. In considering these attacks both past and present, we have observed that the opponents of God's purpose (to return His presence to earth) have also been the opponents of God's people, the Jews (who are to serve as a kingdom of priests once God's presence is restored). It should not be surprising, then, that the focus of the world has turned again to the Middle East, to Israel, to Jerusalem, and especially to the Temple Mount. Nor should it surprise us that the conflict that has continued through the ages and has renewed itself today is moving inexorably toward a final confrontation in the future. People at every corner of the globe are becoming more and more aware of this, but nowhere as keenly as in Israel, the prophesied focal point of the future battle. Gershon Salomon, director of the Temple Mount Faithful movement in Israel, expressed this when he observed:

> Since that time [the rebirth of the State of Israel in 1948]
> the Arab enemies of Israel, together with their allies all
> over the world, have tried [seven times] to destroy Israel.
> Those wars and the determination of the Arab and
> Islamic countries to destroy Israel were the first black
> clouds indicating the first steps of the end-time war....As
> we watch the events in Israel, the Middle East, and all over
> the world, it strengthens the feeling that the next step is
> the great end-time war.[2]

As we have surveyed the modern-day hostility toward Israel and the threat of war over the Temple Mount, we have only been able to speculate as to what events may occur next. That is why, in this chapter, we will turn our attention to "the sure word of prophecy" (2 Peter 1:9), which details for us in explicit terms what will one day take place on the Temple Mount. According to prophecy, the wars to come will break foreign dominion over the Temple Mount, bring the people of Israel to repentance, and establish them as God's nation and the bearer of the light of God's Word to the world. The terrible judgment upon those who have so defiled God's holy house will be of such a severe and unparalleled nature as to convince the nations that the God of Israel alone is God and that He has returned to rule (Zechariah 14:9,12-16)!

The Battle of the Future Begins

Apparently the first of the future battles that will be fought in the Land of Israel will be a battle known as the "War of Gog and Magog," which is described in Ezekiel 38–39. However, since "Gog" is the ruler of the place "Magog," it is better termed "the Gog prophecy." This war appears to belong to the eschatological future, for the biblical text states, "It shall come about in the last days..." (Ezekiel 38:16). However, exactly *when* in the last days this occurs is a matter of debate. The placement of the Gog and Magog account in the restoration section of Ezekiel (chapters 33–48) could mean it occurs in the Millennium (see Revelation 20:8) or in a time that immediately precedes it, in which case it could be pre-Tribulational, Tribulational, or post-Tribulational. For this reason, the chronological placement of this war is one of the most difficult issues in prophetic interpretation.[3] I have opted for a pre-Tribulational setting on the basis that this best satisfies the majority of the temporal conditions described in Ezekiel 38:8-11 in relation to a people "in the latter years" "gathered from many nations" to a Land that "had been a continual waste" but is now inhabited and which was "restored from the sword [domination]" and is now "living securely" with enviable economic resources. All these descriptions can apply to modern-day Israel.[4]

In addition, this time frame resolves the problem of how Israel disposes of the captured weapons and the slain bodies of Gog and his allies (Ezekiel 39:9-16). According to Jewish law, the dead must be buried immediately because exposed corpses are a source of ritual contamination. However, because of the vast number of corpses, the burials will take "seven months" (Ezekiel 39:12). And the destruction of the weapons will take "seven years" (Ezekiel 39:9). If this battle were to take place at any point during the Tribulation (even during the initial 42 months of pseudopeace), the people would run out of time to complete the latter task before the Antichrist's persecution drives the Jewish population of the area into the wilderness (Matthew 24:16-22; Revelation 12:6) or forces others to wage a defense against his assault on the holy city (Zechariah 12:7-8; 13:1; 14:2; Revelation 11:2). However, if this war occurs before the Tribulation begins, there would be ample time and freedom of movement to accomplish this job according to *halachic* regulations.

Regardless of the specific time of this eschatological conflict, it is clear that the stage for the war is the Land of Israel (Ezekiel 38:9-12,14,16,18-19; 39:11), and specifically "the mountains of Israel" (Ezekiel 38:8; 39:2,17). The invaders are an alliance of foreign nations from "the remote parts of the north" (Ezekiel 38:6,15), the land of Gog, the prince of Rosh, Meshech, and Tubal (Ezekiel 38:2-3). "Rosh" (a proper noun)[5] was originally associated with the tribe of Ros/Rus, which lent its name to a variety of topographical

features in what is now the Ukraine and Russia. On historical, geographical, and toponymic grounds, this identification is best made
with the modern-day Russian people.[6] Linguistically, even the very
name *Russia* appears to have been derived from this term *Rosh*.[7]
Therefore, despite the objection of modern critics to this position,
it seems the prophecy of Ezekiel 38–39 remains a prophecy of the
Russian invasion of Israel.

The other northern nations allied with Gog in the invasion
(Meshech, Tubal, Gomer, Togarmah) are joined with nations that
may represent the other three areas of the compass: Persia (Iran)
from the east, Cush (northern Sudan) from the south, and Put
(Libya) from the west, constituting this as a worldwide attack.
Additional nations that support the war against Israel in this text
are Sheba (Yemen), Dedan (Saudi Arabia), and Tarshish (far west)
with its merchants (an economic union).

The Gog Prophecy and Current Conditions

Just as the modern Israeli state fits the description given by
Ezekiel for the Israel of the last days that will experience this battle,
so these modern countries fit the details as Israel's enemies (or
potential enemies) who can and have formed alliances and have
economic incentives for invasion. If the Gog war was predicted for
a time such as this, and Russia and the Islamic nations are to be
involved, it may explain why Russia today is so economically
dependent and why Islam has risen to dominate the Middle East
economically through its control of vast oil reserves. Russia's economic hardships and political instability have made it attractive to
establish economic and military alliances with Islamic powers—
the same powers that continually call for Israel's destruction.[8]

For example, since the collapse of the communist Soviet
Union, six of the former Soviet republics in the south (but north
of Israel) have become independent *Islamic* nations: Azerbaijan,
Kazakhstan, Uzbekistan, Kyrgyzstan, Turkmenistan, and Tajik-
istan). As *U.S. News & World Report* editor-in-chief Mortimer
Zuckerman has observed,

> Russia is an economic free fall that threatens the coher-
> ence of the central state and the ability of the government
> to control its arsenal of nuclear, chemical, and biological
> weapons. Any time now they might become black-market
> items for rogue buyers....And if the state disintegrates
> altogether, we could face the apocalyptic scenario of ultra-
> nationalists or some other faction challenging the com-
> mand and control of nuclear weapons spread over 39
> different Russian districts....Russia is a tragedy on the
> way to a catastrophe that could envelop us all.[9]

Israel is without a doubt one of the most highly developed[10] and westernized countries in the Middle East, and its technological achievements (Israel is the Silicon Valley of the Middle East) and natural resources (water, valuable chemicals and minerals in the Dead Sea, and untapped oil reserves) could make it the "great spoil" Ezekiel 38:13 says these nations will seek to capture. Today Turkey (Togarmah) has a military alliance with Israel, and Turkey's million-man army is one of the factors keeping both Egypt and Syria (with whom Israel shares a border) at bay. However, Turkey is an Islamic country, and if it were called to participate in an Islamic alliance of the magnitude predicted by Ezekiel, it would be compelled to join.

In the recent past, an axis was thought to have been formed between Russia and the Middle Eastern countries of Iraq, Iran, Syria, Sudan, and Ethiopia with the goal of overthrowing the United States and its Zionist ally in the Middle East, Israel. Russia has already forged alliances with Iran, Syria, Pakistan, Libya, and Turkey. Moreover, the Central Asian republics of Kazakhstan, Turkmenistan, Tajikistan, Uzbekistan, and Kyrgyzstan have signed a military assistance pact with the Russian Federation.

These countries are all Islamic, and many have been confirmed to possess nuclear weapons. Libya is supposed to have made the greatest progress in the Middle East with respect to its nuclear arms program, and Iran has a less-developed program. Pakistan has tested nuclear weapons, and other countries have reportedly acquired weapons of mass destruction supplied by Russia, North Korea, and China. Iraq, too, once had a developing nuclear arms program until invaded by the United States. These facts demonstrate that conditions exist at present to fulfill the Gog prophecy. Could the war on terrorism, now being waged in this region, be a catalyst that will draw many of these countries together toward a future invasion of Israel, the object of their present hatred?

Will Gog Attack Jerusalem?

Motivated by a desire to plunder Israel's economic resources, Gog's invasion is stated to be against those "who live at the center of the world" (Ezekiel 38:12). Ezekiel 5:5 employs this expression in reference to the holy city: "This is Jerusalem; I have set her at the center of the nations, with lands around her." Following this idiomatic usage, *Tanhuma* 106 declares: "Israel lies at the center of the earth, and Jerusalem lies at the center of the Land of Israel." Based on this association, traditional Jewish interpretation has accepted the Gog prophecy as the same attack on Jerusalem and the Temple Mount as that described in Zechariah 12–14.

However, it is difficult to decide if this expression is used by the enemy in mockery of Israel's confidence based on its accumulated wealth, or in reference to the object of their attack being Jerusalem. If the former, the sense might be "[Israel] thinks it is the best in the world," an accusation made against Israel by its enemies today. If the latter, it might be speculated that the source of the wealth could be connected with the Temple Mount. Although such a suggestion is attractive in light of the present discussion concerning the battle for the Temple Mount, it fails, in my opinion, to find support in the biblical context. Ezekiel 38:11 specifically states that the invasion is launched against "the land of unwalled villages...all of them living without walls, and having no bars or gates." Jerusalem, however, is the exception, being characterized since earliest times as a walled city with gates, towers, and ramparts (Psalm 24:7; 48:12; 51:18; 100:4; 122:2,7; Isaiah 62:6), a distinction that continues today with respect to the Old City. Moreover, while the "mountains of Israel" where the invaders fall in defeat (Ezekiel 39:4; see also 38:21) may include the mountain range that encompasses Jerusalem, these mountains are also in the northern part of Israel. Since the attack is from "the remotest parts of the north" (Ezekiel 39:2), it seems more reasonable that the destruction occurs where the invasion would first occur—in "the [northern] mountains of Israel."[11]

The Prophecy's Connection with the Temple Mount

While I do not find sufficient support for the idea that the war of Gog is aimed at Jerusalem and the Temple Mount, I believe it could bear a crucial connection with the Temple Mount, and that it may initiate the prophetic process that leads to the rebuilding of the Temple. In support of this, notice that the Gog prophecy appears between two other important prophecies about the future Temple (Ezekiel 37:26-28 and 40–48). This arrangement is not artificial, as some have suggested (being the out-of-sequence intrusion of a later author or editor). Rather, it provides theological assurance that the new Temple introduced in Ezekiel 37, and detailed in chapters 40–48, will never again be violated (as past Temples have been). The fact Gog will be defeated is proof that Israel's God has pledged to defend His Land from future invasion, as will occur in the Tribulation and again in the final end-time invasion (Revelation 20:6-9).

The Transition to the Tribulation Temple

The Gog prophecy may also provide a transition to the Tribulation period mentioned in Daniel's 70-weeks prophecy as well as a possible motive for the enigmatic "covenant" predicted in this text (Daniel 9:24-27). To explain, if the next war is that of Gog and Magog, and divine intervention takes place on behalf of Israel, the Islamic world is likely to retreat from further hostile actions toward Israel and withdraw to deal with its public disgrace. That's exactly what happened after each of the massive Arab invasions of Israel in past wars met with humiliating defeat, and especially after the Six-Day War, in which the air forces of both Egypt and Syria were destroyed. In fact, President Nasser of Egypt attempted to resign as a result of his nation's losses in this war. After the war of Gog and Magog, then, the Islamic threat may well be removed from the world scene, and there will also be a political power vacuum as a result of the rapture of the church. Consequently, there will also be power shifts among the nations of the world at that time, leading to the wars which establish the Antichrist in power (Daniel 7:23-25; 11:40-45; Revelation 6:2).

As stated earlier, the war of Gog and Magog may provide the transition to the Tribulation period mentioned in Daniel's 70-weeks prophecy (Daniel 9:24-27). One result of the war would be a new world alliance that could assume responsibility for restoring global stability in the wake of the political and religious crises caused by the destruction of the Russian and Islamic armies. Daniel 7:23-24 indicates that at first, a one-world government will arise, but then it will divide into ten governments. If, as we suggest, the Gog and Magog war occurs before Antichrist's rise to power, there will be no central figure to sustain a one-world government, and it will soon become reorganized into the ten-nation confederation. Another result of the Gog and Magog war may be a global recognition of Israel that leads to negotiations that bring about normalized relations between Israel and the rising leader of the world government, the Antichrist. After all, Israel's stunning victory over the Russian-Arab alliance would cause Israel to be perceived as a force to be reckoned with. And because Israel's miraculous deliverance was made possible by Israel's God (at least from the Israeli perspective), Antichrist's global policy would have to include concessions to Israel that honored the God of Israel. What more appropriate tribute to Israel's God could be imagined than that of rebuilding the Jewish Temple, which represented His divine presence among His people? The "covenant" of Daniel 9:27a between the Antichrist ("the prince of the people," verse 26) and Israel ("the many") seems to result in the rebuilding of the Temple, and Daniel 9:27b implies that the same covenant will be broken through the Antichrist's desecration of the Temple, which will force a cessation of the Temple service.

The Antichrist's purpose in making this covenant with Israel is surely part of a deceptive scheme to politically position himself in Jerusalem in order to introduce the "abomination of desolation" in the Temple and usurp divine authority (Matthew 24:15; Mark 13:14; 2 Thessalonians 2:4; cf. Revelation 11:2), and to carry out the satanic goal of Jewish genocide (Matthew 24:16-22; Revelation 12:13). However, the Antichrist's desire to establish a covenant with Israel may also be good political strategy at the time (for him), since Israel will have gained a position of worldwide respect as a result of her "miraculous" victory in the Gog and Magog war. Any future move the Antichrist would make to consolidate his leadership would be improved with Israel in his pocket. Therefore, like a mobster running a protection racket, the Antichrist may offer, through this covenant, a special guarantee of security that would enable Israel to act with an independence never previously known. It will also be the first time in modern history that Israel will come away from the international negotiating table *getting* something instead of *giving up* something! This covenant will usher in for Israel a time of pseudopeace that, in contrast to the warfare, pestilence, and famine suffered by the rest of the world (Revelation 6:1-6), could deceive many Jews into believing the promised messianic era had arrived.

Under the covenant with the Antichrist, Jerusalem could gain a new status as a "world capital." Over the past few decades, various peace proposals, including a plan from the Vatican, have proposed internationalizing the city of Jerusalem. Rabbi Nachman Kahane, who was one of the spiritual forces behind the organizers of the modern Temple movement, stated to me in a 1989 interview that he thought the best solution for the current controversy over Jerusalem was for Jews, Christians, and Muslims to come

PART III: THE FUTURE BATTLES

together on common ground and make Jerusalem a religious world capital.[12] In like manner, in July 2003, Prime Minister Shimon, head of Israel's Labor party, when asked by Russian diplomats-in-training how he would resolve the Israeli-Palestinian conflict, cited his plan "to declare the holy sites sacred to Jews, Christians and Muslims in Jerusalem as a world capital."[13] Under this plan, the Temple Mount would be governed internationally with the U.N. secretary-general serving as mayor. I offer these examples only to suggest the form the covenant with Jerusalem might take in light of current events. Whatever form it takes, it will likely leave the Orthodox Jews in charge of the Temple Mount and enable them to rebuild their Temple and resume the sacrificial service.

During this time, the Antichrist will consolidate his power by declaring war on the ten kings of the confederation (Daniel 11:40-45), and killing three of them (Daniel 7:24b; Revelation 17:12-13). Once he has reached the apex of his political power, he will move to assume a comparable religious power through the activities of his false prophet (Revelation 13:11-17). In order to make the greatest possible statement to a world that had only a few years earlier witnessed the power of Israel's God, the Antichrist will apparently try to defame Him by an open assault upon the symbol of His authority, the Temple.

The Antichrist's Assault on the Temple Mount

The Old and New Testaments alike predict the desecration of the rebuilt Temple and an all-out battle by the armies of the Antichrist to conquer Jerusalem and maintain control of the Temple Mount. The Antichrist's initial assault on the Holy City, the Temple Mount, and the Holy of Holies in the Temple will apparently come as a surprise and shock to the Jewish people. The Antichrist may come to Jerusalem on a pretext, perhaps on an inspection tour, with his usual military entourage. Then, perhaps while the priests are carrying out their daily tasks, a unit of the Antichrist's soldiers will invade the Temple Mount, expel the priests and Levites, and secure the area. Texts such as Isaiah 66:1-6, Daniel 9:27, Matthew 24:15, Mark 13:14, 2 Thessalonians 2:4, and Revelation 11:1-2 tell us that the Antichrist will trample the Holy City for 42 months (the last half of the Tribulation), drive out the Temple priesthood and worshipers, stop the sacrificial system, and position himself in the place of deity in the Holy of Holies. The Antichrist's action will render the Temple inoperative due to ritual impurity, which will manifest itself in the cessation of the sacrificial system as predicted in Daniel 9:27. The Antichrist's installation of himself within the Temple is called "the abomination of desolation" (Matthew 24:15; cf. Daniel 9:27). The apostle Paul, in 2 Thessalonians 2:4, predicts this same event, and describes the abomination of desolation in terms of its action of desecration. Paul states that the Antichrist (referred to in 2 Thessalonians 2:3 as "the man of lawlessness") will commit the ultimate offense of self-elevation above the only true God by enthroning himself in the place of deity within the Temple of God. This act is alluded to in Daniel 11:36, where we read that the Antichrist "will exalt and magnify himself above every god and speak monstrous things against the God of gods."

Daniel 11:45 notes that as a result of this invasion, "He [the Antichrist] will pitch the tents of his royal pavilion between the seas and the beautiful Holy Mountain." This describes the Antichrist's setting up a military and political base in Jerusalem (between the Mediterranean Sea and the Dead Sea) and particularly on the Temple Mount ("the beautiful Holy Mountain"). Once the Antichrist takes over the Temple Mount, it is possible that Jerusalem becomes the political and religious center of his rule and the place from which the false prophet issues and enforces the mark of the beast as a sign of allegiance to the Antichrist's government and godhood (Revelation 13:16-17). For Orthodox and messianic Jews of this time, the Antichrist's actions will, on the one hand, commence the persecution of their Jewish people (Isaiah 66:5-6; Matthew 24:16-22) that will characterize the remainder of the Tribulation (provoking national repentance and the return of the Messiah to rescue His righteous remnant), and on the other hand, will begin an underground resistance of the Antichrist's policies by a dedicated band of Jewish rebels whose main objective may be to retake the Temple Mount (Zechariah 12:8–13:2; 14:4). The details of this resistance and its climatic conclusion in the Battle of Armageddon are recorded in Zechariah 12–14.

The Tribulation Battle for the Temple Mount

As we harmonize the events of Zechariah 12–14 with those in the book of Revelation, it appears that as the Antichrist rallies his army in the Valley of Jezreel (Revelation 16:14-16), his enemies will launch an attack against his commercial center, Babylon, and destroy it (Revelation 18:1-24). Next, motivated by a desire to destroy the people of God, the Antichrist will move his troops south to join an international coalition assembled to attack Jerusalem (Zechariah 12:1-3; 14:1). This will be the final campaign of the battles of Armageddon, and it appears to be focused on the eastern section of the city, which includes the Temple Mount, where the Antichrist had earlier established his religious base (Daniel 11:45a).

From the description of the battle as recorded in Zechariah 12 and 14, it seems that the Jewish resistance will recover the eastern portion of the city and the Temple Mount (Zechariah 12:5-9; cf. Micah 4:11–5:1), and they will lose the western half, which will be exiled (Zechariah 14:2). Even though the text is not explicit about which part of the city will be held by the Jewish remnant, I believe it will be eastern Jerusalem and the Temple Mount for several reasons: 1) because of the presence of the Temple, this area would be the most fiercely defended and the last to fall; 2) the fact the text mentions the part of the Mount of Olives that "is in front of Jerusalem on the east" directly across from the Temple Mount; and 3) the Mount of Olives will split in two and the two sides will move north and south, creating a east-west escape route for the Jews (Zechariah

14:5). This east-west escape route would go directly from the eastern side of the city, and probably directly from the Temple Mount, across the Kidron Valley and through the Mount of Olives toward the Judean desert. The only way to access this route would be from the eastern part of the city, so it seems reasonable that this is the area that would be in the possession of the Jewish remnant.

Still another evidence that this battle may include the Temple Mount is implied by the contrast between the nations gathered against Jerusalem *for battle* (Zechariah 12:3; 14:2) and the nations gathered to Jerusalem *for worship* (Zechariah 14:16; cf. Isaiah 2:2; 56:7). In the latter instance, the focus of *adoration* is the Temple Mount. To complete the contrast, the former instance should have, as its focus, an *assault* on the Temple Mount.

And finally, we must keep in mind that the Messiah will descend upon the Mount of Olives directly across from the Temple Mount (Zechariah 14:3-4). Once His feet touch the mountain, it will split open to both provide a way of escape for the Jewish remnant (cf. Joshua 3:6-17) and simultaneously cut off the Antichrist's armies' escape to the north and south, leaving them alone in the Kidron Valley, also known as the Valley of Jehoshaphat ("God will judge"), to be destroyed (Zechariah 14:12-15; cf. Isaiah 14:3-21; Joel 3:12-13; Revelation 19:11-16). Messiah will then destroy the Antichrist's armies by plague (Zechariah 14:12-15; Revelation 19:17-21), and the escape route will provide His repentant people with a passage to Himself on the Mount of Olives.

This act will fulfill the promise Jesus made from the Mount of Olives when He said that the Temple would be desolate and the leaders of Jerusalem would not see Him until they said, "Blessed is He who comes in the name of the Lord!" (Matthew 23:38-39), and it will fulfill His prediction concerning the desolation of the Temple and the judgment on those who desolated it (Matthew 24:15; Luke 21:28; cf. Daniel 9:27). After the conclusion of this battle for the Temple Mount, the Lord will enthrone Himself in a new Temple (Zechariah 14:9,16; cf. Jeremiah 3:17) on a greatly restored Temple Mount (Zechariah 14:10; cf. Isaiah 2:2-3) that will stand all through the Millennium (Ezekiel 37:26-28).

The Final Battle for the Temple Mount

The ancient prophets and Revelation 20:1-15 portray the Millennium as a period of unthreatened holiness during which Israel enjoys a theocratic government under the rule of the Messiah. Ezekiel 40–48 further depicts this age as one of unparalleled worship and spiritual service around the Millennial Temple (Isaiah 2:2-4; 66:18-23; Ezekiel 36:25-36; 37:25-28; 43:7; 44:3,24; 45:8-10). This era will be marked by longevity, harmony in nature, true peace, bountiful prosperity, and a universal knowledge of the Lord as well as fellowship with Him on earth (Isaiah 11:6-9; 65:18-25; Jeremiah 31:27-33). It may come as a surprise, then, to read in Revelation 20:7-9 of another future attack by the Gentile nations against "the beloved city" (Revelation 20:9), reminiscent of the earlier "Gog war" (Ezekiel 38–39). However, while the Gog war was launched from and fought in the north, the Revelation 20:7-9 attack is centered in the south on Jerusalem, and they will surround "the camp of the saints and the beloved city" (Revelation 20:9).

For 1000 years (Revelation 20:6), the Millennial Temple will serve as the Lord's throne (Jeremiah 3:17), and the world will make annual pilgrimages to it in worship of the Messiah who reigns within (Zechariah 14:16-19). At the outset of the millennial age, weapons will be banished and Israel and the nations will abandon the art of warfare (Isaiah 2:4). According to Revelation 20:7-8, the reinstatement of war at the end of the Millennium will have its origin in Satan, who will be released from his bondage (Revelation 20:1-3) to foster a final deception before the close of earth's history. Knowing that the source of all fighting is the evil resident within mankind (James 4:1-3), Satan will gather to himself all of those who, on the outside, may appear to have conformed outwardly to the New Covenant rule of the Messiah, but are inwardly still rebellious. These will be the offspring of the regenerate peoples that entered the millennial kingdom after the judgment of the nations at the end of the Tribulation (Matthew 25:31-46).

God's purpose for allowing this final rebellion at the end of the Millennium may be to reveal to mankind that even in the most perfect environment—with an undeniable, visible witness of the Lord's own presence and 1000 years of instruction in God's Word—the unregenerate will still rebel against God. Whatever the reason, Satan, in the guise of Gog, will lead his worldwide allied army against the Lord at the Millennial Temple. The text identifies this place as "the broad plain of the earth...the camp of the saints and the beloved city" (Revelation 20:9). According to Zechariah 14:10, this "broad plain" was the result of a divine transformation of the topography around Jerusalem "from Geba [10 miles north of the city] to Rimmon [35 miles southwest of the city]." Isaiah 2:2 implies this land was flattened in order for the Temple Mount to stand out at the center (see Ezekiel 48:21). Ezekiel 48:10-22 describes the "camp of the saints" as the divisions of land around the sanctuary where the priests, Levites, and workers of the Holy City will dwell.

Just as the Gog war described in Ezekiel had revealed God's glorious power to Israel and the nations and His ability to protect His own during the Tribulation, so will this final demonstration in human history prove to the nations His power and to God's people their need of His protection. As in the war of Gog, God's divine intervention on behalf of His people will be unmistakable, in the form of "fire [that] came down from heaven" (Revelation 20:9). However, after this final battle, the devil will join those whom he deceived in the judgment by fire, joining the Antichrist and False Prophet in the Lake of Fire for all eternity (Revelation 20:10). With this final showdown, the battles of the Temple Mount will forever cease, and the world will be renewed along with the heavens (Isaiah 65:17; 66:22; 2 Peter 3:10-13) for the eternal state.

In our survey of the last battles of earth, which will center on Israel and its Temple Mount, we have seen that the Lord will triumph as His prophetic program comes to completion.

However, you and I must continue to live in this present day of escalating troubles on the Temple Mount—troubles that menace our lives with political and religious maelstrom. How can we prepare ourselves to engage the issues of our time and the coming day in which the dire prophecies of the future become a part of our present? In the next chapter, we will explore how you can be ready for whatever may come, and how, even now, you can experience the heavenly blessings that lay beyond the earthly battles.

14

Are You Ready
for the Future?

*All who mourn for Jerusalem will merit to see
its rejoicing.*

BABYLONIAN TALMUD, TA'ANIT 30B

Israel and the Arab world are on a collision course over the
Temple Mount. Muslims have declared that no sharing will
ever be possible and that the site must remain under Islamic
control. On the Temple Mount, Muslims continue to transform
the site into a mosque, and in the process are destroying remnants of the past in order to support their denial of Jewish history. At the same time, Jewish activists have declared that the time
of Islamic domination is coming to an end and predict that the
mosques will all be moved and the Third Temple built. Both sides
today claim sovereignty over the Temple Mount, but at some
point in the future, only one side will prevail.

How long can the current standoff continue? Will escalating
violence against Israel force the Israeli government to finally move
against the Palestinian Authority to put an end to terrorism? Will
such a crackdown by the Israelis force a similar move against the
Palestinian-controlled Waqf to reclaim full Israeli sovereignty over
the Temple Mount? Would this provoke the Islamic world to
attack Israel? Would other nations get involved, leading to the
need for an international solution to end the conflict? Would this

then bring about an international control of the Temple Mount? Could this lead to the rebuilding the Third Temple? So many questions about the future! But, the most important question is this: Are *you* ready for that future?

The War Is Coming!

The present struggle over the Temple Mount will one day become a battle for the Temple Mount. In this war, it should not be expected that the nations of the world will comprehend the significance of the Temple Mount except as an obstacle to peace and a problem to be resolved. The Jewish Midrash states, "If the nations of the world had only known how much they needed the Temple, they would have surrounded it with armed forces to protect it" (*Bamidbar Rabbah* 1:3). But, the nations of the world have not known and will not know this until they are regenerated and brought under Messiah's reign in the millennial kingdom (Zechariah 14:16). Therefore, until that time, they will increasingly view the Temple Mount as a source of international controversy and conflict, and in the end times they will launch attacks against it. The Arab world, as part of these nations, is likely to be the leading force against Israel and Jerusalem. In fact, Palestinian leader Jeries Soudah predicts that Israeli intransigence over East Jerusalem and the Temple Mount has made war inevitable:

> When it comes to that sensitive point, Jerusalem, I think there will be another war. The Islamic and the Arab world just cannot compromise concerning Jerusalem. They just can't....[1] United Nations Resolution 242, which states that Israel has to pull out from the occupied territories, from the West Bank and Jerusalem, has to be taken into consideration. If this will not happen or if they will not at least negotiate about Jerusalem, another Civil War, another *Intifada*, will start....This time the entire Arab world will participate in that *Intifada*. It will be Arabs, Muslims, Christians—a huge *Intifada* that Israel cannot resist. Arabs are not going to give up the holy place that

easily. Palestinians and the whole Arab world are ready to go for a new civil war....But talking about the Temple, Israelis say that it has to be built on the site of the Dome of the Rock. The Muslim community will not allow anything to happen to the Dome [of the Rock]....[2]

The renewed intifada that Soudah threatened back in 1997 came to reality three years later in 2000, and it is certain that other parts of his prediction will also come to pass in time. This can be seen in the following report concerning the Islamic agenda in relation to Israel. Its frightening description of the Arab world's current preparation for the next great war in the Middle East seems comparable to the descriptions given by the biblical prophets concerning the invasion of Israel and Jerusalem in the end times:

The Arab countries (and Iran) are frantically arming themselves with the most dreadful weapons of mass destruction. As the world knows, it is for one purpose only—their only political objective and their relentless obsession—namely the destruction of Israel. Two or three nuclear weapons would wipe Israel off the map once and for all. Retaliation by Israel, the destruction of major Arab cities, and millions of Arab casualties would not deter the Muslim fanatics from pursuing their goal. For them, it would be a small price to pay. With Israel dismembered, with five or six Arab states poised to attack with weapons of mass destruction, with 40,000 Palestinian "police" armed to the teeth in Israel's midst, can anybody really doubt that a second Holocaust, even more terrible than the first one, is just about upon us?[3]

Is it really as bad as this? Are we on the brink of unparalleled days of trouble for the Jewish people in the Middle East? Consider for a moment the words of Israeli Yochanan Ramati, who serves as director of the Jerusalem Institute for Western Defense. Ramati is a man who has seen it all. He served in the British Army during World War II, and witnessed from his home—near the Old City of Jerusalem—every war fought in Israel since 1947. He has known personally all of Israel's past and present leaders, and is himself an expert on the Arab/Muslim world. In his opinion, circumstances have never been worse, and his sobering words below were spoken to me as words of hopeful warning:

> Well, if I'm allowed to hope, I want to hope that we have at least as many years in front of us as we have behind us. [But] I'm not sure of that at all. If I'm allowed to hope, let me hope that western civilization will survive another 30 or 40 years, which at the moment I rather doubt. That is so much for hopes. I'm not giving any scenarios. All the scenarios I can see are too pessimistic to give. One thing I promise you: there is not going to be any peace here [in Israel]. There may be peace treaties [but] there will be not peace because the Arabs do not want peace with us. They are using the peace treaties as a means to create a situation in which they can wage a victorious war....I don't know whether the Temple Movement in Israel has any future. I can visualize an imaginary situation in a war where things could happen, but if that is to be, we have to be in a situation to win a war....[However,] everyone concerned, not only the Arabs, but [also] the [international] powers seem to be determined to put us in a situation in which we cannot win a war. Obviously this cannot have a good end.[4]

When Will the End Come?

Based on the storm clouds gathering in the Middle East, we can discern that the days of fulfillment for the Temple Mount are closing in fast. But who can predict the future with any amount of accuracy? God can! His predictions, while not dependent upon current events, may be revealed by them. Through the ages, students of Bible prophecy have watched for certain events that would help them to discern the times and determine whether the

Art by Larissa Lando and used with permission

An artist's depiction of the Gentile nations gathered around Jerusalem for battle in the last days.

end times were approaching. By understanding these signs and the stage that is being set for their fulfillment, we can gain some insight into the future and prepare ourselves accordingly. Indeed, there are four events in the Bible that center on Israel—the key to understanding the fulfillment of prophecy—and serve as an indication that the last days are near.

1 When Israel Is Regathered and Restored to the Land

The first of these four events was a regathering of the Jewish people to '*Eretz-Yisrael* (the "Land of Israel") from out of the Diaspora [Hebrew, *Galut*], the Jewish exile to lands under Gentile dominion as a result of divine discipline. Most scholars see this regathering occurring in progressive stages with an indeterminate amount of time between stages. Ezekiel's famous prophecy of the "valley of dry bones" coming to life (Ezekiel 37:1-14) illustrates the two phases of Israel's regathering and restoration as do other Bible passages (Ezekiel 11:17-19; 36:24-27; 37:21,23). The first stage of the

Art by Larissa Lando and used with permission

An artist's depiction of the Jewish people receiving their Messiah, who will descend upon the Mount of Olives and be victorious in battle over the Gentile nations.

regathering will be to the *Land* (geographical); the second stage of restoration will be to the *Lord* (spiritual). This was the pattern established by the previous Jewish exile and return. Rabbi Nisan Aryeh Novick explains:

> *Hashem* [God] never said that both forms of *Galus* [exile] have to end together at the same exact moment—they certainly do not even begin in the same instant. Isn't it true that *first* the Jews acted inappropriately and then some time later they were exiled from the Land; this phenomenon has occurred twice....Isn't it also true that there were two forms of *Galus* [exile] in Egypt which were cast-off at two different points of time? *The geographical Galus [exile] ended* the moment the Jews left Egypt. The estrangement, *the spiritual Galus [exile] ended* in a very slow and deliberate fashion....But both *Galuyot* [exiles] did not end at the same moment. Both ended in a serial fashion—first the physcial *Galus* [exile] and later the spiritual.[5]

This two-stage operation—the first by man, the second by God—has been observed to correspond to the early efforts of Zionism to prepare the Land to receive a Jewish population (the first stage), which will be followed at the end of the biblical Tribulation by God's spiritual revival of national Israel (the second stage). The return *(aliyah)* by Jewish immigrants to the Land of Israel today from all over the world, including large populations of Jews from foreign lands such as Eastern Europe, the Soviet Union, and Ethiopia, have served as signs in our day that God is working out His plan and moving His people toward the fulfillment of His restoration promise.

2. *When Israel Is Again Established as a Nation*

The biblical prophecies about the Tribulation period reveal that during that time, Israel is not only in her Land, but that the Land is in her control. In Ezekiel 38–39, it is clear that Israel is both regathered to the Land and secure in the Land. Ezekiel 38:8 says, "After many days you will be summoned; in the latter years you will come into the land that is restored from the sword, whose inhabitants have been gathered from many nations to the mountains of Israel which had been a continual waste; but its people were brought out from the nations, and they are living securely, all of them." From this verse we can see that following a worldwide regathering (the first stage), there will arise a "land that is restored from the sword." This describes the establishment of a Jewish nation (state), and the initial fulfillment of this prophecy may have been the establishment of the modern State of Israel in 1948—the first time Israel had been an independent national entity since the Roman period. This verse's connection to the regathering seems to be affirmed by the statement that the people "are living securely, all of them." The Hebrew term *betach* ("safety, security") refers to Israel's freedom in the Land (whether premillennial or millennial) and could have in view a security derived from military strength (consider the modern Hebrew term *bituhōn*, which means "military security").

The timing for the establishment of this nation may also be noted as a time after the Land "had been a continual waste." When Zionist pioneers began arriving in Palestine in appreciable numbers early in the twentieth century, they drained the swamps and revived a region that had been described by pilgrims through the centuries as a desolate wasteland. The 70-year exile in Babylon did not fulfill the prophecy regarding a "continual waste," for at the time, the Land did have inhabitants, and it was not a "continual waste." The fact that the physical Land of Israel is today under independent Jewish control makes possible the end of physical exile for all of the Jewish people, thus setting the stage for the final fulfillment of Israel as a revived nation under Messiah in the millennial kingdom.

3. When Jerusalem Comes Under Jewish Control

The fulfillment of many end-times prophecies centers on Jerusalem. For example, Zechariah 14:2 states, "I will gather all nations against Jerusalem to do battle, and the city will be captured, the houses plundered, the women ravished and half of the city exiled, but the rest of the people will not be cut off from the city." The "Jerusalem" described here is clearly a Jewish Jerusalem, meaning it is under the control of the Jewish people and not simply inhabited by Jews. The fact that people can be exiled from their city and that some still defend themselves and remain, reveals that the city is under their control. The Jerusalem in view in the biblical text refers to the present-day "Old City" of Jerusalem, which was the only Jerusalem that existed until about 150 years ago. While Israel has had control of the western section of Jerusalem, the "New City," since 1948, it was not until 1967 that the eastern section (with the Old City and the Temple Mount) came under Jewish control. While it may argued that Israel does not fully control the Old City, and controls the Temple Mount to an even lesser extent, it nevertheless has exercised sovereignty over a united Jerusalem for over a third of a century. Therefore, regardless of the degree of control exercised, it's clear that the city of Jerusalem is again a Jewish city under Jewish control. This, of course, has set the stage for the fulfillment of end-time events.

4. *When the Third Temple Is Rebuilt*

As we have already seen, numerous Bible passages predict that before the time of the end the Jewish Temple will be rebuilt in Jerusalem. This fourth event requires the previous three events to have already occurred, for the Jewish Temple cannot be rebuilt except 1) by Jews, 2) in the Land of the Jews, 3) in a Jerusalem under Jewish control. Daniel 9:27 reveals the Temple is rebuilt by Jews, while Revelation 11:1-2 shows the Jerusalem in which it is built is under Jewish control, for the nations "trample it" (verse 2), which these nations wouldn't do if they were in control of Jerusalem. Another passage that possibly implies a Jewish control at the time of the building of the Temple is Matthew 24:15-20, which notes that Jews live in their own houses throughout the city, observe the Sabbath, and are free to flee from persecution (all benefits of independence). As we have also seen, preparations to build the Third Temple are already under way, and the only obstacle standing in the way of rebuilding is the presence of the Muslim mosques on and Islamic control over the Temple Mount. But all of this could change tomorrow, and we could find ourselves nearer than ever before to the fulfillment of end-times events.

As I mentioned earlier, students of Bible prophecy in past ages have expected these events to take place in the future. In their day, the Jewish people were scattered among the nations, and the Land of Israel, Jerusalem, and the Temple Mount were desolate and under the control of foreign Islamic regimes, with non-Muslims being punished by death if they attempted to enter the sacred site of the Temple Mount. If those Bible students of the past could see what is now happening with the Jewish people and these places in our day, would they not tell us that we are "blessed"? Surely they would not understand our lack of excitement at the evidence that God is fulfilling His Word, nor would they excuse

us for our lack of spiritual preparation in light of the nearness of
the hour!

From Darkness to Light

On one of my trips to Jerusalem, as I walked through the historic Jewish Quarter on the eve of *Tisha B'Av*, I noticed posters
prominently placed throughout the area to catch the attention of
passersby. The Hebrew words read *'Ein 'or me'ir 'ele' metok ha-
choshek* ("Light will not shine except from the darkness"). The
New Testament has a similar statement: "The Light shines in the
darkness, and the darkness did not comprehend it" (John 1:5).
The meaning intended by the poster's message—for these Jews
who daily live in sight of a Temple Mount under control of Muslims who deny their history and existence—was that the situation at present is truly dark. Yet the shining hope of a brighter
future will burst forth from just such darkness. This brighter
future holds the promise of messianic deliverance with a glori-
ously rebuilt Temple served by a restored Israel and visited by
redeemed Gentile nations. Yet, as we have seen, this hope cannot
be realized until after the dark days of the Tribulation.

What I have sought to do in this book is to show that from the
present darkness that is the Middle East conflict—a conflict that
may usher in the Tribulation—the light of the glory of the Lord
will one day shine. It will shine in the coming of the Messiah to put
down oppression and reign in righteousness (Psalm 2:6-9; Zechariah 14:9-14). It will shine as Israel is regenerated and restored and
fulfills its mandate to be a light to the nations (Isaiah 49:6). It will
shine through the Temple, which will again house the presence of
God and welcome the world to worship (Isaiah 2:2-3; 56:7).

Have You Seen the Light?

In the book of Proverbs we read that "the way of the wicked is
like darkness" but that "the path of the righteous is like the light of
dawn, that shines brighter and brighter until the full day" (Proverbs

4:18-19). As we watch events unfold on the map of the Middle East, that small ray of hope that is piercing the darkness is the sure promise of the Word of God. At present it is just a glow on the horizon, "the light of dawn." Even so, it reveals the way in the darkness to the light, and furnishes proof that one day the darkness itself will be dispelled. Today we may see only the faint beginning of that dawn, but there will soon come a time as Israel's future fast unfolds that the promised "full day" will shine upon us.

Let me ask you: Have you seen the light? Have the events of the Middle East conflict, the threats of terrorism in your own country, and the difficulties of daily life darkened your hope? Look again! As you consider what you've learned about the Temple Mount and the prophetic messages about it, do you not see the hand of God in the unprecedented preservation of the Jewish people, and their return to the Promised Land after so many centuries even after so much intense persecution at the hands of their enemies? Do you not see that the ray of hope promised by the prophets is shining and getting a little brighter every day? The prophet Isaiah declared, "Arise, shine; for your light has come, and the glory of the LORD has risen upon you. For behold, darkness will cover the earth and deep darkness the peoples; but the LORD will rise upon you and His glory will appear upon you. Nations will come to your light, and kings to the brightness of your rising" (Isaiah 60:1-3).

The darkness of doubt will be dispelled only by the light of God's truth. The Messiah of Israel 2000 years ago proclaimed concerning Himself: "I am the Light of the world; he who follows Me will not walk in darkness, but will have the Light of life" (John 8:12). Believing God's truth requires us to recognize and accept not only God's Messiah, but to respect God's plan for the Jewish people—a recognition that includes a prayerful concern for their present problems and a petition to God for their future restoration. In the context of this book, it also includes at least an understanding of the Jewish struggle for the Temple Mount and a prayer "for the peace of Jerusalem" (Psalm 122:6), which is a prayer not only for Israel's peace, but for the peace of all the world (Isaiah 2:2-4). In concert with this the Babylonian Talmud says, "All who mourn for Jerusalem will merit to see its rejoicing" (*Ta'anit* 30b). Once you have taken the step of faith and believe God's truth, you will come to see more clearly the future God has promised.

15

What Should
We Do?

What should our response be to the battle being waged today by Islam against both the history and heritage of the Temple Mount? For Muslims, it is incumbent upon them to discover the truth of the issues, such as that given by the Egyptian Muslim writer Ahmad Muhammad 'Arafa (see chapter 7). There is no historical or religious reason for accepting that Jerusalem has any original sanctity for Islam, that Muhammad made his Night Journey to this site, nor that the mosques subsequently built there were erected for other than political purposes. With this, the Muslim must consider the record of the Palestinian usurpation of Jordanian jurisdiction on the Temple Mount and the Palestinians' continued occupation of the site in order to further their own political ambitions. They must consider that since 1967 when Israel captured the Old City, they returned control of the site to Muslims and have protected and preserved Muslim religious demands at the site ever since—even to the point of arresting its own Jewish citizens who attempted to violate Islamic law by praying on the Temple Mount. In what Islamic country have Jewish rights been so regarded?

They must also consider the regard Jews have had toward the site since before the advent of Islam, the sacred concern they continue to exercise toward the site today, and the religious expectation they have of its being the center of their worship in the future.

For Jews and Christians, it is important to insist upon the historical accuracy of the *Tanach* (Jewish Scriptures) and the New Testament as a means of contending with Islamic propaganda and outright attacks on the factual basis of faith. Most of the major media will probably continue in their reports on the Middle East conflict to adopt a revisionist view of history and favor the Palestinian position by interpreting acts by the Israeli government and its military as acts of aggression and occupation, especially with respect to the Temple Mount. Jews and Christians alike are in an ideological war with Islam over the authority and truth of the Bible. Muslim denials of Jewish and Christian history, such as those surrounding the existence of the Jerusalem Temple, directly attack both the foundations of Jewish heritage and hope and the Christian gospel of the death, burial, and resurrection of Jesus. The only means to effectively countering such persuasive deception is with an understanding of the unchangeable grounds of the Jewish people's right to the Land of Israel—namely, the historical and unconditional covenants made by God with the Jewish people. For this understanding, the Scriptures must be known and made known, as Elwood McQuaid has charged:

> As Christians, we must be discerning and not allow the media or politicians to sway our commitment to Israel and the Jewish people despite the constant, dishonest, and manipulative depiction of Israel as the persecutors of helpless Arabs. Our defense of the integrity of the Word of God, both Old and New Testaments, is critical in these days of denial. We must be biblically literate discerners of the times and be prepared to fight the good fight in these last days.[1]

However, for Christians in particular there exists opposition within the Christian camp itself toward those who view the promises to the Jewish people as having abiding validity and who expect a literal fulfillment of redemption and restoration on a national scale. For example, a recent "Open Letter" issued by two covenant theologians promoting the position of Replacement Theology, called for "evangelicals and other interested parties" to reject such "false claims" that are "mislead[ing]" "large segments of the evangelical community, our fellow citizens, and our government…with respect to the Bible's teachings regarding the people of God, the land of Israel, and the impartiality of the Gospel."[2]

This "false teaching," the letter asserts, is in relation to "two fatally flawed propositions." The first being "that God's alleged favor toward Israel today is based upon ethnic descent," and the second growing from the first, or that "the Bible's promises concerning the land are fulfilled in a special political region or 'Holy Land,' perpetually set apart by God for one ethnic group alone." The letter then states, "Bad Christian theology regarding the 'Holy Land' contributed to the tragic cruelty of the Crusades in the Middle Ages…[and] is today attributing to Israel a divine mandate to conquer and hold Palestine, with the consequence that the Palestinian people are marginalized and regarded as virtual 'Canaanites.'" In keeping with what the covenant theologians consider to be theological error contributing to abuse in the political sphere, they offer this proposition concerning the Temple:

> Jesus taught that his resurrection was the raising of the True Temple of Israel He has replaced the priesthood, sacrifices, and sanctuary of Israel by fulfilling them in his own glorious priestly ministry and by offering, once and for all, his sacrifice for the world, that is, for both Jew and Gentile. Believers of all nations are now being built up through him into this Third Temple, the church that Jesus promised to build.[3]

The arguments presented here are too complex to be dealt with in this context,[4] however, they are sufficient to show that a segment of Christians radically disagrees with those Christians who believe in a future for ethnic Israel that is distinct from the church (as presented in chapter 1). Christians have unfortunately been divided among themselves while fighting the true enemy in spiritual warfare. Even so, it is critical in the face of such denials of the prophetic promises to Israel that each of us become more able students of the prophetic scriptures in order to discern and defend the truth and to maintain our responsibility in waging spiritual warfare to "pray for the peace of Jerusalem" (Psalm 122:6), the Israeli city to which our Savior, the Messiah of Israel, has promised to return to rebuild His Temple and reign (Zechariah 6:12-13; 8:3; 14:3, 9-11; cf. Matthew 19:28; 23:37-39; 25:31; Luke 21:27-28; Acts 1:6,11; 3:19-21).

The battle for the last days' Temple is escalating. And the call to battle is getting louder as the Middle East conflict moves closer to the Temple Mount. The near future holds conflict, compromise, and still greater conflict, but also the final conquest of the Temple Mount by the Lord, whose light will rise upon a restored Israel and to whose light the nations will come. As that battle intensifies in the days to come, may we remember that "the battle is the LORD's" (1 Samuel 17:47). As such, He and we (who are His) cannot fail to win the day.

> The battle is the Lord's!
> Not ours is strength or skill,
> But His alone, in sovereign grace,
> To work His will.
> Ours, counting not the cost,
> Unflinching to obey;
> And in His time His holy arm
> Shall win the day.[6]

Chronology of Battles over the Temple Mount

Part 1: The Temple in History

Pre-Temple Mount Conflicts

C. 1200 B.C. Tabernacle at Shiloh destroyed, Ark taken (Psalm 78:60-61; Jeremiah 7:12; 26:6; 1 Samuel 4:10-11, 22).

990 B.C. Divine destruction of Jerusalem averted. David purchases threshing floor of Araunah the Jebusite as site for the First Temple (2 Samuel 24:18-25; 1 Chronicles 21:18-26).

Conflicts During the First Temple

910 B.C. Temple treasures taken by Egyptian Pharaoh Shishak (1 Kings 14:25-28; 2 Chronicles 12:1-11).

826 B.C. Jehoash (Joash), king of Israel, attacks Judah, breaks down the walls of Jerusalem, and plunders the Temple, removing the Temple treasury to Samaria (2 Kings 14:13-14).

720 B.C. Ahaz closes Temple, empties Temple treasury, breaks up Temple furnishings and vessels to pay tribute to the Assyrian king Tiglath Pileser, and defiles Temple with a pagan Syrian altar (2 Kings 16:10-16, 2 Chronicles 28:21,24).

711 B.C. Hezekiah is forced to give up Temple treasuries and strip gold off Temple doors to pay tribute to the Assyrian king Sennacherib (2 Kings 18:15-16).

700 B.C. Hezekiah foolishly shows the treasures of the Temple treasury and of the king's house to Berodach-baladan, a prince of Babylon and his envoys—an act the prophet Isaiah predicted would lead to the eventual plunder of the Temple by the Babylonians (2 Kings 20:12-21; 2 Chronicles 32:31).

695-642 B.C. King Manasseh of Judah places idols within the Temple, including the Holy Place and the Holy of Holies. The Ark and the other Temple treasures were probably removed by the faithful Levites, whom Manasseh deposed, to prevent their defilement. Manasseh repents, but does not restore these treasures to the Temple (2 Kings 21:4-7; 2 Chronicles 7-9,15).

605 B.C.   Babylonian King Nebuchadnezzar pillages the Temple, taking articles and depositing them in the Babylonian temple at Shinar (2 Chronicles 36:7).

598–597 B.C.   King Nebuchadnezzar returns and further plunders the treasures of the Temple (2 Kings 24:13; 2 Chronicles 36:7).

586 B.C.   King Nebuchadnezzar invades Jerusalem a third time and destroys the Temple.

538 B.C.   Daniel receives prophecy of the defiling of the Second Temple by an "abomination that makes desolate" (Daniel 11:31).

Conflicts During the Second Temple

OCTOBER 11-12, 539 B.C.   Babylonian king Belshazzar desecrates Temple vessels at a pagan feast (Daniel 5:1-4) and Persian monarch Cyrus the Great conquers Babylon.

332 B.C.   Alexander the Great conquers Jerusalem but spares the Temple from destruction (*Ant.* xi. 392–339).

175–165 B.C.   Antiochus IV (Epiphanes), Seleucid king of Syria, pillages Temple; soldiers of Antiochus defile Temple; the king stops Jewish sacrifices and institutes worship of Olympian Zeus in Temple (1 Maccabees 1:10-63; 2 Maccabees 5:1–7:42).

67 B.C.   Aristobulus besieges Jerusalem and substitutes pig for sheep in attempt to end Temple sacrifices (which were stopped on the 17th of *Tammuz*). The result of this fratricidal war between Aristobulus and his brother Hyrcanus led to the intervention of Rome and the end of Jewish independence.

63 B.C.   The Roman emperor Pompey conquers Jerusalem and enters the Temple's Holy of Holies on horseback.

20 B.C.   The rabbis fear the Roman-appointed Judean king Herod is plotting the destruction of the Temple through a ruse to rebuild the structure. Herod's workmen totally dismantle the Temple of Zerubbabel; work continues on new Temple until c. A.D. 64 (Matthew 24:1; Mark 13:1; Luke 21:5; John 2:20).

A.D. 33   Jesus predicts destruction of Second Temple (Matthew 23:37-38; 24:2; Mark 13:2; Luke 21:6,20-24).

A.D. 40   Roman emperor Caligula fails in his attempt to defile Temple by erecting a statue of himself.

A.D. 70   Roman general Titus destroys Second (Herodian) Temple and carries off Temple vessels to Rome to be paraded before his father, Emperor Vespasian.

Post-Temple Conflicts

A.D. 132–135   Roman emperor Publius Aelius Hadrianus reneges on Temple pledge to Jews and sparks Bar Kokhba rebellion. Hadrian retakes Jerusalem after three years and desecrates the Temple Mount by erecting an equestrian statue of himself at site of the Holy of Holies. He later constructs on the Temple Mount a Roman pagan temple of Jupiter.

A.D. 135   Tinneis (Turnus) Rufus, Roman governor of Judea, plows up the site of the Temple Mount on the Ninth of *Av* (*Tisha B'Av*) to signify the utter destruction of the Jewish city and signal the change of Jerusalem into the Roman colony *Aelia Capitolina.*

A.D. 363   Pagan emperor Julian (the Apostate) allows Jews to attempt rebuilding of Temple to counter Byzantine Christianity; effort fails as earthquake destroys building materials stored in Solomon's Stables.

A.D. 638   Muslims conquer Jerusalem and Caliph Omar Ibn el-Khattab is shown Temple Mount and site of Temple (Rock) by Jerusalem patriarch Sophronius.

A.D. 691   Caliph 'Abd al-Malik Ibn-Marwan erects Dome of the Rock on the Temple Mount.

A.D. 715   The Muslim caliph al-Walid completes the Al-Aqsa Mosque on the site of a Byzantine church (on southern portion of Temple Mount). This is the Al Aqsa *el-Qadimeh* underneath the present structure.

A.D. 940   The Karaite writer, Solomon Ben-Yerucham, writes about a synagogue on the southern side of the Temple Mount and the arguments between the rabbis and Karaites that caused the Jews to lose their foothold on the Mount.

A.D. 1099–1118   Crusaders capture Jerusalem after bloody battle and transform Muslim Dome of the Rock into Christian church (*Templum Domini*, "the Temple of the Lord") and the Al-Aqsa Mosque into headquarters of the Order of the Knights Templar.

A.D. 1165   The Rambam visits Jerusalem and prays on the Temple Mount.

A.D. 1187   The Muslim caliph Saladin recaptures Jerusalem from the Crusaders and restores the *Templum Domini* and the Al-Aqsa to the status of mosques.

A.D. 1845   Crimean War (Turkey, France, England, Russia), fought to resolve guardianship of Jerusalem's holy places (especially the Temple Mount).

Conflicts in the Modern Period

1917–1947   Jerusalem is conquered by British; continual struggles and riots between Arabs and Jews over access and control of Western Wall of Temple Mount.

MAY 14, 1948   Israeli independence granted and country invaded by Arab armies; both Dome of the Rock and Al-Aqsa Mosque are damaged by bombs during the war.

MAY 25, 1948   The Old City falls to the Jordanians and Jews are forbidden access to the Western Wall of the Temple Mount for the next 18 years. Jordan destroys 58 synagogues in the Jewish Quarter.

1951   King Abdullah of Transjordan is assassinated at the Al-Aqsa Mosque.

JUNE 7, 1967   Israel, in the Six-Day War, liberates the Temple Mount and places an Israeli flag on top of the Dome of the Rock to signify Israeli sovereignty over the Temple Mount. However, Defense Minister Moshe Dayan orders the flag removed to avoid provocation.

JUNE 17, 1967   Moshe Dayan meets with leaders of the Supreme Moslem Council in Al-Aqsa Mosque and returns control of the Temple Mount to the Waqf as a gesture of peace; Muslims agree to Jews visiting the site, but Jews are forbidden to conduct prayers or religious activities.

AUGUST 16, 1967   Israel Defense chaplain Rabbi Shlomo Goren leads group to pray on Temple Mount, causing Muslim protest to the Israeli government.

DECEMBER 19, 1968   Prayers are offered on the Temple Mount at Hanukkah by nationalistic Jewish group.

APRIL 15, 1969   The Temple Mount Faithful file legal action against police minister Shlomo Hillel to allow Jewish prayer services on Temple Mount; refused on basis of national security and political concerns.

AUGUST 23, 1969   Australian tourist Denis Michael Rohan sets fire to the Al-Aqsa Mosque; Muslim officials accuse Israel of deliberately setting the blaze in order to rebuild the Temple.

AUGUST 27, 1969   Waqf closes the Temple Mount to all non-Muslims for two months.

MARCH 11, 1971   Gershon Salomon, leader of Temple Mount Faithful, leads group of students to pray on Temple Mount; results in minor disruption.

JANUARY 30, 1976   Lower Court (magistrate) acquits Betar youths arrested for holding prayer service on Mount and effects ruling that Jews are permitted to pray on the Temple Mount.

FEBRUARY 9-23, 1976   Arab East Jerusalem schools protest the court ruling; Arab shops close in strike; riots in West Bank result in over 100 arrests.

MARCH 11, 1976   Muslim councils in Ramallah, El Bireh, and Nablus protest police action against Arabs who demonstrated in response to the court ruling permitting Jewish prayers on the Temple Mount, and ruling is overturned (**MARCH 17**) by district court but upholds the historical and legal right of Jews to pray on the Temple Mount if the Ministry of Religious Affairs can regulate such activity and maintain public order.

MARCH 25, 1979   Rumors that Meir Kahane and Yeshiva students would hold prayer service on Temple Mount provokes a general strike among West Bank Arabs; 2,000 Arab youths brandishing stones and staves riot at Temple Mount and struggle with Israeli police.

AUGUST 10, 1980   Ultra-right activist group, *Gush Emunim* ("Bloc of the Faithful"), with 300 supporters, attempt to force their way onto the Temple Mount and are dispersed by police.

SEPTEMBER 2-10, 1981   Yeshivah students of Rabbi Getz break down Arab wall erected to prevent Jews from getting into the area under the Temple Mount that was excavated by Rabbi Getz and Shlomo Goren when in search of the Ark of the Covenant; Arabs clash with Jewish students and police intervene, and ancient gate entrance to the area is sealed in response to threats from the Waqf.

APRIL 11, 1982   Alan Goodman, an American immigrant in the Israeli army, opens fire on the Temple Mount "to liberate the spot holy to the Jews." The incident sets off week-long Arab riots in Jerusalem, the West Bank, and Gaza, and draws international criticism against Israel.

APRIL 25, 1982   Kach party member Yoel Learner attempts to sabotage a mosque on the Temple Mount. He is arrested and later sentenced to two-and-one-half years in prison.

DECEMBER 9, 1982   Geula Cohen, a member of Israel's Knesset, raises the charge that Muslim Arabs have caches of ammunition sequestered on the Temple Mount.

MARCH 10, 1983   Rabbi Israel Ariel and a group of more than 40 followers, planning to pray on the Temple Mount (via the Solomon's Stables, adjacent to the Al-Aqsa Mosque), are caught breaking into the area. Weapons and diagrams of the Temple Mount are recovered in a police search, and numerous arrests are made.

JANUARY 27, 1984   Temple activists are arrested for attempting to "attack" the Temple Mount.

JANUARY 8, 1986   Several members of the Knesset, led by Geula Cohen, seek to hold a prayer service in the Temple area. The incident provokes a riot and an altercation with Arabs on the Temple Mount.

OCTOBER 16, 1989   Gershon Salomon, with Yehoshua Cohen dressed in priestly garments and with members of the Temple Mount Faithful, attempt to lay a cornerstone for the Third Temple at the entrance to the Temple.

OCTOBER 8, 1990   Second attempt by the Temple Mount Faithful to lay a cornerstone for the Third Temple provokes a riot on the Temple Mount. At the Western Wall, where more than 20,000 Jews are assembled for Feast of Tabernacle services, 3,000 Palestinians pelt the Jewish crowd with stones from above and Israeli police intervene, killing 17 Arabs. Saddam Hussein uses incident to call for *jihad* against Israel and fires Scud missiles at Israel.

OCTOBER 31, 1991   At the Middle East peace conference in Madrid, Spain, Syrian foreign minister Farouk Al-Shara accuses Israel of attempting to blow up the Al-Aqsa Mosque and proclaims there will be no free access to the religious sites on the Temple Mount unless Israel returns all of East Jerusalem to the Arabs.

SEPTEMBER 25, 1995   Temple Mount riot occurs when Israeli government opens an exit tunnel to the Hasmonean aqueduct at the end of the Western Wall Tunnel, and 58 deaths result in Jerusalem and the territories.

SEPTEMBER 1997   Israeli Orthodox Jew Yehuda Etzion is arrested for attempt to pray on the Temple Mount; appeals to Supreme Court, which upholds his right (and Jewish right) of access to the Temple Mount for worship. However, attempts by his organization, Chai VeKayam, continue to be rebuffed by police fearing Arab riots.

MAY 14, 1998   Arsonist throws firebomb at wooden gate leading to Temple Mount.

NOVEMBER 14, 1998   PLO chief Yasser Arafat threatens war if Palestinians are prevented from praying in Jerusalem. At the same time, the Palestinian mufti prevents Jews from praying on the Temple Mount.

SEPTEMBER 1999   Islamic construction within underground remains of the Second Temple-period Huldah Gates to build new mosque within Solomon's Stables is reported to have illegally excavated and destroyed archaeological artifacts. Archaeologists and other officials are prohibited from inspecting the damage and debris.

DECEMBER 1999   Palestinian mufti Ikrima Sabri moves his office onto the Temple Mount, stating that the area is only for Islam.

SEPTEMBER 28-29, 2000   Likud leader Ariel Sharon, accompanied by Knesset members and security guards, visits the Temple Mount to investigate reports of destructive activity and of illegal construction by the Waqf. In response, riots break out the next day and are used as a justification by Yasser Arafat for renewing the intifada, now called the Al-Aqsa Intifada because of the focus on gaining Palestinian Muslim sovereignty over the Temple Mount.

OCTOBER 2000   Waqf issues a ban on Jewish entrance to the Temple Mount and Israeli government extends closure to tourists. The Waqf continues construction of new mosques on Temple Mount and maintains ban for the next three years.

APRIL 2002   Waqf begins repairs on bulge in southern wall of the Temple Mount—a bulge caused by the construction work done to build the al-Marawani Mosque. Israeli authorities stop the repair work on the bulge, which is on Israel's side of the wall, fearing that improper repair techniques will hasten the collapse of the wall and Israel will be blamed and a conflict will ensue. Eventually, a Jordanian team undertakes the restoration work.

AUGUST/SEPTEMBER 2003   Israeli government ends closure of Temple Mount to Jews and other tourists. Yasser Arafat and the Waqf protest the move. Access is still denied to the Dome of the Rock and the Al-Aqsa Mosque.

SEPTEMBER 23, 2003   A wall in an Islamic museum near the Al-Aqsa Mosque collapses on the Temple Mount, leading to fears that more structures may collapse, leading to extensive destruction and increased conflict between Israelis and Palestinians.

NOVEMBER 2003   Muslim authorities complain that some of the Jewish groups entering the Temple Mount have attempted to pray. Police arrest violators, but Yasser Arafat and Mufti Ikrima Sabri declare Israel's permitting Jewish visitation a crime against Muslims and insist that the site is strictly for Muslims. Palestinians stone Jews praying at the Western Wall after a sermon at the Al-Aqsa Mosque calls for the Jews to be stopped from defiling the mosques.

JANUARY 2004   Plans are announced by the Israeli Western Jerusalem Development Company to soon begin construction on an underground tunnel to stretch from the Western Wall Tunnel to the Silwan area in the south. The purpose of the tunnel is to protect Jews from violence against them at the site. Muslim authorities contend this is an Israeli government plot to cause the collapse of the mosques on the Temple Mount so that the Temple can be rebuilt.

Part 2: The Temple in Prophecy

A massive invasion of nations to the north of Israel, called by Ezekiel "Gog of Magog," allied with other enemies of Israel, attempts to plunder the country and is destroyed as a result of divine intervention. The results of this war may lead to the Antichrist making a covenant with the leaders of Israel.

The Jewish Temple is rebuilt in Jerusalem, perhaps as a part of the provisions of the covenant made with the Antichrist—a covenant predicted in Daniel 9:27.

The Antichrist breaks his covenant with Israel by desecrating the Temple and stopping the sacrificial system (Matthew 24:15; Mark 13:14; 2 Thessalonians 2:4).

The Antichrist invades Jerusalem and tramples the Temple Mount, making the city his military headquarters (Daniel 11:40-48; Isaiah 28:14-22; Revelation 11:1-2). During this time the abomination of desolation occurs in the Temple (Daniel 9:27; 12:11; Matthew 24:15-16; 2 Thessalonians 2:3-4, 8-12; Revelation 13:11-15), and the Antichrist forces his godless worship on Jerusalem and the world (Daniel 11:36-39; Revelation 13:1-18), perhaps making the Temple Mount his religious center.

The Two Witnesses don sackcloth to mourn for the Temple's desecration and then remain to oppose the Antichrist's persecution of Jews in Jerusalem and permit the remnant to flee (Revelation 11:3-6).

The Antichrist will move against Jerusalem to destroy the Jews (Zechariah 12:1-3; 14:1). Briefly, Jewish forces will control the city (Zechariah 12:4-9; Micah 4:11–5:1), possibly with the help of the Two Witnesses. But ultimately, half the city will be taken (Zechariah 14:2) and the Two Witnesses will be killed and their bodies put on display in the streets of Jerusalem (Revelation 11:7-10). A Jewish remnant apparently occupies the eastern part of the city, along with the Temple Mount.

The Messiah appears and defends the remnant of Jerusalem in the battle for Jerusalem (Malachi 3:1; Isaiah 37:32,35; Zechariah 12:4,9; 14:2; Revelation 19:11-21). He will triumphantly descend onto the Mount of Olives (Zechariah 14:3), and a great earthquake will split Jerusalem, creating a valley leading from the Temple Mount to the desert—a valley through which the Jews will flee to safety (Joel 3:14-17; Zechariah 14:4-5; Revelation 16:18-19).

At the end of the Millennium, the Temple Mount will be attacked a final time by Satan and a multitude of rebellious nations (Revelation 20:6-9).

Notes

A Word from the Author

1. J. Randall Price, *The Desecration and Restoration of the Temple as an Eschatological Motif in the Tanak, Jewish Apocalyptic Literature, and the New Testament* (Ann Arbor, MI: VMI, 1994).

2. See chapter 14: "Historical Problems with Preterism's Interpretation of Events in A.D. 70" and chapter 15: "Historical Problems with a First-Century Fulfillment of the Olivet Discourse," Tim LaHaye and Thomas Ice, eds., *The End Times Controversy: The Second Coming Under Attack* (Harvest House Publishers, 2003), pp. 355, 377.

3. *The Coming Last Days Temple*, filmed in Israel, is a 60-minute documentary available in both video (NTSC or PAL format) and DVD and can be ordered for $19.99 plus $3.95 shipping & handling from World of the Bible Ministries, Inc., P.O. Box 827, San Marcos, TX 78667-0827 or at http://www.worldofthebible.com.

4. See Timothy P. Weber, *On the Road to Armageddon: How Evangelicals Became Israel's Best Friend* (Grand Rapids: Baker Book House, 2004) and Stephen R. Sizer, "Whose Promised Land: Israel and Biblical Prophecy Debate between Neil Cornell (CMJ & ITAC) and Stephen Sizer," Guildford Diocesan Evangelical Fellowship St. John's, Woking (Surrey, March 18, 1997).

5. Barry Chamash, *Save Israel!* (Modiin, Israel: Modiin House, 2002), p. 153. Mr. Chamash is an Israeli author and contributor of articles on the Internet. His first book, *Who Murdered Yitzhak Rabin?* was also a conspiracy piece. His thesis in *Save Israel!* is that many of Israel's leaders are willing players in an international plot against their country. In naming "Christian fundamentalist leaders" to this plot (the list in which I appear), especially those who support Israel and write concerning God's promised future for Israel, it is my opinion that Mr. Chamash has misunderstood not only our intentions but has become too obsessed with the conspiratorial view, finding enemies where he should find friends.

Introduction—The Focal Point of the Battle

1. Gershon Gorenberg, *The End of Days: Fundamentalism and the Struggle for the Temple Mount* (New York: The Free Press, 2000) [ ].

2. Reported in the Egyptian newspaper *al-Shaab* and cited in Aviel Schneider, "Jihad for Jerusalem," *Israel Today* (March 2003): 11.

3. As reported in Haim Shapiro, "Poll: 53% of Israelis want a Third Temple," *Jerusalem Post*, July 18, 2003.

4. *Internet Jerusalem Post* homepage (www.jpost.com), July 7, 2003.

5. As provided by Ammon Ramon of the Institute for Israel Studies and reported by Aaron Lerner, "Most Jews want Jewish Prayer on Temple Mount Permitted," *Institute for Middle East Reporting Agency* (imra@netvision.net.il), July 24, 1997.

6. Yossi Lein Halevi, Special Report: "The Battle for the Temple Mount," *The Jerusalem Report* (October 3, 1996).

7. As cited in story "Secular Jews for the Temple," posted on the Web site of the Temple Mount Faithful Movement (http://www.templemountfaithful.org).

8. James Bennet, "Jerusalem Holy Site a Tense Crossroads Again," *New York Times* (August 29, 2003).

Chapter 1—The Precepts of Prophecy

1. Interview with the Honorable Benjamin Elon (Jerusalem, August 19, 2003).

2. Rob Richards, *Has God Finished with Israel?* (Milton Keynes: Authentic Publishing, 2000), p. 103.

3. Accusations that the actions of fundamentalists (Jewish, Muslim, and Christian), including myself, with respect to the Temple Mount would bring about self-fulfilling prophecies were made by *Jerusalem Report* journalist Gershon Gorenberg, *The End of Days: Fundamentalists and the Struggle for the Temple Mount* (New York: The Free Press, a division of Simon & Schuster, Inc., 2000).

4. The "unbelief," from an Orthodox Jewish perspective, is that the regathering was a secular rather than spiritual return. From a Christian and messianic perspective, it is the possession of an unrepentant heart toward Yeshua as Messiah (see Acts 3:17-26).

Chapter 2—Temple 101

1. The Hebrew word *hekal* is derived from the root *ykl* or *kwl*, which has the basic meaning "to contain," cf. Brown, Driver and Briggs, *Hebrew-English Lexicon of the Old Testament*, s.v. "hekal," p. 228. For further definition of the term see W. B. Kristensen, *The Meaning of Religion* (The Hague: Martinus Nijhoff, 1960), p. 369. If the literal idea of the root is retained in the noun (*hekal*), it has been proposed that the term may connote the idea of the Temple as a "container" for the name of God, cf. Lorne Meisner, "The Temple Motif: God's Witness Unto Himself" (Th.M. thesis, Dallas Theological Seminary), p. 4.

2. In its most general sense, *hekal* sometimes was used to refer to a royal palace (1 Kings 21:1; 2 Chronicles 36:7), although its primary reference is to the "house of God." The more general word for "palace" is *'armon*, which signifies a *fortified* part of the royal complex (1 Kings 16:18; 2 Kings 15:25), but is never used with reference to the Temple. Cf. Menaham Haran, *Temples and Temple Service in Ancient Israel* (Oxford: Clarendon Press, 1978), p. 13.

3. Cf. Anton Deimel, "Erdaufschuttung, "*Sumerisch-Akkadisches Glossar Sumer-isches Lexikon* (Rome: Verlag Des Papstl. Bibelinstituts, 1934) 3/1, p. 206.

4. Liddell & Scott, *A Greek Lexicon*, p. 1774. Refers specifically to a clearly marked area where a theophany once occurred and was again expected on the ground of tradition. Usually, it is a place distinguished by nature, e.g., the grotto of Zeus on Crete, the rock cleft at Delphi, or the holy grove at Olympia.

5. Haran concludes that the expression "arises from the basic concept of a divine residence and expresses the inherent, intrinsic nature of the institution, which primarily was conceived of as the god's dwelling place." "Temples and Cultic Open Areas as Reflected in the Bible," *Temples and High Places in Biblical Times* (Jerusalem: The Nelson Glueck School of Biblical Archaeology of Hebrew Union College—Jewish Institute of Religion, 1977), p. 31.

6. The Hebrew term *mishkanot* (rendered in the English versions "tent," "dwellings") is used once in connection with shepherds (Song of Songs 1:8), and generally describes the dwellings of nomadic groups (Judges 6:3-5; cf. Ezekiel 25:4). The term is used in biblical poetry in parallelism with *'ohel* ("tent") Numbers 24:5; Isaiah 54:2; Jeremiah 30:18; Psalm 78:60; cf. Job 21:28), and also in the Ugaritic texts (though here as mythological residences of the gods, cf. 2 Aqht v. 31-3); C. H. Gordon, *Ugaritic Textbook* (Rome, 1965), p. 128, and Y. Avishur, *Semitics* [Pretoria] 2 (1971-2), pp. 19-20. Hillers has discovered the word *miskana'* in the Aramaic inscriptions of Hatra, D. R. Hillers, *Bulletin of the American Schools of Oriental Research* 206 (1972): 54-56; however, as Haran points out, *Temples and Temple Service*, p. 196, n. 12, its meaning in these inscriptions appears to be "abode," or "dwelling place," rather than "tabernacle," or even "shrine."

7. The modern term apparently developed from the Mishnaic *beit miqdash* ("house of holiness"), the common phrase for the Temple, which has one biblical occurrence in 2 Chronicles 36:17.

8. The noun *miqdash* is not used exclusively of a temple, but also of any article or object possessing sanctity (e.g., the tithe, Numbers 18:29).

9. For example, Homeric usage in *Iliad* 1, 39; Odessey 6, 10; 12, 346.

10. Moulton and Milligan, *The Vocabulary of the New Testament and Literary Papyri*, suggest that Koine Greek, following classical usage, may have distinguished between the use of *heiron* (neuter of *heiron*, "holy [place]," used as a noun) and *naos*. The former may have had a wider and more general use, with reference to the entire edifice (i.e., the Temple complex with all of its courts), while the latter may have been restricted to the most sacred part of the Sanctuary (i.e., the *Devir*)—see Moulton and Milligan, *The Vocabulary of the New Testament and Literary Papyri*, s.v. "naov," p. 422. This distinction may hold true for the New Testament, since the older term for the site of a "temple," which is "temenov," is not used—cf. Otto Michel, *Theological Dictionary of the New Testament* 4, s.v. "naov," p. 887. One example usually cited for support is Matthew 27:5, where *naov* apparently refers to the Holy of the Holies. However, this distinction is contested, since in other instances the two terms appear to be used interchangeably; e.g., John 2:20, where *naos* is here apparently used of the entire Temple—cf. Bauer, Ardnt, Gingrich, and Danker, *Greek-English Lexicon of the New Testament*, s.v. "naov," p. 300.

11. See W. von Meding, *New International Dictionary of New Testament Theology*, s.v. " naov," p. 783.

12. While *naos* can sometimes refer to both the Temple complex and the inner sanctuary, it generally bears a technical distinction from *heiros*, which always appears to denote the general structure. The 45 occurrences of *naos* in the New Testament are divided among the historical books (nine times in Matthew; three in Mark; four in Luke; three John; two in Acts), the Pauline corpus (four times in 2 Corinthians; two in 2 Corinthians; once each in Ephesians and 2 Thessalonians), and the Apocalypse (16 times in Revelation). For further discussion on this distinction, cf. Bauer, Arndt, Gingrich and Danker, *Greek-English Lexicon of the New Testament*, (1979), pp. 373.2, 535.1a; *Exegetical Dictionary of the New Testament*, s.v. "naov," by U. Borse, p. 457, and A. T. Robertson, *Word Pictures in the New Testament* (Nashville: Broadman Press, 1932), 4:377; 5:38.

13. Note especially in Revelation 11:1-2 that the Temple is referred to as *ton naon tou theou*, and then in the next part of the verse reference is made to *ten aulen ten exothen tou naou* ("the court which is outside the Temple") as something separate. This outer precinct was thus *outside* the *naos*, but still *within* the *heiros*, indicating the specificity given to the terms.

14. Some English versions may use the translation "shrine," or "sanctuary," to distinguish pagan cultic installations.

Chapter 3—The Purpose of the Temple

1. Shaye J. D. Cohen, *From the Maccabees to the Mishna*, Library of Early Christianity, ed. Wayne A. Meeks (Philadelphia: The Westminster Press, 1987), p. 106.

2. Ephraim E. Urbach, *The Sages: Their Concepts and Beliefs*, transl. Israel Ahrah uis, 2 vols. (Jerusalem: Magnes Press, 1975) 1: 50.

3. Cf. R. E. Clements, *God and Temple* (Oxfd. Basil Blackwell, 1965), pp. 63-78 (esp. 71, 83).

4. Cf. the brief discussion of this concept in Lucius Nereparampil, "Biblical Symbolism of the Templ," *Journal of Dharma* 9:2 (April-June, 1984), pp. 164-66.

5. The reason for the specificity of Deuteronomy 12:9, the first such use of the Hebrew term *haminuchah* with a definite article, is that in Numbers 10:33, *minuchah* had described the *temporary* "resting places" where Israel was to camp during their wilderness sojourn, but with entrance to the Promised Land in view (Deuteronomy 12:10), *haminuchah*, a *permanent* resting place, is envisioned—i.e. a divine, God-given "rest."

6. Note in 1 Chronicles 22:9 that Solomon, before his birth, was appointed as a man of *minuchah* ("rest"), which in this text apparently parallels the bestowal of his name (cf. *shalom*, "peace"). The very next verse (verse 10) predicts Solomon's task as Temple-builder for the Lord's "name," thus making the connection mentioned in the two passages discussed above.

7. For references to "rest" during the time of the conquest/judges, cf. Joshua 21:43-45; 22:4-5; 23:1; Nehemiah 1:26-28. Second Samuel 7:10-11 cites the first promise of a central sanctuary made to Moses in Exodus 25:9, mentioning the temporary rest experienced during the period of the judges, and then linking the whole promise to fulfillment in the house of David. David appears to have believed this rest was experienced in part during his reign (1 Chronicles 23:25-26), and Solomon recognized it as existing during his time with relation to the Temple (1 Kings 5:18 [5:4 in English]). Rest is also mentioned during the period of the monarchy during the reigns of Asa (2 Chronicles 14:4-6 [14:5-7 in English]; 15:15), Jehoshaphat (2 Chronicles 20:29-30), and Hezekiah (2 Chronicles 31:10).

8. Such a loss of rest was predicted in Deuteronomy 28:65 as a result of covenant unfaithfulness (cf. Psalm 95:10-11; Micah 2:7,10).

9. *Jerusalem to Jabneh: The Period of the Mishna and its Literature* (Ramat-Aviv: Everyman's University, 1980), Unit I.3, p. 15.

10. Mishna *Avodah Zarah* 8b and *Sanhedrin* 14b (the ruling is based on Deuteronomy 17:8).

11. All legal matters were decided by the Sanhedrin, who had their full prerogatives of office only when seated in the Temple, and only when the sacrificial system was operational.

12. Cf. for additional discussion on this concept, Jon. Levenson, "The Jerusalem Temple in Devotional and Visionary Experience," *Jewish Spirituality 1: From the Bible through the Middle Ages*, ed. Arthur Green (New York: Crossroad Publishing Co., 1988), pp. 53-57.

13. Cf. TP, *Berakot* 4, 5; cf. *Tosefta Berakot* 3, 15; *Pesiqta Rabbati* 149b.

14. TP, *Berakot* 4, 5.

15. While only a speculation, it may be that for a similar reason sacrifice was acceptable on the barren foundation stone within the Second Temple. Perhaps also because the Ark of the Covenant was thought to be buried in a hidden chamber directly below the Pen of Wood, and therefore directly below the Holy of Holies (cf. *Shekalim* 6:1-2), it thereby transferred sanctity to the region above, aligned with the true Ark in the heavenly Holy of Holies.

16. Cf. R. Aha, *Tanhuma*, Exodus; *Exodus Rabbah* 2,2; *Midrash*, Psalms 11, 3.

Chapter 4—Ancient Battles for the Temple Mount

1. For the published report of the Channel 2 interview, see Etgar Lefkovits, "Likud MKs who want to ascend Temple Mount flunk history quiz," *Jerusalem Post* (August 7, 2003): 4.

2. As cited in *The Jerusalem Temple: A Summary of its Site, Structure, Service, and Abuse* (http://www.users.iafrica.com/I/II/lloyd/1-IsraelTimeLine/temple.htm): 4.

3. Tacitus, *Historiae* 5, 9: 1.

4. R.M. Smallwood, *The Jews under Roman Rule: From Pompey to Diocletian* (Leiden: E.J. Brill, 1976), pp. 434-36.

5. Rabbi Leibel Reznick, *The Mystery of Bar Kokhba: An Historical and Theological Investigation of the Last King of the Jews* (New Jersey: Jason Aronson Inc., 1996).

6. *Paschal Chronicle* P.G. 92, 613; cf. also Benjamin Mazar, *The Mountain of the Lord* (New York: Doubleday & Co., 1975), p. 236.

7. Dio Cassius, *Roman History*, lxix: 12.

8. Philip C. Hammond, "New Light on the Nabateans," *Biblical Archaeology Review* (March/April, 1981), p. 23.

9. Ammianus Marcellinus in *Ammianus Marcellinus*, trans. John C. Rolfe (London: William Heinemann, 1939), 2: 23.1,3.

Chapter 5—Modern Battles for the Temple Mount

1. For more details on the Mufti's Nazi connection, see Joseph B. Schechtman, *The Mufti and the Füehrer: The Story of the Grand Mufti of Jerusalem and His Unholy Alliance with Nazism* (New York: Thomas Yoseyoss, 1965).

2. Treaty of Peace between the State of Israel and the Hashemite Kingdom of Jordan, October 26, 1994 (http://www.mfa.gov.il/mfa/go.asp?MFAH00pa0).

3. Hussein's forfeiture of the guardianship of the Al-Aqsa Mosque and the Dome of the Rock was a significant blow to him.

4. Abraham Rabinovitch, "Making History Happen," *Jerusalem Post International Edition* (July 29, 1995): 21.

5. Mordecai Gur, *The Temple Mount Is in Our Hands* (Tel-Aviv: Defense Ministry Publishing House, 1968) as cited in Abraham E. Millgram, *Jerusalem Curiosities* (Philadelphia: The Jewish Publication Society, 1990), p. 291.

6. As cited by Martin Gilbert, *Jerusalem in the Twentieth Century* (New York: John Wiley & Sons, Inc., 1996), p. 287.

7. Ehud Sprinzak, *The Ascendance of Israel's Radical Right* (New York: Oxford University Press, 1991), p. 279.

8. For details, see *In Search of Temple Treasures* (Eugene, OR: Harvest House Publishers, 1994) and interviews with rabbis Goren and Getz on the companion video documentary of the same name. Both items are available from World of the Bible Ministries, Inc., P.O. Box 827, San Marcos, TX 78667-0827 or from http://www.worldofthebible.com.

9. See "Rabbi Wants to Destroy Mosque, Wanted Mosque Leveled," *Ha'aretz* (December 31, 1997).

10. For my discussion of the content of these speeches with respect to Jerusalem and the Temple Mount, see *Jerusalem in Prophecy: God's Stage for the Final Drama* (Eugene, OR: Harvest House, 1998), pp. 145-47, 164, 278-79, 338-39.

11. See Joshua Brilliant, "Arsonist Targets Jerusalem Temple Mount," *Arutz Sheva* news service (Friday, May 15, 1998).

12. See "Damage to Temple Mount 'Under Discussion'," *Arutz Sheva* news service (Wednesday, May 26, 1999), pp. 1-3.

13. Cited in Arutz 7 News, Sunday, October 13, 1996.

14. As cited in *Artifax* (Winter 1999): 8.

Chapter 6—Muslims on the Mount

1. As cited in Aref el-Aref, *Al Mufassal fi Tarikh al-Quds* (Jerusalem, 1961).

2. Emanuel A. Winston, "The Imminent Collapse of the Jewish Temple Mount," *Tzemach* news service (March 11, 2002): 4.

3. Paul Fregosi, *Jihad in the West: Muslim Conquerors from the 7th to the 21st Centuries* (New York: Prometheus Books, 1998), p. 67.

4. On this identification see al-Waqidi, *Kitab al-Maghazi* (Oxford: Oxford University Press, 1966), 3: 958-59. For discussion on the location and the political basis for the construction see Mordechai Kedar, "How Did Jerusalem Come to Be So Holy to the Moslems?," Department of Arabic Studies, Bar-Ilan University, Ramat Gan, Israel. Published online and cited in Richard Benkin, "The Modern Destruction of the Temple Mount, May 2003 (http://www.antiantisemitism@comcast.net).

5. Shlomo Dov Goitein, "The Historical Background of the Erection of the Dome of the Rock," Journal of the American Oriental Society 70:2 (April-June, 1950), p. 107.

6. Ya'qubi (writing in A.D. 874) in G. Le Strange, *Palestine Under the Moslems,* reprint of the 1890 edition (Beirut: Khayats, 1965), p. 116. While repeated by later Muslim authors and accepted by most Western historians, the account suffers by virtue of the fact that no other contemporary historians are aware of Ya'qubi's story, but instead offer entirely different explanations.

7. See I. Goldziher, *Muslim Studies II* (1890): 44-45.

8. See S.D. Goitein, "The Sanctity of Jerusalem and Palestine in Early Islam," *Studies in Islamic History and Institutions* (Leiden: E.J. Brill, 1966): 135-37.

9. See Ahmad Muhammad 'Arafa, *Al-Qahira* (Egyptian Ministry of Culture, August 19, 2003).

10. Emanuel A. Winston, "The Imminent Collapse of the Jewish Temple Mount," *Tzemach* news service (March 11, 2002): 4.

11. Miriam Ayalon, "Islamic Monuments In Jerusalem," in *Jerusalem: City of the Ages,* p. 82.

12. *Al-Muqaddasi: Description of Syria, including Palestine,* translated from the Arabic and annotated by G. Le Strange, Palestine Pilgrims Text Society 3, reprint of 1896 edition (New York: AMS Press, 1971), pp. 22-23, as cited in F.E. Peters, *Jerusalem,* p. 198.

13. As cited in Moseh Gill, "The Political History of Jerusalem During the Early Muslim Period," in Joshua Prawer and Haggai Ben-Shammai, eds., *The History of Jerusalem: The Early Muslim Period,* 638–1099 (New York: New York University Press, 1996): 7.

14. Ibid.

15. Ibid, p. 13.

16. Berel Wein, "The 'Two' Jerusalems," *Jerusalem Post* (www.jpost.com), May 29, 2003, p. 1.

Chapter 7—Islamic Revisionist History and the Temple Mount

1. A Gallup Poll of 9924 adults throughout the Muslim world conducted during December 2001 and January 2002 revealed that a majority believed this historical lie. See Andrea Stone, "In poll, Islamic world says Arabs not involved in 9/11," *USA Today,* February 2003 (cover story).

2. Ronald S. Hendel, "Was There a Temple in Jerusalem? Wartime reports from Jerusalem mask the truth," *Bible Review* 6:5 (October 2003): 8.

3. As cited in Charles Enderlin, *Shattered Dreams: The Failure of the Peace Process in the Middle East, 1995–2002,* reviewed in *New York Times Book Review* (May 4, 2003): 11.

4. Sermon in the mosque (the most important in Mecca), April 2002.

5. Aired on Palestinian television November 3, 2000.

6. As cited by Professor Huston Smith in his introduction to Cyril Glasse, *The Concise Encyclopedia of Islam* (San Francisco: Harper & Row Publishers, Inc., 1989), p. 5.

7. Ibid.

8. Altaf Ahmed Kherie, *Islam: A Comprehensive Guide-Book* (Pakistan, 1993), p. 28.

9. Ibid, p. 29.

10. Emanuel A. Winston, "The Imminent Collapse of the Jewish Temple Mount," *Tzemach* news service (March 11, 2002): 4.

11. Stated in an interview in January 2000 with the German paper *Die Welt* and reported in *Jerusalem Post* (January 26, 2000).

12. As cited in *The Jerusalem Report* (December 16, 1993).

13. *Independent Media Review and Analysis,* December 25, 1996.

14. Yasser Arafat, speech to the Organization of Islamic Conference Summit in Teheran, Iran, December 9, 1997.

15. Interview with Jeries Soudah by Irwin Baxter, "Arafat and Jerusalem from a Palestinian Perspective," *Endtimes* magazine 7:5 (September/October 1997), pp. 9-10.

16. PA information ministry press release, December 10, 1997.

17. Interview by Etgar Lefkovits, "Mufti again denies Wall's Jewish link," February 21, 2001.

18. *Ma'ariv,* October 11, 1996.

19. *Independent Media Review and Analysis,* November 23, 1997.

20. As cited by Jeffrey Goldberg, "Israel's Y2K Problem," *The New York Times Magazine* (October 3, 1999): 52.

21. As cited in *Unholy War* (Eugene, OR: Harvest House Publishers, 2001), p. 263.

22. Interview with Ikrima Sabri, office of the grand mufti, Jerusalem (November 1998).

23. Quoted from *Palestine: History, Case and Solution* as cited in the newspaper *Al Qaida,* June 21, 2001.

24. As cited by Etgar Lefkovits, "1930 Moslem Council: Jewish Temple Mount ties 'beyond dispute,' " *Jerusalem Post* (January 26, 2001).

25. Ibid.

26. *Al-Qahira* (August 5, 2003).

27. Translation by MEMRI (Middle East Research Institute) and cited in their publication *Special Dispatch Series* No. 564 (September 3, 2003): 1-2.

28. *Al-Qahira* (August 19, 2003).

29. Translation by MEMRI in *Special Dispatch Series* No. 583 (October 3, 2003): 1-2.

30. Ibid., p. 2.

31. Ronald S. Hendel, "Was There a Temple in Jerusalem? Wartime reports from Jerusalem Mask the Truth," *Bible Review* 6:5 (October 2003): 8.

Chapter 8—How Israel Lost the Temple Mount

1. Nadav Shragai, "A cause for lament—situation on Temple Mount," *Ha'aretz* (July 29, 2001).

2. Cited by Avraham and Judith in Ramot <endtimes-news-events@egroups.com> (July 30, 2001).

3. It should be remembered that in this civil war, both Syrian and Iraqi troops supported and aided in the Palestinian invasion of Amman in an attempt to overthrow Hussein.

4. Moshe Dayan, *Moshe Dayan: Story of My Life* (New York: William Morrow and Company, Inc., 1976), pp. 386-88.

5. Ibid., p. 389.

6. Ibid.

7. As cited in "Conflicting Claims," *Artifax* (Winter 2000): 1,3.

8. Ariel Sharon, "Towards a National Agenda of Peace and Security," address to the Palestinian Authority Policy Conference (Washington, D.C., March 19, 2001), p. 1.

9. As cited in the *Baltimore Sun* Service and Associated Press report "Israel Closes Holy Site, Fearing Reprisal Attack," March 5, 1994.

10. Aaron Lerner, "Museum Exhibit That Sums It All Up," *Jerusalem Post*, February 17, 1997.

11. See Elaine Ruth Fletcher, "Arafat warns Jews not to visit Temple area" (Religion News Service), *San Antonio Express & News* (October 6, 2003); "Waqf Rejects Israeli Actions Permitting Non-Muslims into Al-Aqsa," Palestine Media Center (July 1, 2003).

12. As cited by Matti Friedman, "Morning on the Mount," *The Jerusalem Report* (September 22, 2003), p. 10.

13. Ibid.

14. For more information on the rabbis and their organizations, see my book *The Coming Last Days Temple* (Eugene, OR: Harvest House Publishers, 1999) and the video of the same title, in which they are interviewed.

15. This is not to say that the Waqf has not permitted visits from l on its own authority. Under special arrangement, some Christian individuals have been admitted to the Dome of the Rock accompanied by Waqf representatives since the re-opening.

16. As cited by Matti Friedman, "Morning on the Mount," *The Jerusalem Report* (September 22, 2003), p. 10.

17. Ibid.

18. Gershon Gorenberg, *The Jerusalem Report* (August 14, 2000): 15.

Chapter 9—Welcome to the Al-Aqsa Mosque!

1. For more on these decisions, see Ruth Lapidoth and Moshe Hirsch, eds., *The Jerusalem Question and Its Resolution: Selected Documents* (Dordrecht, Netherlands: Martinus Nijhoff Publishers, 1994), pp. 465-66.

2. Emanuel A. Winston, "The Imminent Collapse of the Jewish Temple Mount," *Tzemach* news service (March 11, 2002): 3.

3. Interview with Eilat Mazar, Shalom Center, Jerusalem (August 8, 2003).

4. Ibid.

5. Ibid.

6. Ibid.

7. Cited in a posting (no longer available) from an Islamic professor in the Department of Religious Studies at Stiring University, Scotland at http://www.stir.ac.uk/Departments/Art/ReligiousStudies/afa/jerusalem/News.htm.

8. Interview with Eilat Mazar (August 8, 2003).

9. *Arutz Sheva* news service, Thursday, December 26, 1996.

10. Cited in Nadav Shragai, "Settlement rabbis mull ending the ban on Jews on Temple Mount," end times-news-events, July 18, 2001.

11. Interview with Eilat Mazar (August 8, 2003).

12. Ibid.

13. "The Destruction of the Temple Mount Antiquities" http://www.har-habayt.org/destruct.html (June 2001).

14. Etgar Lefkovits, "Covert contacts led to Temple Mount reopening," *Internet Jerusalem Post* (August 22, 2003): 1.

15. As cited in Joseph Farah, "Temple Mount reopens to non-Muslim visitors," *G2 Bulletin* (July 1, 2003): 1.

Chapter 10—The Battle of the Bulge

1. As cited in Mark Ami-El, "The Destruction of the Temple Mount Antiquities," Jerusalem Letter/Viewpoints, *The Jerusalem Center for Public Affairs* 483 (August 23, 2002): 8.

2. This make-believe scenario was adapted from *Byline with Dan Betzer*, Program #2049: "Revising History" (aired August 9, 2001).

3. See Stephen J. Adler, "Israeli Court Finds Muslim Council Destroyed Ancient Remains on Temple Mount," *Biblical Archaeological Review* (July/August 1994): 37.

4. As reported to me in a conversation with Gershon Salomon, Jerusalem, October 1998.

5. Interview with Eilat Mazar, Shalom Center, Jerusalem, August 8, 2003.

6. Rabbi Chaim Richman, *Newsletter of The Temple Institute* (January 16, 2000), p. 2.

7. "Furor over Temple Mount construction," *Biblical Archaeology Review* (March/April 2000), www.likud.nl/press21.html.

8. Interview with Eilat Mazar, August 8, 2003.

9. Zachi Zweig, "What can we learn from this destructive dig?" (August 29, 2000), http://www.har-habayt.org.

10. See Mark Ami-El, "The Destruction of the Temple Mount Antiquities," Jerusalem Letter/Viewpoints, *The Jerusalem Center for Public Affairs* 483 (August 23, 2002): 6.

11. As cited in James Bennet, "Jerusalem Holy Site a Tense Crossroads Again," *New York Times* (August 29, 2003): 2.

12. Gerald M. Steinberg, "Playing out a familiar script," *Jerusalem Post* (July 29, 2001).

13. Joseph Farah, "Destruction of Holy Places," *WorldNet Daily* (August 2, 2001).

14. Interview with Eilat Mazar (August 8, 2003).

15. Chris Mitchell, "The Battle of the Bulge at Israel's Temple Mount," *Christian World News* (November 15, 2002), http://cbn.org/CBNNews/CWN/111502temple.asp.

16. "The 'Earthquake' Caused by the Cornerstone on Tisha b'Av 5761," *Voice of the Temple Mount Faithful* (Winter 2002/2003): 10.

17. Shafika Matta, "Jordanian Expert: Mosque Wall Safe," *Miami Times Herald* (Nov. 10, 2002).

18. Interview with Eilat Mazar (August 8, 2003).

19. As reported in *Israel Today* 45 (October 2002): 11.

20. As reported in *Los Angeles Times* and cited by Jerry Golden, "Report" (November 22, 2002): 4.

21. Jerry Golden, "Jordanian architects will fix Al-Aqsa bulge," *Report* (Jerusalem, November 22, 2002): 1.

22. Interview with Eilat Mazar (August 8, 2003).

23. Eilat Mazar as quoted by WorldNetDaily and cited in Stephan J. Bos, "Temple Mount wall collapses amid concern about anti-Israel world opinion," Assist News Service (ANS), September 27, 2003, p. 1.

24. Ibid.

25. As cited in "Temple Mount Wall Collapses," http://www.elijahlist.com (September 25, 2003): 2.

26. As cited in Ryan Jones, "The coming fall of the Temple Mount," *Jerusalem NewsWire* (October 15, 2002), http://www.jnewswire.com/analysis/02/10/021015_temple_mount.asp.

27. Ibid.

28. Dan Ephron, "Jerusalem's Armageddon Wall," *The Bulletin with Newsweek* (October 30, 2002), http://bulletin.ninemsn.com.au/bulletin/EdDesk.nsf/All/4BAF29BEB06A8DC9CA256C60007FF1DF.

Chapter 11—The Battle to Rebuild

1. Interview with Rabbi Nachman Kahane, Young Israel Synagogue, Jerusalem, 1989.

2. Yisrael Ariel and Chaim Richman, *The Odyssey of the Third Temple* (Jerusalem: Israel Publications & Productions Ltd., 1994), p. 102.

3. A full-color spread of some of these items was first introduced to the public through Richard Ostling's article "Time for a Temple?" in *Time* magazine (October 16, 1989), pp. 64-65. A framed copy of this article has graced the wall of The Temple Institute office ever since.

4. Chaim Odem, a craftsman who immigrated to Israel from Soviet Georgia, constructed the wax replica that now stands in the exhibition center. According to *Jerusalem Post International Edition* (August 31, 1991), the estimated cost of constructing the actual menorah, which will require 94.6 pounds of gold for the electroplating, has been estimated at $10 million.

5. As reported in the *Sunday Telegraph*, April 2002, and cited in "Red Heifer" (see the website discoverrevelation.com/43.html).

6. See Ehud Sprinzak, *The Ascendance of Israel's Radical Right* (New York: Oxford University Press, 1991), p. 283.

7. Statement by founder Gershon Salomon in the first newsletter produced by the organization, October 1995.

8. This may, in part, be because of an early ideological dispute after beginning together under the seminal influence of Rabbi Nachman Kahane, or consequences arising from The Temple Institute's Rabbi Chaim Richman's early work with, and then departure from, the Temple Mount Faithful, or simply the competition inherent in keeping a high profile and demonstrable production in keeping with fundraising need. This, however, is not to impugn the motives of either organization, both of which are essentially religious and dedicated to God.

9. As cited in a brochure published by the Temple Mount Faithful, Jerusalem, p. 2.

10. Ibid.

11. The evidence for this is 1) only 20 TMF members were marching to the Siloam, hardly constituting a threat; 2) Arabs had been stockpiling stones and weapons on the Temple Mount above the Western Wall since 3:00 A.M. the morning of the attack; 3) Waqf security personnel were absent; and 4) the event was planned regardless of whether or not the Temple Mount Faithful made their march. For the documentation in connection with this see *The Real Story: The Attack on the Western Wall Plaza* (RTF Film Associates—Mattus Heritage Institute Productions, 1991), and Richard J. Andrews, "The Political and Religious Groups Involved with Building the Third Temple in Jerusalem" (unpublished thesis, Indiana University, June 30, 1995), pp. 51-54.

12. The death toll varies according to the source. According to Israeli reports the toll was 17, and according to Palestinian reports it was 20.

13. Emanuel A. Winston, "The Imminent Collapse of the Jewish Temple Mount," *Tzemach* news service (March 11, 2002): 1.

14. "Exciting Events on the Temple Mount and in Jerusalem," online edition of the newsletter of the Temple Mount Faithful (http://www.temple-mount-faithful.org), September 17, 2003, p. 4.

Chapter 12—Setting the Stage for the Last Days' Temple

1. Sheikh Ibrahim Idris as cited in Khaled Abu Toameh, "Palestinian preachers accuse Israel of destroying Aksa Mosque," *Jerusalem Post* (August 3, 2003): 3.

2. As cited in *Artifax* (Winter 1999): 8.

3. As cited by Ulf Carmesund, *Two Faces of the Expanding Jewish State: A Study on How Religious Motives Can Legitimate Two Jewish Groups Trying to Dominate Mount Moriah in Jerusalem* (Sweden: Uppsala University, 1972), pp. 86-87.

4. See "Damage to Temple Mount 'Under Discussion,'" *Arutz Sheva* news service (Wednesday, May 26, 1999), pp. 1-3.

5. Statement by Hasan Tahboub, Head of Religious Affairs in the Palestinian Authority, as cited in Arutz-7 News on Sunday, October 13, 1996.

6. Arutz-7 News on Monday, October 14, 1996.

7. Bernard Wasserstein, *Divided Jerusalem: The Struggle for the Holy City* (London: Profile Books Ltd., 2001), x.

8. *Arutz Sheva* news service (August 4, 1998), p. 2.

9. Yisrael Medad, "The Temple Mount problem of Zionism," *Jerusalem Post* (August 3, 2003): 6.

10. Berel Wein, "The 'Two' Jerusalems," *Jerusalem Post* (www.jpost.com), May 29, 2003, p. 1.

11. "End Talk of a Third Temple," Letters to the Editor, *Ha'aretz* (August 14, 2003): 8.

12. Hillel Halkin, "Farewell, Temple Mount," *Jerusalem Post* (August 8, 2003): B9.

13. As cited in Stuart Winer, "Mounting tensions," *In Jerusalem* (a weekend supplement to *Jerusalem Post*), 11:99 (August 1, 2003): 1.

14. The Temple was built on Mount Moriah, and Mount Zion was originally the site of King David's city. When the Temple was built, the name Zion became attached to this site, and, in the Psalms, Mount Zion is said to be the place of God's presence.

15. From her report in the *Galilee Experience Update* 25, Friday, May 14, 1999, p. 3.

16. The statement of West Bank resident Sameeh Abu Ramila as cited by Associated Press writer Jason Keyser in "Jerusalem's New Wall," *Israel and Global News* (July 28, 2003), p. 4.

17. As cited by Maha Abdul-Hadi and Suleiman Besharat, "Israel to Dig New Tunnel Under Aqsa Mosque," *IslamOnline* (January 4, 2004): 1.

Chapter 13—The Future Battles for the Temple

1. Gershon Salomon, "The Arab and Islamic Countries and Their Allies Continue to Prepare for the End-time War against Israel," *Voice of the Temple Mount Faithful* (Winter 2002/2003): 35.

2. Ibid.: 35.

3. At least six different chronological placements have been suggested. For these, see my book with H. Wayne House, *Charts on Biblical Prophecy* (Grand Rapids: Zondervan Publishing Co., 1999).

4. For my arguments, see *The Coming Last Days Temple* (Harvest House Publishers, 1999), pp. 452-54. Arnold G. Fruchtenbaum, *The Footsteps of the Messiah: A Study of the Sequence of Prophetic Events*, also gives a good defense of the pre-Tribulational placement. Revised edition (Tustin, CA: Ariel Ministries, 2003), pp. 106-26.

5. The absolute state of the Hebrew *Rosh* indicates it should function as a proper noun rather than a "noun-adjective" in the construct chain. For the grammatical argument in favor of this option see James D. Price, "Rosh: An Ancient Land Known to Ezekiel," *Grace Theological Journal* 6:1

(Spring 1985): 67-89. The earliest translation of *Rosh* as an adjective ("chief, head") was by the Jewish translator Aquilla, probably based on the nongrammatical use of the term in this text by the first-century Jewish historian Flavius Josephus. Jerome, the translator of the Latin Vulgate, adopted Aquilla's incorrect translation and through his influence it has passed into many modern translations.

6. For the arguments in support of this identification see Clyde E. Billington, "The Rosh People in History and Prophecy" (Parts 1-3), *Michigan Theological Journal* 3:1-2 (1992): 54-64, 142-174, and 4:1 (1993): 38-62, and Mark Ruthven with Ihab Griess, *The Prophecy that Is Shaping History: New Research on Ezekiel's Vision of the End* (Fairfax, VA: Xulon Press, 2003), pp. 55-116.

7. For the evidence for this conclusion see the pertinent discussions in the above references. However, the term *Meshech,* although similar to the term *Moscow,* cannot be identified with the modern city on the basis of the available evidence.

8. For Russia's long time backing of Syria and its recent support of a Palestinian State see *Jerusalem Post International Edition* (April 30, 1999).

9. Mortimer B. Zuckerman, "Coming to Russia's Rescue," *U.S. News & World Report* (February 8, 1999): 68.

10. Significant technologies and industries include (with export figures for 1998): Israel Aircraft Industries ($1.44 billion), Teva Pharmaceutical Industries ($863 million in exports in 1998), ECI Telecom ($780 million), Formula Systems ($259 million). So significant are hi-tech firms in the Israeli economy that some have jokingly said that the Jaffa orange, which serves as the symbol of Israel's produce, should be changed to a microchip!

11. Some argue from the place of burial being in the region of the Dead Sea that the destruction occurred in the mountains near this area; i.e., the Judean mountains that descend from the area of Jerusalem to the Dead Sea. However, the enemy is said to "be like a cloud covering the land" (Ezekiel 38:9), and divine destruction even extends to the land of Magog and the coastlands (Ezekiel 39:6). Apparently the wilderness is selected to serve as a burial ground because it is removed from the cities and thus prevents Israelis from being exposed to corpse impurity.

12. This interview was conducted at the Young Israel Synagogue in the Muslim Quarter, Jerusalem. *Day of Discovery* reporter Jimmy DeYoung was also present during this interview.

13. "Peres raises 'world capital' solution for Jerusalem," Zionist News Releases, eretz-yisrael@shamash.org (July 22, 2003).

Chapter 14—Are You Ready for the Future?

1. Interview with Jeries Soudah by Irwin Baxter in "Arafat and Jerusalem," *Endtimes* magazine 7:5 (September/October 1997), p. 11.

2. Ibid., p. 9.

3. Excerpt from an advertisement by Facts and Logic about the Middle East in *Jerusalem Post International Edition* (March 26, 1999): 22.

4. Interview with Yochanan Ramati, Jerusalem, November 4, 1990.

5. Rabbi Nisan Aryeh Novick, *Fascinating Torah Prophecies Currently Unfolding* (New York: Netzach Yisrael Publications, Inc., 1997), p. 72 (emphasis in the original).

6. Second stanza from the Christian hymn "The Battle is the Lord's" by E. Margaret Clarkson, 1962, set to a synagogue melody and arranged by Meyer Lyon, 1770.

Chapter 15—What Should We Do?

1. Elwood McQuaid, "How Important is the Temple Mount Controversy," *Israel My Glory* 61:5 (September/October 2003): 8.

2. "An Open Letter to Evangelicals and Other Interested Parties: The People of God, the Land of Israel, and the Impartiality of the Gospel," posted on the website of the Knox Theological Seminary (http://www.knoxseminary.org/Prospective/Faculty/WittenbergDoor/index.html), a reformed school in Ft. Lauderdale, Florida. Drafted by two Knox Seminary professors, Fowler White

and Warren Gage, in December 2002, its ten propositions are followed by signatures of semi-nary professors, pastors, and public and lay leaders who have endorsed its propositions.

3. Proposition VII, Ibid., p. 2.

4. I have dealt in general with the views of Replacement Theology in my books *Jerusalem in Prophecy* (Eugene, OR: Harvest House Publishers, 1998) and *The Coming Last Days Temple* (Eugene, OR: Harvest House Publishers, 1999). For a specific point-by-point critique and refutation of the ten propositions of the "Open Letter" see Mike Stallard, "A Dispensational Response to the Knox Seminary Open Letter to Evangelicals" (delivered to the Conservative Theological Society, August 2003).

Person Index

Subject Index

Scripture Index

Jeremiah

Lamentations

Ezekiel

Nonbiblical Texts

Photo Index

Charts and Diagrams Index

About the Author

Randall Price is regarded as one of the leading evangelical authorities on biblical prophecy and is recognized as an expert on the Middle East. He holds a master of theology degree from Dallas Theological Seminary in Old Testament and Semitic Languages, a Ph.D. from the University of Texas at Austin in Middle Eastern Studies, and has done graduate study at the Hebrew University of Jerusalem in the fields of Semitic Languages and Biblical Archaeology. He has taught undergraduate and graduate courses on biblical archaeology at the University of Texas, biblical languages at the Central Texas Bible Institute, and biblical theology at the International School of Theology.

As President of *World of the Bible Ministries, Inc.*, a nonprofit organization dedicated to reaching the world with a biblical analysis of the past, present, and future of the Middle East, Dr. Price speaks to international audiences through conferences and lectureships each year. He also serves as director of the Qumran Plateau excavation project in Israel, is a certified pilgrim tour guide in Israel, and through his tour company *World of the Bible Tours* has directed 45 tours to the Bible lands. Dr. Price has authored or co-authored some 20 books on the subjects of biblical archaeology and biblical prophecy, is general editor of *The Messianic Prophecy Bible* (in progress), and is a contributor to the *New Eerdmans Dictionary of the Bible*.

He has appeared on numerous television documentaries, including the "Ancient Secrets of the Bible" series, the "Thief in the Night" series, and "Uncovering the Truth about Jesus," has been the executive producer and on-screen host of five video productions based on his books, and is featured regularly on television and radio talk shows. Dr. Price and his wife, Beverlee, have five children and reside in Texas.

World of the Bible Ministries

World of the Bible Ministries, Inc., is a nonprofit Christian organization dedicated to exploring and explaining the past, present, and prophetic world of the Bible through an analysis of archaeology, the Middle East conflict, and biblical prophecy. Three ministries comprise this organization to accomplish this practical purpose:

World of the Bible Productions—produces new books, online studies, and documentary films on biblical backgrounds and biblical prophecy for international outreach through distribution and media, and publishes the *World of the Bible News & Views* newsletter.

World of the Bible Seminars—the speaking ministry of Dr. Randall Price through conferences in churches and organizations, and college, university, and seminary lectureships.

World of the Bible Tours—Offers customized annual pilgrimages and study tours that allow participants to experience the reality of the world of the Bible.

To find out more about our products, request a free subscription to our newsletter, or receive a brochure of current tours to the Bible lands, or to contact Dr. Price for speaking engagements, you can reach us at:

Website:	www.worldofthebible.com
E-mail:	wbmrandl@itouch.net
Address:	World of the Bible Ministries, Inc.
	P.O. Box 827
	San Marcos, TX 78667-0827
Toll free (in US):	(866) 604-7322
Phone:	(512) 396-3799
Fax:	(512) 392-9080

Other Books by J. Randall Price

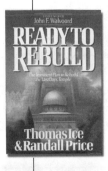

Ready to Rebuild

A fast-moving overview of contemporary events which indicate that a significant move to rebuild the Temple is gaining momentum in Israel. Includes important pictures and charts. Co-authored with Thomas Ice. (Video also available.)

In Search of Temple Treasures

Does the Ark of the Covenant still exist? Why is it so important? *In Search of Temple Treasures* takes you on a remarkable expedition into the ark's mysterious past, its explosive significance today, and its implications in the timing of last days' events. Meticulous research and dozens of interviews with leading authorities in the Middle East provide a factual inside view of one of history's most fascinating quests. (Video also available.)

The Coming Last Days Temple

Rebuilding the temple? Surveying the plans, furnishings, priesthood, and research to replicate ancient Temple functions, Randy gives readers an up-close glimpse into preparations for prophecy fulfillment. Includes interviews with key officials. (Video also available in NTSC, PAL, and DVD.)

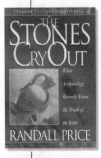

The Stones Cry Out

Recently uncovered ancient artifacts shed light upon the lives of the patriarchs, the Ark of the Covenant, the fall of Jericho, the existence of King David, and more. A fascinating survey of the latest finds in Bible lands, with more than 80 photographs affirming the incontrovertible facts that support biblical truth. (Video also available.)

(more on next page…)

Secrets of the Dead Sea Scrolls

Discover the new technology that helps translators with previously unreadable Scroll fragments, supposedly "secret" Scrolls in hiding, the furious debate about who rightfully owns the Scrolls, and the newest efforts to find more Dead Sea Scrolls. Includes never-before-published photographs. (Video also available.)

Jerusalem in Prophecy

Jerusalem has an incredible future in store, and it's at the very center of Bible prophecy. This book reveals what will happen, who the key players will be, and what signs indicate we're drawing close. (Video also available.)

Unholy War

Why does strife continue in the Middle East? How is it connected to terrorist attacks on Western nations? Dr. Price provides a concise, fascinating look at the problems and the players in the Middle East.

Fast Facts® on the Middle East Conflict

In a helpful Q-and-A format with maps, charts, and side-bars, bestselling author and expert in Middle Eastern studies Randall Price counters misconceptions with truth behind the headlines and a fascinating timeline of the conflict.